Teaching Music

Teaching Music

James P. O'Brien
The University of Arizona

Holt, Rinehart and Winston
New York Chicago San Francisco Philadelphia Montreal Toronto London Sydney
Tokyo Mexico City Rio de Janeiro Madrid

Library of Congress Cataloging in Publication Data

O'Brian, James Patrick.
Teaching music.

   Includes indexes.
   1. School music—Instruction and study. I. Title.
MT1.02 1983   372.8'7   82-12076

ISBN 0-03-057718-7

CBS COLLEGE PUBLISHING
Holt, Rinehart and Winston
The Dryden Press
Saunders College Publishing

Preface

Who is the music educator? Anyone who provides on-going learning experiences for children in and through music is a music educator. Often, this is the classroom teacher. The music educator, however, may be a music specialist whose primary task in the school is to teach music. In addition, it may be a private music teacher or parent.

This book is for all music educators. It is directed especially to elementary classroom teachers with knowledge of musical fundamentals who wish to provide meaningful musical experiences in their classrooms on a regular basis. Music education majors who are preparing for a career as elementary music specialists will find the material equally worthwhile.

To develop as a music educator, a person must feel comfortable with music in order to have enthusiasm for it and a commitment to sharing it with others. This requires an understanding of the concepts and materials of music. A person must also possess at least modest skills of singing and playing instruments, be able to read musical notation and, above all, must enjoy music and have insight into bringing this enjoyment to pupils. A single book cannot provide everything needed to reach this goal. It can, however, provide the inspiration, the organizational model, and suggest sufficient materials and strategies to initiate a viable music program. This is indeed the intent.

This is a comprehensive text that covers diverse subjects related to elementary school music. It is designed to lead the reader from general considerations in elementary music education to specific techniques. Part One provides the rationale for teaching music and a look at the psychological basis of learning as postulated by Piaget and Bruner, which leads naturally into chapters on objectives, planning lessons and motivation for learning in Part Two.

Part Three, Musical Experiences, explores the procedures which are used in elementary classroom music for singing in unison and in harmony, listening to music, playing instruments, moving to music, reading music, and creating music. Program objectives charts in these chapters identify the specific objectives to be taught coordinating the theory and techniques at each level for teaching music. Part Four presents evaluation, Part Five provides alternate experiences and techniques including musical games, special subjects of relating the arts, providing music for the exceptional child, adapting the Kodály, Orff and Manhattanville methods, and finally, establishing and maintaining good classroom discipline. Sample lessons and activities are dispersed throughout the text. The appendices provide review material in music fundamentals, a glossary of terms and concepts, criteria for evaluating series texts, recorder fingering and guitar chords. A song index and general index follow.

The basic, well-proven and traditional approaches to music are included as are many curricular trends and tendencies of the last decade. Supplementary texts should not be necessary unless greater depth, beyond the usual limits of an introductory music methods course, is desired.

This text is specifically designed for an elementary music methods class meeting at least twice a week for one semester or three times a week for one quarter (term). It can be expanded by attention to the exercises at the end of each chapter. Conversely, it may be abbreviated by using Chapters 14 through 18 selectively. It may be used flexibly by following other than a chronological order of presentation.

Although this work is authored by a single writer, like any book, it is the collective effort of a compatible team. I wish particularly to thank all the elementary classroom teachers, music specialists and elementary children, spread across three continents, with whom I have worked during my career. They have responded to my ideas in music and have shared so many of their own. Their inspiration gave me reason to write this text. I wish to thank all the following critical reviewers who have provided valuable ideas on content and form during the preparation of the manuscript.

John Batcheller   *University of New Mexico/Albuquerque*
Robert Borg   *University of Minnesota/Minneapolis*
Carole J. Delaney   *California State University/Sacramento*
Joseph Farruggia   *Humbold State University*
Annette George   *Murdoch Center/Butner, North Carolina*
Betty Kanable   *University of Texas/Austin*
Nancy Matheson   *University of Tennessee/Martin*
James Scholten   *Ohio University/Athens*
Robert F. Shambaugh   *Louisiana State University*
Jean Signor   *Indiana State University/Bloomington*
C.R. Varner   *William and Mary College*
Robert Weiss   *Southern Illinois University/Carbondale*
Virginia Whitfield (Professor Emerita)   *University of Oregon*

I would also like to thank the helpful professionals at Holt, Rinehart and Winston, particularly Cherrie Schmierer, Carolyn Viola-John, Project Editor, Nancy Myers, Senior Production Manager, and Gloria Gentile, Design Supervisor, who have maintained their dedication to quality publishing without ever losing the personal touch. Finally, I wish to thank Shirley, who understood what I was doing since she was buried under her own manuscript at the same time.

James P. O'Brien

Contents

CONTENTS

Part Three   Musical Experiences   53

Teaching Music

PART ONE

Teaching Children Music

Music in the Elementary School

The place of music in the framework of education has been a subject of discussion for thousands of years. The ancient Greek philosopher Aristotle believed that music should both educate and entertain the individual. During the Middle Ages in the Western world, music was the equal of mathematics and astronomy in the medieval curriculum, the *quadrivium*. The educated Renaissance person was as much at home in the world of music as in the world of politics and science. In the early twentieth century in the United States, music was included in the school curriculum because it was thought to develop citizenship and responsibility.

The teaching of music has, in fact, been used to serve many purposes in American society for more than three centuries. In Colonial times, training in music was necessary so a church congregation (including the children) could sing psalms and hymns reasonably well in tune. Traveling singing masters with their rudiment books met this challenge, conducting singing schools in local churches and moving from town to town like circuit riders. In the early nineteenth century Lowell Mason considered music "a sure means of improving the affections; and ennobling, purifying, and evaluating the whole man."[1] In the early twentieth century music was included in the curriculum because it gave children something to do with their leisure time, would make them healthier, and—as already suggested—developed their civic pride. Music educators in the past have therefore had to teach for various purposes.

[1]Arthur Rich, *Lowell Mason: The Father of Singing Among the Children* (Chapel Hill: University of North Carolina Press, 1946).

Music continues to be included in the school curriculum today for a number of reasons. First, it provides an aesthetic experience that can be realized in music's unique way—through sound. It is, too, a framework for looking at our culture and at the cultures of other regions and nations. It provides mental and emotional diversion regardless of the level or type of involvement of the participants. It also develops responsibility and provides a positive outlet for filling the increasing hours of leisure that are available to many of us. In the process, much more is required of today's music educator than of his or her Colonial counterpart. Today's teacher of music in the schools must be perceptive educator, sociologist, psychologist, recreational therapist—and musician.

Although its purposes and applications are diverse, music has been justified in education through many centuries for both nonmusical and musical purposes. When its significance is nonmusical, the values are often referred to as *secondary*. On the other hand, whenever music is used for musical purposes only, its values are considered *primary*.

What *is* the primary musical value of music; does it even exist? Or is music subservient to other disciplines or needs? Indeed not! Music has a unique contribution to make in the educative process. It enables people to feel good about hearing or making sound. Anyone who has made music knows what this means and what it is: an aesthetic feeling evoked in music's own way, through sound. This contribution is quite sufficient to justify music's inclusion at any educational level, and is referred to as music's *primary* or *musical* value. In the simplest terms, it is feeling satisfaction from a musical experience.

Aesthetic response to sound is difficult to measure, however. It is not clearly delineated and is different things to different people. To the young child, it is the excitement of striking a triangle on "Twinkle, twinkle." To the budding guitarist, it is mastering three chords. To the trained violinist, it is mastering a difficult concerto and successfully performing it in public. For all, it is a response to music that defies verbalization. Although it can rarely be measured, it can be frequently observed and includes the following:

the satisfaction of listening to a beautiful symphony or of participating successfully in a musical group
the joy of musical activities such as writing or making music, attending concerts, or listening to records or the radio
the realization that music is a basic enhancer of life that enriches and deepens it
an absence of negative feelings such as reticence or fear, whether in discussing, listening to, or creating music.

The use of music we most frequently observe is undoubtedly for secondary purposes. Television and radio present many commercials with music, the purpose of which is to attract attention to a particular product. Some regular members of audiences at concerts and opera may attend more out of civic and social responsibility or to be entertained at a sophisticated level than to experience the aesthetic import of the sound. The same may be said for the music one finds in the elementary school. How often is the stress in music on preparing the holiday or PTA show? Secondary values generally outweigh the purely musical ones in many cases.

Aesthetic response can occur in music without a musical performance, at least in a public sense. It takes an awareness on the part of the teacher to provide for the aesthetic qualities of music. Aesthetic response cannot be seen, touched, or measured. Its presence, however, can be inferred.

If music is being taught for its unique contribution to the curriculum, musical purposes should ultimately predominate. Music education allows people to feel good about music. Music teaches music best. Everything else is a bonus. If everything attributed to music could be accomplished in another way, would there be a need for music education? The only subject that teaches children to understand and respond to music *is* music. This is its unique contribution—aesthetic response to sound.

This book will present material that will enable the reader to use music in both primary and secondary ways. The emphasis, however, will always be on the aesthetic nature of music.

The Music Specialist and the Classroom Teacher

Two people often share responsibility for providing music education for elementary children—the music specialist and the classroom teacher. In an ideal program both cooperate in providing musical experiences for a classroom.

The music specialist is likely to have majored in music at the university level, understands how to read it and to listen to it, knows its theoretical structure and historical development, and is proficient on one or more instruments, can sing well, and can think through musical situations and problems quickly. He or she has had some college-level courses in how to teach music as well as the traditional educational psychology courses that deal with learning in general.

The classroom teacher, however, has majored in elementary education and has taken courses in a variety of subjects as well as many methods courses in how to teach them. The elementary major usually has had a course in the content of music (music fundamentals) and its methods and has studied the overall learning process in many psychology courses.

The specialist is thus trained in depth in one subject—music—while the elementary teacher is trained broadly in many, including music. Each is important in the elementary school and can accomplish much through a cooperative effort. The role of both is shaped by the individuals involved, the administrators, and the policies of the school districts. The following description represents a norm.

The music specialist generally meets with the children for twenty to thirty minutes once or even twice a week. Rather than seeing each child every day the specialist plans long-range objectives for each classroom, perhaps in a district curriculum guide, and implements them in weekly lessons with the children.

The classroom teacher often helps plan the long-range objectives in music but in any event is responsible for implementing lesson objectives on the days the specialist is not present. (This implementation could include reviewing a song, repeating a record for listening, or drilling on a skill introduced by the specialist.) In some districts, specialists leave written lesson plans and ideas for the classroom teacher, who often introduces new songs or recordings or follows through on creative activities in progress.

The role of each kind of teacher is further shaped by individual personality and ability. In some districts there is no specialist and classroom teachers are responsible for the entire music program. A resource person from the district or state level may be available for consultation; if not, the elementary teacher has to rely on college courses, a good series book, and much initiative and imagination. In these circumstances, there will be no music for the children if the classroom teacher does not include it.

There are many advantages in having a music specialist available. A specialist can oversee musical activities and direct the overall program, knows music well, is aware of a variety of resources, and thinks musically and can consequently teach it more quickly and with a finer ear. Built-in motivation exists because of his or her skills in playing instruments and singing. Since the specialist is a visitor to their classroom or they travel to a music room, the children are often more attentive than they are to the regular teacher, whom they see day in and day out.

There are also some drawbacks to having a specialist who must teach music to a given grade at a certain time because there is usually a rigid schedule that sometimes involves several schools. The itinerant specialist usually has little involvement with the children outside music. As a result, among both children and classroom teachers there may be a sense that the specialist is not truly part of the real educational scene. The facility of many specialists in music can also overwhelm the children and the classroom teacher. Although this is a motivation in some cases, it can be a disadvantage because it places too great a distance between the specialist's skills and those the children (or the classroom teacher) can hope to obtain. In addition, the music specialist may have musical standards that are totally unrealistic for many elementary classrooms. When this happens, little music is taught and children are led to believe that music is only for the highly trained.

Music specialists need to bridge the gap between their art and the art of music in the classroom. This requires that they see children in nonmusical situations to understand how each learns. Doing so could include visiting the classroom at times other than for music or assisting the classroom teacher in nonmusical instruction. It could mean being involved with the total school; attending a nonmusical event such as a play or ball game; sitting in on parent-teacher conferences; providing a music report card; and being a viable even if transient faculty member of each school.

The classroom teacher has many advantages when it comes to teaching music: Knowing the children well, he or she can program musical activities that are highly suitable both to the class as a whole and to individuals, schedule the music lesson so it is always appropriate within the day and integrate music with other subjects so that mutual meaning develops.

Disadvantages to be faced when the classroom teacher handles music include the fact that this teacher's musical skills and discrimination are often not as sophisticated as the specialist's and children may learn music incorrectly. The program may not be balanced to include all possible facets of singing, listening, playing instruments, moving, and reading and creating music. The classroom teacher may require a longer preparation time. The flexibility of scheduling music at any time in the day may result in its being forgotten or being taught only on Friday afternoons.

In the ideal situation, of course, both the music specialist and the classroom teacher are cooperatively involved to present a valid music program for their children and to assist one another in personal and professional growth. The classroom teacher can give insight into children and the specialist can provide insight into music. Each is able to see the other work with the class and develop new perceptions. It is a matter of joint responsibility and satisfaction.

Exercises and Activities

1. Observe a music lesson in an elementary classroom. What activities seem to be of secondary value? How do you know? What activities promote the primary value of music? Why? How could you change those activities which are non-aesthetic to ones that contribute to aesthetic development?
2. Interview a music specialist on the advantages and disadvantages of the position. Discuss possible solutions with him or her.
3. If you were a music specialist, what things could be done to make your position more credible in the school? What things could you do to make the principal, classroom teachers, and children more comfortable with music?
4. Interview a classroom teacher or elementary principal on the advantages and disadvantages of using a music specialist versus the classroom teacher.
5. What things could a classroom teacher do to involve a music specialist in the total educational goals?

Key Terms and Concepts

Primary value   Music specialist
Secondary value   Classroom teacher
Aesthetic response

Professional Readings

Hughes, William O. *A Concise Introduction to School Music Instruction, K–8*, 2nd edition. Belmont, Calif.: Wadsworth, 1981.

Landis, Beth, and Polly Carder. *The Eclectic Curriculum in American Music Education. Contributions of Dalcroze, Kodály and Orff*. Washington, D.C.: Music Educators National Conference, 1972.

Linderman, Earl W., and Donald W. Herberholz. *Developing Artistic and Perceptual Awareness*. Dubuque, Iowa: Wm. C. Brown, 1974.

Reimer, Bennett. *A Philosophy of Music Education*. Englewood Cliffs, N.J.: Prentice-Hall, 1970.

Strunk, Oliver (ed.). *Source Readings in Music History*. New York: W. W. Norton, 1950.

How Children Learn Music

2

Elementary children may be only four years old when they begin kindergarten and are often twelve or thirteen on completion of the sixth grade, an age span of eight or nine years. They have different physical and mental characteristics as well as different social and emotional needs from one end of the age spectrum to the other. Involvement in music is likewise somewhat different at either end of the range. The way music is presented changes according to social and emotional adjustment, as do the activities.

This chapter first explores some of the characteristics of children at each age in the elementary school—the physical, mental, and social-emotional characteristics of early elementary children (ages 4–7), middle elementary (7–9), and upper elementary (9–12). Two recent and applicable learning theories are then discussed and applied to the development of musical concepts in the elementary school.

Characteristics of Elementary Children

Ages 4–7: The Early Elementary Years

The ages of four to seven roughly correspond to kindergarten through second grade. The child who is a preschooler at the beginning of this period can be expected to become a well-adjusted elementary student by the completion of the second grade.

Children grow rapidly during this period. Their rounded baby visages change to faces with the distinctive features they will bear most of their lives.

8

They become taller and heavier. Their coordination improves because the large muscles of their bodies are now well developed. They are capable of many activities that involve these large muscles, such as running and hopping. Their small muscles also continue to develop during this period, which allows good eye-to-hand coordination and enables them to play some musical instruments.

The child's mental development during these years is also rapid, with vocabulary expanding to at least two thousand words. Learning through imitation continues, but a vivid imagination and creative bent also lead to flights of fantasy. The child mentally begins to sort objects, people, and phenomena into tentative categories. He or she enjoys naming colors and animals or arranging shapes and sizes as well as identifying people and determining their relationships.

The child begins this period with little social orientation, is quite egocentric at the outset, and may want to play alone. Through the social contacts of the school, however, he or she begins to achieve a concept of self as well as to seek friends. Boys and girls in this period still play together and have similar interests.

The child in the early elementary grades has many physical and mental skills but is usually neither ready to study a musical instrument that requires extremely fine muscle coordination and mental distinctions nor capable of making abstractions to the extent required by music reading. Activities that employ the large muscles and which allow cooperative work with others can nevertheless be enjoyed.

Ages 7–9: The Middle Elementary Years

These ages correspond to grades three and four. The child's physical change is not as startling as it has been in earlier periods. The growth rate is slow and steady. The large muscles are generally fully under control. Small-muscle coordination continues to improve. Most children in this age group have good manual dexterity and can master many skills, including musical tasks that require fine muscular coordination.

Mental development in the middle years is remarkable. The child masters many academic tasks; vocabulary expands to more than eight thousand words and reading usually improves markedly. Many symbolic systems, particularly numbers, are now mastered. The child of this age is more able to classify objects and ideas abstractly than his or her early elementary counterpart. This is when the sense of pitch develops and some of the abstractions of musical notation can be understood.

In the middle years the child moves away from a strict family orientation and begins to identify with peers, typically in a sex-aligned fashion. Boys play with boys and model adult male roles; girls play with girls and model adult female roles. The child develops loyalties to a particular group, as well as an ability to empathize with those who are part of this group.

Children in the middle years can acquire many musical skills and concepts. They should participate in a variety of activities that keep their social structures from becoming highly polarized and inflexible.

Ages 9–11: The Upper Elementary Years

Children in the upper elementary years—grades five and six—generally refine all the mental and physical skills of the middle years. Their small muscles become highly coordinated and they are capable of mastering skills that require minute coordination. Toward the end of the period, they experience a spurt of physical growth as the body enters puberty. These changes occur faster in girls than in boys and it is typical to find sixth-grade classes in which many of the girls tower over the boys.

Abstract thought in this period is present to a degree not possible in earlier years. Children can manipulate mentally such symbols as numbers and musical notation. Many children reach mental maturity in these years, their ability to abstract approaching that of most adults.

The peer group continues to be a strong force in the upper elementary years. There is often open antagonism to the opposite sex. Songs and activities the boys like will automatically be disliked by the girls. During this period, children usually become highly competent and confident of their abilities. They develop a great deal of learning independence. They are more autonomous in their activities and thoughts and begin to make moral judgements. In addition, many children develop a strong sense of humor during this period.

We will now look at two theories of learning to see how and *why* children's differences can be accommodated in the elementary school.

The Theories of Jean Piaget

Jean Piaget (1896–1980), a Swiss educator, studied cognitive development in children, and his ideas attracted many educators in recent times because of the logic with which he described the learning process. His theories account for the child's physical and mental maturation, interaction with the environment, and equilibration, that is, self-regulation as a result of sensory input.

Piaget divides childhood into four stages of development: sensory-motor intelligence; preoperational thought; concrete operational thought; and formal operational thought.

Sensory-motor Intelligence (Ages 0–2)

According to Piaget, children begin to learn as soon as they are born. For the first two years of life their behavior is motor. During the first month of life, a child's behavior is reflexive: it cries, sucks, and moves eyes and limbs. These are automatic responses. In the next three months, there is a modification of such reflexes. Crying will occur because the child is hungry. The eyes follow a moving object and the head turns toward a loud sound. Between the fourth and eighth months, the child begins to do physical acts intentionally—crawls across the room to grab a toy or shakes a rattle to hear the sound. Up to one year of age, this intentionality becomes refined. When the child begins to walk, movement across the room is for a reason: someone has called or the child is hungry. In the second year, the child begins to solve problems internally as long as the object in question is in his or her physical presence. A ball seen under the table invites thinking of a way to retrieve it by reaching or crawling under the table. If the same ball cannot be seen, the child will not be concerned with retrieving it. What cannot be perceived in the child's immediate environment cannot be constructed mentally and does not exist.

Preoperational Thought (Ages 2–7)

This level is important to teachers since children are generally at this stage when they enter school, whether kindergarten or the first grade. This is the period when concepts are formed and language develops. Words begin to represent objects and are used as symbols when the object is no longer present. Most language usage among two- to four-year-olds is, as Piaget terms it, egocentric. There is no real communication. It is a verbal thinking process by the individual. However, the speech of five- to seven-year-olds becomes socialized; it is designed to communicate with others.

Children in the preoperational stage can learn more quickly because of the words they already know. (Words accelerate the process of gathering information and storing it in their minds.) Children demonstrate an egocentric manner of thinking during this period. They believe everyone thinks as they do and therefore never question the way they do things. As the child enters school and has heightened social interaction, he or she begins to seek verification of thoughts and actions, begins to accommodate personal behavior to something of a group norm. (This does not mean children function as a group but that they do things similar to what those around them are doing.)

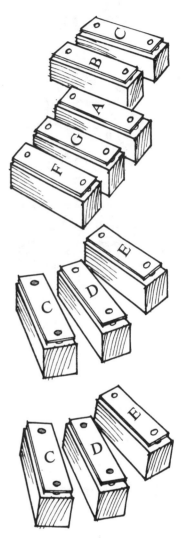

The child in this stage is no longer limited to object permanence, as was the case in the sensory-motor period, and can see what might happen to an object if it is acted upon. However, this thought process is limited by the inability to see the steps between the beginning and the end. Piaget refers to this as inability to transform. If resonator bells are set up as a scale and a tonal pattern is then extracted one tone at a time, the child will see these as a group of bells, not as a pattern that has been transformed from the original scale. In the same way, a bell that is high in one case cannot be seen as low in a second example. This lack of logical thought process is characteristic of the child at this age. Similarly, the preoperational child cannot see all the aspects of a given stimulus at once. Given a large drum to play, the child will probably play it one way, such as loudly with one hand, if this is the way he or she has seen it done. This child will probably not discover it can be played softly as well as with varying degrees of intensity or that two hands, the fingertips, or a mallet can be used to strike the surface. Piaget refers to this as centration, the inability to perceive all the aspects or possibilities of a stimulus.

Another characteristic of preoperational thought is the inability to reverse operations. Playing bells from high to low may be accomplished, but playing low to high is, to the child, a disassociated operation, not the reverse of the former. A crescendo (soft to loud) is considered different from a decrescendo (loud to soft), not the reverse. The child is perception-bound because his or her decisions are based purely on perceptual cues. A big drum will play "big" and a small one "little"—not loud and soft, respectively.

There are numerous applications for teaching music in early childhood years. Group activities should not be forced. The child is not able to concentrate on something that does not involve him or her. Watching another child play an instrument is not appealing; one must play it personally. Small music groups and individual work at this age level may be preferable to large groups. The child is limited in the ability to discover techniques and relationships too, imitation being a more viable way to learn. Relational concepts are not easily perceived either, such as opposites like loud–soft, fast–slow, and high–low. Instruction should provide rich experiences without interrelating all of these into a conceptual framework.

Period of Concrete Operations (Ages 7–11)

In grades three to five, children gradually learn to decenter their perceptions, concentrating on many attributes of a stimulus simultaneously. They also begin to attend to transformations, the steps leading from one stage to another. They also see reverse operations, recognizing that adding and subtracting are inverse operations, high is the opposite of low, and water can become ice yet return to its liquid state again. This remains true as long as reasoning is not purely verbal nor hypothetical. A child at this stage can see that the C chord = C E G but not that all I (tonic) chords = *do–mi–sol.*

During this stage, language becomes clearly communicative; the child becomes very social, yet realizes others think differently. For this reason, he or she seeks constant verification of ideas and operations. Unlike a younger sibling, the child at this level can conserve—that is, see that number, area, mass, and volume remain the same if transformed. The pitch of a given-tone bell does not innately change because it is high in one context, low in another; it remains a middle C. This child becomes aware of the relational aspects of objects and is able to arrange objects serially by increasing or decreasing size, shape, length, or width. He or she can arrange pitches from low to high, organize like timbres into groups, and understand soft to loud as a series of changes of intensity. It is now possible to grasp the elements of music as categories—melody, rhythm, harmony, timbre, intensity, and form—since taxonomical classification is another characteristic of this cognitive stage. This is the period during which children appear to learn the most in school. Their natural curiosity seems insatiable, their newfound mental skill in organizing allows learning to occur in geometrical proportion to stimulation. Learning is still experiential in this period but relationships—conceptual frameworks—are being formed to last a lifetime.

Period of Formal Operations (Ages 11–15)

Children reach the formal-operations stage of cognitive development near the sixth grade. Cognitive structures become highly established if not totally refined in this stage. Although their social and emotional needs are still child-like, children begin to think very much like adults. They are capable of using scientific reasoning and of establishing, testing, and refining hypotheses. They can solve purely verbal problems, as in mathematics, as well as understand proportions and formulas.

In the study of music, children are able to deal most effectively with the relationships of music reading, its shorthands and symbols. They are able to explore the creative endeavors of composing with traditional and graphic notation as well as with electronic means. They are able to relate music to such other arts as painting and sculpture, and to other disciplines like mathematics and science.

The Theories of Jerome Bruner

Jerome S. Bruner, Professor of Psychology and Director of the Center for Cognitive Studies at Harvard University, has presented a model of learning similar to that in Piaget's work. He has articulated three levels representing the stages whereby children form concepts.

At the first level, which applies mostly to preschoolers, children learn by responding to the stimuli around them. This Bruner calls the *enactive* stage, the experiential part of learning. During this time, children receive and act upon the sensory input in their environment. This type of representation is the basis of learning responses and habits. Children experience music through singing, listening, moving, creating, and playing instruments.

In the second phase of conceptual development, the *iconic* stage, children begin to summarize their images into mental categories or concepts: for example high and low; long and short; loud and soft; fast and slow; and winds, strings, and percussion. Patterns or paths are formed in their minds based on the perceptions acquired in the enactive phase. These categories rarely are named or defined upon first acquisition. Children can, however, mentally manipulate concepts they have formed without the objects or ideas being

ENACTIVE	ICONIC	SYMBOLIC

Instrument Classification

Fast vs. Slow Music

ALLEGRO

VS.

ADAGIO

High vs. Low Music

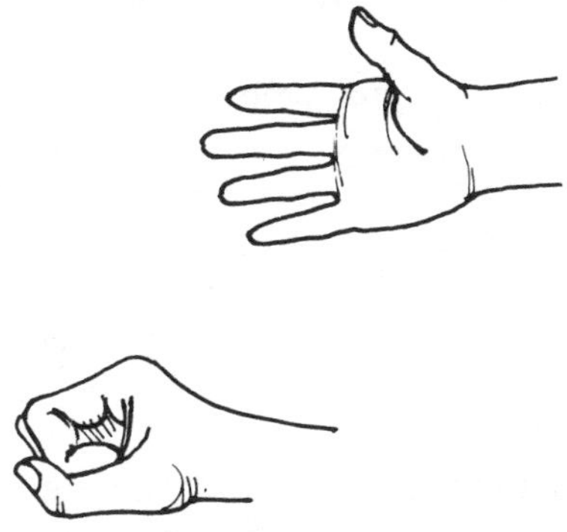

Loud vs. Soft

present. Children are typically in the iconic phase at kindergarten or the first grade.

The final stage of conceptual development, according to Bruner, is the *symbolic*. The child applies a label to a learned concept, whether it is a word or a number. In music, he or she uses correctly terms such as melody, harmony, tempo, and beat. These labels or symbols thus become a means of thinking. The child enters this phase soon after beginning school. This stage includes not only naming things, but also dealing eventually with objects and ideas in the most abstract fashion, as in reading and writing. This ultimately includes music reading. The ability to operate on a symbolic level is of course the basis for most learning in and out of school. Not all phenomena need to be experienced physically; alternatives can be derived and manipulated mentally. This leads to adult thinking and reasoning.

Unlike Piaget, Bruner has not delineated a rigid time line for stages. Most children and all adults operate in one of the three forms of representation in most types of learning. The two-year-old—involved with learning only on the enactive level—plays with toys and reacts to adults, all the time experiencing objects of various sizes, shapes, densities, and colors as well as people who are male or female, tall or short, or speak loudly or softly. Children absorb the world and its contents through their eyes, ears, fingers, mouths, and noses.

If they hear a loud sound, they may recoil or be startled. If they hear a soft sound, they may lean forward or approach it to hear it better. These experiences with sound dynamics will affect how they continue to learn all of their lives. Four-year-olds, still relying on sensory input, will be aware that the "volume" knob on a television set makes the sound louder or softer, depending on which way it is turned. Although they may not know the words *loud* and *soft*, they will have the difference in sound categorized by experience. They will know there is a difference between a shout and a whisper or between the sound of music played *forte* or *piano*, whether or not they can verbalize the difference. They may simply refer to them as "big" versus "little" sounds.

Eight-year-olds, who have had many experiences involving loud and soft sounds, clearly have the differences sorted out in their minds and use the terms *loud* and *soft* to describe the differences. They are operating at a symbolic level. They can transfer the concept "loud-soft" to a new situation. When they begin to read, if they have not already done so, the words *loud* and *soft* will have meaning. When they discover how *forte (f)* and *piano (p)* are used in muscial notation, these clearly will symbolize experiences they have already had.

Older children and adults continue to experience other examples of "loud-soft" and continually refine and adjust their concept. This may occur either through the senses or symbolically, in vicarious activities such as reading. Thus learning a concept is a spiraling process that involves constant experiencing, recategorizing, and symbolizing. All three levels are necessary for continued learning. The older the child, the more quickly will he or she be able to place an idea into its proper category or to readjust a conceptual framework to accommodate it. Concepts are expanded and refined, however, throughout all of adult life.

A Practical Synthesis for Music Teaching

We have looked at the way children mature physically, mentally, socially, and emotionally. We have also examined the theories of Jean Piaget and Jerome

Bruner. How can this be applied to music education? The following points provide a framework for developing musical concepts:

1. Children learn best *a posteriori,* by experiencing music first. These experiences should always be diverse, since this forms the basis whereby the mental constructs called *concepts* are formed. Concepts are the basis through which a child learns to symbolize or label musical experience and eventually to acquire an ability to deal with it in a notational scheme. To repeat, music is best learned through experiencing music. The younger the child, the more important a lengthy and rich experience.
2. Children have developmental levels that must be acknowledged and accommodated in music classes. The young child has control of his large muscles but probably not of his small ones. He or she should experience music in a way which is compatible with this physical development. Children should not be asked to do something for which they have not developed the muscular coordination.
3. Children have varying social and emotional needs. The young child is more egocentric and may not enjoy group music activities. The older child becomes highly socialized and will enjoy group participation. Music instruction should provide for these various social organizations.
4. The ideal music program uses the concrete elements of music—melody, rhythm, harmony, timbre, intensity, and form—to build mental categories or musical concepts that in turn are eventually labeled and possibly even symbolized in notation, which is the epitome of dealing with music at an abstract level. Good instruction follows the scheme of: experiencing; categorizing; symbolizing; and notating.

The teacher, as may be seen in the left-hand column of Chart 2–1, first provides children a variety of experiences in the musical elements (melody, rhythm, harmony, timbre, dynamics, and form). These experiences include singing, listening to music, playing classroom instruments, moving to music and even creating music. Through these experiences, the teacher leads the

CHART 2–1

New experiences enable children continually to refine and adjust their concepts in music.

Experience level	Category level (Realizations from the experience)	Symbolic level	Notational level
The teacher provides the children with a variety of musical experiences in melody, rhythm, harmony, timbre, dynamics, and form through singing, listening to, playing, moving to, and creating music.	The teacher leads the children to discover and establish relationships in music so they become aware of its elements. That music consists of a horizontal element (melody), a durative element (rhythm), a vertical element (harmony), a color element (timbre), an expressive element (intensity) as well as an overall interrelationship of these elements (form).	The teacher leads the children to apply labels to the categories as needed. No term and word 's introduced before the children have experienced it sufficiently and understand its meaning. Labels are not presented as definitions, but *a posteriori*	The teacher introduces notation as a written form of the labels. This is a shorthand for identifying and remembering a concept and for creating new musical experience.

children to discover the elements and structure of music, as seen in the second column. As experiences become formulated, terms and labels are gradually introduced *after* the children have clearly categorized the concept (third column). Finally, as seen in the right-hand column, written symbols are casually introduced when it becomes apparent the children have a clear mental category of what the symbol now represents. Chart 2–1 (which represents neither what occurs in any *one* grade level or *one* year nor a strict time line) is a model of concept formation for the entire elementary school. Many teachers are needed for its realization. Early experiences are intended as appropriate for the lower elementary grades, the formation of categories for the middle grades, and the introduction and use of symbols for the upper grades. However, in the event an upper elementary class has not formed a certain concept, the experience level is still the point with which the teacher should begin. Older children will grasp the significance of the experience much more quickly and be able to form a mental construct or concept in a shorter period of time. Good instruction does not begin with "A melody is . . . ," but rather allows the children—whatever their age—to experience many types of melodies in

CHART 2–2 Melody Concepts

Overall Principle: Melody is the linear element of music created by playing tones in succession.

Experience level	Category level (Realizations from the experience)	Symbolic level Words & Terms	Notational level
	The tones of a melody are called pitches.	Pitch names (C,D,E)–(*do, re, mi*)	Placement of pitch on staff. Clefs, ledger lines
Children sing, listen to, play, move to, and create songs and musical compostions that provide a wide variety of melodic experiences.	Tones may be high or low.	High–low	
	Tones in a melody may go up, fall down, or stay put, or combinations of these.	Ascending–descending	
	Tones may move by steps, skips, or leaps, or combinations of these.	Intervals (conjunct–disjunct)	Observation and identification in music with some group and independent reproduction
	The range of a melody may be wide or narrow.	Wide–narrow	
	A melody may be grouped into breathing units called phrases.	Phrase and cadence	
	Phrases may incorporate smaller units called motives.	Motives	
	Words are set to music in various ways, including syllabic and melismatic settings.	Syllabic and melismatic	
	A tonal pattern is a smaller unit within a melody of two to six tones.	Tonal pattern (in pitch names)	
	Tonal patterns with characteristic rhythms are called motives.	Motives	
	Motives repeated at different pitch levels are called sequences.	Sequences	
	Melodies are often organized around scales and tonal centers. Common scales include the major and minor diatonic, the pentatonic, and the chromatic.	Key, tonic, scales, major, minor, pentatonic, chromatic, half-step, whole-step	Key signatures
	Melody is visually represented through direct symbolism by points on a graph to show the degree of highness or lowness with varying degrees of precision.	Music reading	Synthesis of above points

16

many ways. In schools in which learning follows this logical sequence, definitions are seldom necessary.

Each element of music should be developed in a similar fashion. Melody (Chart 2–2) is experienced through singing and listening to songs. To cite an example, children gradually develop the realization that it is necessary to take a breath at certain points in each song and that everyone breathes at the same time. Eventually the teacher calls the unit between breathing points a *phrase* and the actual point of breathing a *cadence*. When music books are used, phrases and cadences can eventually be identified visually.

Rhythm (Chart 2–3) develops in a similar manner. Pulse (beat) is experienced by marching, clapping, stamping, and playing instruments. Gradually, children sort out the beat from the tempo, accent, or melody-rhythm. It is now appropriate to use the term *pulse* or *beat* to describe this category. Eventually, an actual note value may be used to represent the underlying pulse.

Harmonic (Chart 2–4) experiences, too, are first provided before children are asked to respond to symbols. By listening to the teacher's guitar or autoharp accompaniment as they sing, they soon realize that different chords may be used to accompany a song and that one chord, the tonic, has a stronger pull in most songs. Gradually, the terms *tonic* (I), *dominant seventh* (V7), and *subdominant* (IV) are introduced in the classroom to identify the chords the children have distinguished aurally. Finally, the symbols of I, V7, and IV have meaning to the children when they see them in written notation.

Charts 2–5 (timbre), 2–6 (dynamics), and 2–7 (form) represent additional elements of music. The development of concepts in each follows the sequence outlined above—experiencing, categorizing, symbolizing, and notation.

CHART 2–3 Rhythm Concepts

Overall Principles: Music is governed by a forward impulse, a series of sounds and silences, grouped or not grouped, and generally controlled by an underlying pulsation.
There are many rhythms operating in a composition at the same time—pulse, accent, and melodic rhythm.

Experience level	Category level (Realizations from the experience)	Symbolic level Words & Terms	Notational level
	Music may be fast or slow.	Tempo—fast– moderate– slow	Italian tempo terms*
Children sing, listen to, play, move to, and create songs and musical compositions that provide a wide variety of rhythmic experiences.	Many pieces have an underlying pulse that remains relatively consistent throughout the piece.	Pulse or beat	Notes to represent pulse ♩, ♪, ♫, ♬, etc.
	Other pieces may have a changing pulse or no clearly discernible one.		
	The pulse of a piece may move at the same tempo throughout or it may change.	Tempo changes or deviations	Accelerando, ritardando, rubato
	Pulses may be grouped by accent into twos or fours (duple) or threes (triple).	Accents—duple, triple, quadruple	Meter signatures $\frac{4}{4}$ $\frac{3}{2}$ $\frac{6}{8}$ etc.
	In some music, the pulse may be grouped into unusual meters, such as fives and sevens, or in ways that defy classification and pattern.	Asymmetrical meter; changing meter	Meter signatures $\frac{5}{4}$ $\frac{7}{8}$ etc.
	Rhythm (characteristic) patterns may be even, uneven, or syncopated.	Even, uneven, and syncopated patterns	Accents, dots, ties, note values, proportions
	Patterns may incorporate silences or rests.	Rests	𝄽 𝄾 etc.

*Such as Adagio, Andante, Moderato, Allegro, Presto.

17

CHART 2–4 Harmonic Concepts

Overall Principle: Harmony is the vertical element of music that results from simultaneous combination of two or more tones.

Experience level	Category level (Realizations from the experience)	Symbolic level Words & Terms	Notational level
Children sing, listen to, play, move to, and create songs and musical compositions that provide a wide variety of harmonic experiences.	Harmony may be consonant or dissonant.	Consonant–dissonant	
	Melody is supported in homophonic textures by harmony that is called the accompaniment.	Accompaniment and homophony	Observing in music
	Melodies may be combined simultaneously to form polyphonic structures; melodies having the same harmonic structure may be combined.	Polyphony—rounds and canons	Observing in music
	Harmony may be created by reiteration of a motive—ostinato or drone.	Ostinato and drone	Observing in music
	Chords may be constructed and used according to plan.	Tonic, dominant and subdominant	I, V7, IV
	The function of a chord may depend on its relationship to a tonal center.	Key—major and minor	Key signatures and pitch names

CHART 2–5 Timbre Concepts

Overall Principle: Timbre is the characteristic quality of the sound generator.

Experience level	Category level (Realizations from the experience)	Symbolic level Words & Terms	Notational level
Children sing, listen to, play, move to, and create songs and musical compositions that provide a wide variety of experiences with timbre.	The characteristic quality of a sound source may be varied, depending on how it is played.	Pizzicato, mute, bowing, etc.	Written symbols for special effects
	Timbre is changed by combining various individual instruments and voices.	Band, orchestra, choir, jazz ensembles, etc.	Score order
	Tone color may be categorized as: Vocal Sounds—soprano alto tenor bass	Soprano Alto Tenor Bass	Abbreviations and foreign terms to indicate instruments and special effects
	Instrumental Sounds Strings	Violin Viola Cello Bass Harp Guitar, etc.	Abbreviations and foreign terms to indicate instruments and special effects
	Winds (Woodwinds and Brass)	Piccolo Flute Oboe Clarinet Saxophone Bassoon Trumpet French horn Trombone Tuba, etc.	Abbreviations and foreign terms to indicate instruments and special effects
	Percussion	Snare drum Bass drum Timpani Triangle Cymbals, etc.	Abbreviations and foreign terms to indicate instruments and special effects
	Electronic or Synthesized	Musique concrète Synthesizer	Abbreviations and foreign terms to indicate instruments and special effects

CHART 2–6 Dynamic Concepts

Overall Principle: All musical sounds possess degrees of loudness and softness.

Experience level	Category level (Realizations from the experience)	Symbolic level Words & Terms	Notational level
Children sing, listen to, play, move to, and create songs and musical compositions that provide a wide variety of experiences with dynamics.	Dynamics are related to all other musical elements in subtle ways.	Soft, loud	*pp, p, mp, mf, f, ff*
	Dynamics depend upon three factors: 1. Energy of performer 2. Number of performers 3. Distance from performer to listener		
	Dynamics may change either gradually or suddenly between notes, motives, phrases, sections, or movements.	Crescendo, decrescendo, gradual transition, terraced dynamics	*sfz* (*sforzando*) *subito*

A balanced music program requires attention to all the elements outlined in Charts 2–2 through 2–7. By the end of the elementary school experience, children should be able to deal with *each* element on a symbolic and notational level. This may be the termination of their formal music education,

CHART 2–7 Formal Concepts

Overall Principles: Form or design in music results from the interrelationship of the other elements, particularly melody, rhythm, and harmony.
Form involves repetition (unity) and contrast (variety).

Experience level	Category level (Realizations from the experience)	Symbolic level Words & Terms	Notational level
Children sing, listen to, play, move to, and create songs and musical compositions that provide a wide variety of experiences in form.	The phrase is a small unit that contributes to overall design.	Phrase	Observation in music
	A phrase is analogous to a breath span; it generally ends with a punctuation point.	Cadence	
	Phrases may be alike, similar, or different.		
	Phrases may be constructed from motives.		
	Phrases may be grouped into questions (antecedents) and answers (consequents).	Antecedent–consequent	
	Phrases are often grouped together to form longer sections in musical compositions.		
	SECTIONS AND MOVEMENTS		
	Larger sections and movements of a composition are also based on repetition, repetition with variation, repetition with contrast, or pure variation.	Terms related to these forms	
	Common combinations in music are:		

Repetition (strophic)	Repetition w/variation	Repetition w/contrast	Pure Variation		
Hymn tunes Folk songs Pop music Strophic art songs	Blues Canons Fugues Theme & Variations Jazz Improvisation	Ternary (Song form) Rondos Minuets & trios Sonata-allegro form Da Capo arias	Rags Some electronic composition Through-composed art song	Terms related to these forms	*D.C. al Fine* *D.S. al Fine*

Other arts contain similar principles of design.

19

and such conceptual development will provide them a framework for understanding and appreciating most types of music for the rest of their lives. In the event they elect to study music in junior or senior high school, these elementary experiences will provide an excellent foundation for specialized music training. In either case, their elementary school music program will have served them well.

Exercises and Activities

1. Observe children of different ages in an elementary school during recess or lunch break. What evidence do you see that children at different ages have varying physical and mental abilities? different emotional and social needs?
2. List activities that might allow a child in early elementary school to experience one of the concepts outlined in Charts 2–2 through 2–7.
3. List activities that might allow a child in middle elementary school to categorize and/or symbolize one of the concepts outlined in Charts 2–2 through 2–7.
4. List activities that might allow a child in upper elementary school to symbolize and/or notate one of the concepts outlined in Charts 2–2 through 2–7.

Key Terms and Concepts

Early elementary years
Middle elementary years
Upper elementary years
Jean Piaget
Sensory-motor intelligence
Preoperational thought

Concrete operations
Formal operations
Jerome S. Bruner
Enactive stage
Iconic stage
Symbolic stage

Professional Readings

Andress, Barbara. *Music Experiences in Early Childhood.* New York: Holt, 1980.

Bruner, Jerome S. *Toward a Theory of Instruction.* Cambridge, Mass.: Harvard, 1968.

Garretson, Robert L. *Music in Childhood Education,* 2nd ed. New York: Appleton, 1976.

Land, Lois Rhea, and Mary Ann Vaughn. *Music in Today's Classroom: Creating, Listening, Performing.* New York: Harcourt, 1973.

Newman, Grant. *Teaching Children Music: Fundamentals of Music and Method.* Dubuque, Iowa: Wm. C. Brown, 1979.

Papalia, Diane D., and Sally Wendkos Olds. *A Child's World: Infancy Through Adolescence.* New York: McGraw-Hill, 1975.

Runkle, Aleta, and Mary LeBow Ericksen. *Music for Today: Elementary School Methods,* 3rd ed. Boston: Allyn and Bacon, 1976.

Stone, L. Joseph, and Joseph Church. *Childhood and Adolescence: A Psychology of the Growing Person,* 4th ed. New York: Random House, 1979.

Swanson, Bessie R. *Music in the Education of Children,* 3rd ed. Belmont, Calif.: Wadsworth, 1969.

Wadsworth, Barry J. *Piaget's Theory of Cognitive Development.* New York: David McKay, 1971.

PART TWO

Planning
Music
Lessons

Objectives  3

Objectives are statements of intent or purpose in education, goals to be reached or points of punctuation in individual development. They give focus to our educational effort. Objectives provide both a point toward which to work and a criterion by which to measure development.

Objectives are either long or short in range, and their various levels can be confusing to a teacher. Some are to be realized and evaluated on a day-by-day basis while others take many years to accomplish and are therefore not as easily observed. Let us take a look at the various levels of objectives.

Social Objectives

Social objectives are long-range goals established informally throughout society and assigned to the schools at large. Many times they are responsibilities shared with the home and church. In our complex twentieth-century world, we would assume that everyone in the United States has a command of the English language, competence and comfort in reading, writing, or speaking it. Attaining this is a social objective, fostered and developed by each teacher.

Social objectives are attained over one year or a period of several years. The teacher should facilitate the development of social objectives. These objectives include:

literacy in language (speaking, writing, and reading)
literacy with a variety of symbols (basic mathematical computation, simple
    directions, musical notation, coding)

the ability to reason, to solve problems independently, and to develop a logical thought process
the ability to understand and to work within the democratic process
the ability to be self-actualizing and self-motivating
the development of a positive attitude to the lifelong process of learning and becoming

Every subject in the curriculum probably can or does foster these objectives to a certain degree. The failure of one child to read upon high school graduation is not the failure of the senior English teacher, the sixth-grade remedial reading teacher, or the first-grade teacher who started the whole process. It is the failure of the entire school system as well as of the home and society at large.

Program Objectives

Program objectives are more specific than social objectives and are almost entirely the responsibility of the schools. Usually they deal with one specific subject area. In music, a program objective might be that by the end of the sixth grade, the children will have developed:

1. the ability to sing unison and simple harmony parts reasonably well in tune with musical expression
2. the ability to discern basic forms, timbres, textures, and tempos while listening to standard musical selections by symphony orchestras, jazz or rock ensembles, or choral groups
3. the ability to read and respond as a group to traditional and graphic musical notation with reasonable accuracy, including notation of duration, pitch, and intensity.

This list is not definitive, although *each* teacher of music in *each* grade would be responsible for contributing to the realization of these items. These objectives are termed *broad program objectives.*

For the teacher, it is the *specific program objective* that is important on a yearly basis. Specific program objectives are really the terminal objectives of *one* subject for *one* year; they are limited by shorter time spans than broad program objectives. Most frequently the classroom teacher or specialist formulates the objectives for a grade level.

A few examples may serve to clarify typical specific program objectives.

Grade 1:   The children will demonstrate awareness of:
the difference between high and low through the use of their singing voices and hand levels (pitch);
the differences between fast and slow tempi through bodily movement (duration);
the difference between long and short durations through echo clapping and response to simple rhythmic notation (duration);
the difference between loud and soft sounds through bodily response and the playing of rhythmic instruments (intensity).
Grade 2:   The children will sing twenty-five songs within a one-octave range with reasonable pitch and rhythmic accuracy in a musically expressive manner.
The children will sing simple harmony parts, including rounds, canons, ostinati, and echo and partner songs.

The children will identify simple return forms (ABA, AABA, ABACA) while listening to a live or recorded example.

The children will demonstrate a positive attitude to music through increased participation in musical activities and events.

The children will compose simple sound pictures using graphic and/or traditional music notation.

Specific program objectives are often delineated in the basal music series used in many school districts. These objectives represent *a total picture*, an ideal list, that may or may not apply to one teacher's specific grade level. In other words, for some years and in some schools, these objectives may be realized. In other schools and situations, they may not be realistic. Each teacher should weigh carefully the list of objectives given for any grade level in a basal music series or curriculum guide and then formulate the list of objectives for the specific grade level involved. The individual teacher is the expert on what a given class of children might be able to do. There is no such construct as a *typical fourth-grade class* and therefore no list of objectives for fourth-grade music that can be used year after year without additions or deletions.

The following is a master list of specific program objectives from which a teacher may plan a music program. These are arranged on a continuum by area (early, middle, and upper). Objectives in the early elementary grouping are generally prerequisite to those in the middle grouping, and the middle prerequisite to those in the upper elementary. All lists of objectives are only suggestive, however. When children in the sixth grade are not able to achieve in the upper level, the teacher should move back to the middle or early level to choose skills with which the children can be successful. This may work in the opposite way as well, with a teacher in one level choosing objectives from a more advanced level.

CHART 3–1 Objectives for Singing

	Children will
Early elementary (K–2)	sing unison songs with limited ranges
	sing simple pentatonic songs
	imitate phrases
	sing simple rounds and ostinati
	sing simple partner songs (I chord)
	sing echo songs
	sing conjunct intervals (with the exception of the half-step)
	sing chordal patterns (*do–mi–sol*)
	match pitches
	echo tonal patterns
Middle elementary (3–4)	sing songs with wider ranges
	sing with good tone, diction, and breath support
	sing in tune and stay in the key
	sing independently
	sing advanced rounds
	sing advanced partner songs
	sing descants and two-part harmony
	sing disjunct intervals as well as half-steps
	sing a wide variety of songs
Upper elementary (5–6)	sing songs with expanded ranges in a musically expressive style
	sing with a great deal of independence, both individuallly and as a group

25

CHART 3–1, *continued*

sing three-part harmony

sing harmony by ear

chord vocally

sing in an appropriate style, including attention to articulation, phrasing, and dynamics

CHART 3–2 Objectives for Listening

	Children will
Early elementary (K–2)	identify repeated or contrasting phrases in a composition
	discuss the mood of a selection
	identify the predominant foreground timbres in a general way
	identify musical elements heard, including 1. major dynamic changes (loud to soft) 2. high and low sounds (register) 3. fast or slow tempos 4. beat and accent groupings (2, 3, 4) 5. phrases and cadences in the melody
Middle elementary (3–4)	identify certain timbres as being high or low (flute vs. tuba)
	identify timbres more specifically, including the orchestral families and common instruments by sound (including those in both the foreground and background)
	identify major, minor, and pentatonic sounds, tonality, and modulation
	identify AB, ABA, and variation form
	relate musical elements to the mood of the piece and to extramusical associations
	graph melodic contour
	recognize melodic quality conjunct–disjunct, simple–ornamented, narrow–wide
	recognize-consonance-dissonance
	identify texture (monophonic, homophonic, polyphonic)
Upper elementary (5–6)	identify finer dynamic changes as well as transitions (*pp, p, mp, mf, f, ff, crescendo, decrescendo, subito, sforzando*)
	identify specific forms, such as binary, ternary, rondo, fugue
	identify select musical styles, such as classical, folk, jazz, rock
	identify all orchestral timbres as well as how they are being used (pizzicato, muted, etc.)
	identify asymmetrical meters and tempo deviations (*fives, sevens, accelerando, ritardando, rubato, a tempo*)
	recognize select genres, such as symphony, concerto, suite, opera, lied
	identify select works by name, composer, and historical style
	identify whole-tone, chromatic, 12-tone, and modal sounds
	use musical vocabulary to describe a listening experience

CHART 3–3 Objectives for Moving

	Children will
Early elementary (K–2)	echo clap
	tap, clap, walk, and run to the basic pulse
	move in place through swinging, swaying, etc., to show the mood of the music
	move their bodies to show loud and soft, fast and slow, high and low

CHART 3–3, *continued*

	participate in action songs, finger plays, and singing games
	participate in interpretive movement such as dramatizations
Middle elementary (3–4)	move to even patterns
	skip and gallop to music
	participate in more involved singing games and folk dances
	improvise movements and dances
	show understanding of musical elements through movement, including attention to phrasing, dynamics, articulation, and so on
Upper elementary (5–6)	participate in more involved folk dances
	use conducting patterns (2, 3, 4, 6)
	perform stylized period dances
	use movement to show deviations in tempo and dynamics, such as *accelerando, crescendo, decrescendo,* and so on
	use movement to show the mood and style of the music

CHART 3–4 Objectives for Creating

	Children will
Early elementary (K–2)	make up rhythmic and melodic patterns including simple ostinati
	suggest instruments to interpret the words or mood of a song
	make up phrases and set to music on a pentatonic scale
	set nursery rhymes or poems on pentatonic instruments
	create and interpret sound pictures
	improvise phrases, patterns, ostinati
	discover new ways to play instruments
Middle elementary (3–4)	create and interpret sound pictures
	make up words and notes for ostinati for older songs
	create new verses to songs
	make up tunes in various scales, including the diatonic, pentatonic, and whole-tone
	invent graphic musical notation to represent a sound picture
	transpose songs to a new key
Upper elementary (5–6)	create their own songs and/or lyrics
	notate their own songs, traditionally or graphically
	compose electronically
	invent musical games
	notate electronic compositions
	write in 12 tones
	compose palindromes

There is no prescribed way in which specific program objectives must be stated, nor is the number needed an exact one. Five to ten per year is probably a realistic figure. A balance of the typical musical activities found in the elementary schools—singing, listening, playing instruments, moving, reading, and creating—is to be desired in any statement of specific program objectives.

Lesson Objectives

Lesson objectives, sometimes called behavioral or performance objectives, are highly specific objectives stated and measured for each lesson or lesson component. They are usually behavioral in that a discrete behavior manifests itself. Performance is generally observable, too, since the children are doing something. *Lesson objective* is the best term for this level of planning, since program and social objectives may also be stated in behavioral or performance terms.

Lesson objectives are stated so an overt behavior may be observed and therefore assessed. Common behaviors in music include singing, tapping, chanting, clapping, playing, stating, identifying, and the like. The behavior must be observable.

In addition, a good lesson objective will establish criteria for accepting the behavior. What degree of accuracy will we accept when a child sings? taps? identifies? Common sense dictates these criteria. Songs should be sung reasonably well in tune. Rhythms should be tapped with accuracy. The musicianship of the teacher is very important for knowing when a group is in tune or is playing a rhythm correctly. An example should suffice to clarify the meaning of lesson objectives.

For a given thirty-minute music lesson, a classroom teacher may have planned several activities. These could include a song to be sung, a rhythmic accompaniment to be added, an ostinato to be played, a rhythmic pattern to be identified in the written music, and recognition of the song when it is played by a symphony orchestra. There would be several lesson objectives:

1. The children will *sing* "The Birch Tree" with reasonable pitch and rhythmic accuracy in a musically acceptable manner.

i = E G B
V7 = B D♯ F♯ A

2. The children will accurately *play* a ♩ ♫ rhythmic accompaniment on a drum while singing.
3. The children will *play* an ostinato on the recorder in a musical manner.
4. The children will aurally and visually *recognize* the ♩ ♫ pattern as they look at and listen to the song by pointing to the pattern in the book.
5. The children will aurally *identify* when "The Birch Tree" occurs in Tchaikovsky's "Fourth Symphony" by raising their hands.

All of these are lesson objectives to be achieved within the thirty-minute lesson and all are similar. A discrete, overt behavior is indicated in the verb of each objective—to sing, to play, to recognize, and to identify. In addition, each is stated so it can be measured immediately according to the criteria given. This measurement is generally done informally by the teacher. Did the children sing and play accurately? Did they recognize the pattern by pointing and identifying the tune by raising their hands? If so, the lesson objectives were realized.

Some teachers include highly specific criteria within their lesson objectives. For example, objective 4 could be stated as "The children will aurally and visually recognize the ♩ ♫ pattern with 90 percent (or 50 percent or 75 percent) accuracy as they look at and listen to the song."

In conclusion, all levels of objectives are interrelated in a hierarchy. Lesson objectives are derived from program objectives, which in turn are derived from social objectives. For example:

Social objective: Children will develop literacy in a variety of symbols.
Broad program objective: By the end of the sixth grade, children will develop the ability to read and respond to traditional and graphic musical notation.
Concrete program objective: Second-grade children will clap simple rhythmic patterns composed of | ⊓ and ♪.
Lesson objective: The children will aurally and visually recognize the ⊓ ⊓ | | pattern as they look at and listen to the song "Are You Sleeping?"

Activity
Singing
Level
Early elementary

Specific program objective
The children will sing simple harmony including rounds and echo songs.

Lesson objectives (throughout the year)
The children will sing "Are You Sleeping?".
The children will sing "Little Tom Tinker."
The children will sing . . . .

Activity
Listening
Level
Middle elementary

Specific program objective
The children will identify specific timbres while listening and tell from which orchestral family each comes.

Lesson objectives (through subsequent lessons)
The children will identify verbally which instruments are heard in succession while listening to Ravel's *Bolero* and Britten's *Young Person's Guide to the Orchestra.*

Activity
Creating
Level
Upper elementary

Specific program objective
The children will compose electronically.

Lesson objectives (through successive lessons)
The children will collect ten environmental sounds on reel-to-reel tape.
The children will mutate a sound collected earlier by changing the tape speed.
The children will mutate a sound collected earlier by adding reverberation.
The children will edit a tape to include three original and two mutated sounds.

It is very important for the teacher to state specific program objectives at the beginning of each year for each grade. One in each activity—singing, listening, playing, moving, reading, and creating—is *minimal*. Specific program objectives are the immediate guides for planning the daily musical experiences in the form of lesson objectives. Everything accomplished in the name of music education should relate to a specific program objective.

Exercises and Activities

1. From a basal music series or a state or district curriculum guide, find several examples of each level of objective.
2. Choose a grade level you might teach. Devise at least five specific program objectives related to either musical elements (pitch, duration, etc.) or musical activities (singing, playing, etc.) you believe you could develop with that grade level over a period of one year.
3. Using one of your specific program objectives from Exercise 2, write at least five lesson objectives that would facilitate the development of your program objective.

Key Terms and Concepts

Objective
Social objective
Broad program objective

Specific program objective
Lesson objective

Professional Readings

Bergethon, Bjornar, and Eunice Boardman. *Musical Growth in the Elementary School*, 4th ed. New York: Holt, 1979
Bloom, Benjamin S. (ed.). *Taxonomy of Educational Objectives: Cognitive Domain.* New York: David McKay, 1977.
Boyle, J. David (compiler). *Instructional Objectives in Music.* Vienna, Va.: Music Educators National Conference, 1974.

Gary, Charles L. (ed.). *The Study of Music in the Elementary School: A Conceptual Approach.* Washington, D.C.: Music Educators National Conference, 1967.

Gordon, Edwin. *The Psychology of Music Teaching.* Englewood Cliffs, N.J.: Prentice-Hall, 1971.

Gronlund, Norman C. *Stating Behavioral Objectives for Classroom Instruction,* 2nd ed. New York: Macmillian, 1978.

Holt, Dennis M., and Keith P. Thompson. *Developing Competencies to Teach Music in the Elementary Classroom.* Columbus, Ohio: Charles E. Merrill, 1980.

Hughes, William O. *A Concise Introduction to School Music Instruction K–8,* 2nd ed. Belmont, Calif.: Wadsworth, 1981.

Leonhard, Charles, and Robert W. House. *Foundations and Principles of Music Education,* 2nd ed. New York: McGraw-Hill, 1972.

Mager, Robert F. *Developing an Attitude Toward Learning.* Belmont, Calif.: Fearon Publishers, 1968.

———. *Preparing Instructional Objectives,* 2nd ed. Belmont, Calif.: Fearon Publishers, 1975.

4 Planning Music Lessons

A lesson plan is an organized strategy for stimulating, accomplishing, and evaluating a learning task, either a concept or a skill. It is a mental strategy designed and carried out by the teacher. Writing out plans may help you design the lesson clearly from start to finish as well as provide for contingencies and alternatives. With experience, you can plan and provide valid educational experiences mentally without committing them to paper, since the lesson plan is a *process*, not a sheet of paper. It includes the following components:

1. **Advance planning**
   a. Grade level and subject
   b. Materials and equipment
   c. Specific program objective
   d. Lesson objectives
2. **The lesson**
   a. Motivation
   b. Procedures
   c. Evaluation
3. **Follow-up lessons**

The total lesson plan has three major parts. The first generally represents what a teacher must do *in advance* of the lesson, the second is the *actual presentation* of the lesson, and the third represents what lessons *might follow* as well as alternative strategies for the lesson at hand.

Advance Planning

The four components here require almost total advance planning on the part of the teacher. These components are rather obvious and the two discussed in Chapter 3 will need little elaboration here.

Grade Level and Subject

The working teacher plans a lesson with grade level and a certain subject in mind. For the education student, it is important that this entry be the *first* one on a written plan. This is an excellent reference for the future and also provides an *immediate* reference point for the supervisor who may read the plan or follow its execution in the classroom.

Materials and Equipment

Advance planning for materials and equipment permits the flow of a lesson logically from beginning to end. This is a strong argument against strictly "mental" lesson planning. It is hard to remember exactly what you need for a lesson unless you write it down, put it in a logical place, and have things organized in the order in which they will be used.

Materials might include songs to be sung, visuals to be placed on the board for viewing, and pictures to be used for motivation. There also might be records, transparencies, and handouts. It is important to cite the material in the order in which it is going to be used and then to arrange it in a handy place in the same order.

Material

1. Picture: Kermit the Frog (Personal picture file)
2. Song: "Mister Frog Went A Courtin' " (Making Music Your Own, Book I, page 38).
3. Transparency: Words to "Mister Frog Went A Courtin' " (AV file)

Mister Frog Went A-Courtin'

American Folk Song
Arranged by James Rooker

Sword and pis - tol by his side, Um - hm! Um - hm!

2. He said, "Miss Mouse, are you within?"
   "Oh yes, Sir, here I sit and spin."

3. He took Miss Mouse upon his knee,
   And he said, "Miss Mouse, will you marry me?"

4. Oh, where will the wedding supper be?
   Away down yonder in a hollow tree.

5. Now Mister Frog was dressed in green,
   And Miss Mouse looked like a queen.

6. The first came in was a little white moth,
   He spread out the tablecloth.

7. The next came in was a bumblebee,
   With a fiddle on his knee.

8. The next came in was a little flea,
   To take a jig with the bumblebee.

9. The next came in was a pesky old fly,
   He ate up the wedding pie.

10. The next came in was a little red ant,
    She always says, "I can't, I can't."

11. The next came in was a fluffy yellow chick,
    He ate so much it made him sick.

12. The next came in was an old tomcat,
    He swallowed Miss Mouse as quick as a rat.

13. Then gentleman Frog swam over the lake,
    But he got swallowed by a big fat snake.

14. There's bread and cheese upon the shelf,
    If you want any more you can sing it yourself.

I = G B D
IV = C E G
V7 = D F♯ A C

Arrangement by James Rooker from *Making Music Your Own*, Book 1. © 1964 by Silver Burdett Company. Used by permision.

4. Handout: Chord patterns for playing chords on autoharp to "Mister Frog Went A Courtin' " (File cabinet for ditto masters)

Equipment is equally important. If an overhead projector is needed, it should be placed near the materials. Setting up such equipment in advance, and checking the controls and the focus—particularly when the equipment is unfamiliar to the teacher—is all part of lesson planning. Equipment is easy to use and only takes a bit of preparation on the teacher's part to master. An equipment list might include:

Equipment
Overhead projector (Check out from AV room)
Piano (Roll in from cafeteria)
Three autoharps (Check out from Resource Center)
Assorted rhythm instruments (Available in classroom)

Attention to materials and equipment has many dividends. Time is not wasted and children are not kept waiting. A sense of organization and pre-planning gives the teacher heightened credibility and it is also a deterrent to poor discipline.

Specific Program Objectives

Specific program objectives were presented and discussed in Chapter 3. Each lesson plan should have a central focus around one or two specific program objectives.

Specific Program Objective: Grade 1

Children will identify through listening repeated or contrasting phrases in a composition. (Phrase 1 consists of lines 1 and 2, phrase 2 of lines 3 and 4.)

i = D F A
v = A C E

Wilson et al., *Growing with Music*, Book 8, Englewood Cliffs, N.J.: Prentice-Hall, Inc., 1963. Reprinted by permission.

Lesson Objectives

Each lesson plan needs at least one objective and possibly as many as five, depending on the overall intent of the lesson, the attention span of the children, and the pacing of the lesson. These must be specified by the teacher to keep the lesson clear and sequentially logical. In one thirty-minute music session, the objectives might be:

1. The children will echo clap rhythms in $\frac{4}{4}$ given by the teacher.
2. The children will write select patterns presented by the teacher.
   (| | | | , | | | ? , ⊓ ⊓ | |)
3. The children will sing "Are You Sleeping?" while tapping one of the patterns in Objective 2 as an ostinato.
4. The children will sing the ostinati with the song.

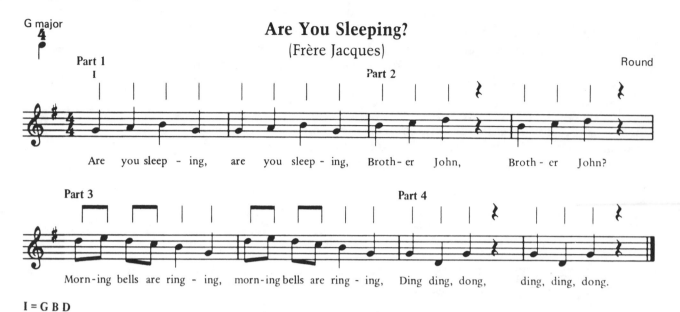

Are You Sleeping?
(Frère Jacques)

Round

G major

Part 1

Are you sleep - ing, are you sleep - ing, Broth - er John, Broth - er John?

Part 3

Part 4

Morn-ing bells are ring - ing, morn-ing bells are ring - ing, Ding ding, dong, ding, ding, dong.

I = G B D

5. The children will identify visually the patterns of Objective 2 in the written music of "Are You Sleeping?"

Each objective emphasizes a slightly different *activity* of music—listening and moving (1), reading and writing music (2), singing and moving (3), singing harmony (4), and reading music (5). This variety is essential to heighten and maintain interest in the lesson. Children are able to attend to one activity for a long time if they are sufficiently motivated. But one activity should never be overworked. Good planning would not allow echo clapping to occupy an entire thirty-minute period, any more than it would allow only singing or tapping. Attention is kept high by moving from activity to activity smoothly and logically. Pacing, the momentum or speed of the lesson, is as important as the variety of activities. Lesson objectives are also discussed in Chapter 3.

In some groups, particularly where exceptional children are involved, fewer or more lesson objectives might be necessary. A group of EMR children might learn from merely singing the song (Objective 3) and tapping the patterns (Objective 1). Gifted children might want to write and perform rhythmic rondos from the patterns presented in Objectives 1 and 2 in small groups. This might be a springboard for individualizing instruction. It is advisable for *any* teacher, novice or experienced, to have more lesson objectives and ideas to develop in a lesson than will be realized ordinarily within thirty minutes. Slightly different objectives, representing varying skill levels, might be needed if the teacher decides to place children in small groups. This is contingency planning.

The Lesson

The actual lesson includes motivation, procedures, and evaluation. It is the overt portion of any lesson plan. This is where the teacher provides the musical experiences that should result in a change of behavior in the students. Learning is not just feeling good (although that is part of it) or enjoying oneself (although learning can be enjoyable).

Each part of the actual lesson—motivation, procedure, and evaluation—will receive detailed attention in subsequent chapters, so an overview of each will suffice here.

Motivation

Motivation builds an excitement for doing something. In the music lesson, motivation can stem from many sources—a change of pace, a different teacher or room, the chance to participate and play instruments, the opportunity to do something creative. A teacher must begin each new lesson with something more exciting than "Let's clear our desks and open our books to page 16. Today, we're . . . !!" The rich musical experience that may or may not follow will never be noticed unless some degree of motivation is present.

Procedures

In music, there is a variety of activities that may constitute a music lesson. A procedure is merely a logical approach for presenting a musical experience to children. If it is a song, the teacher may sing it while the children listen for key words. They may then hum along or tap the melodic rhythm. On the third or fourth repetition, the children may then join in until they can sing the song with accuracy and assurance. If it is a listening experience, the teacher may pose a series of questions before a recording is heard: "What are the timbres in this piece? What type of tempo do you hear?" A portion of the recording might be played after each question, the question answered, and new ones posed until the teacher feels the objectives have been met. In either case, whether the procedure is singing or listening, it should logically present the material and ideas until the lesson objectives are met.

Procedures fall into two categories. Many teachers tell and explain: "Notice the long note in the second phrase." "See how we change to G7 in the third line." Other teachers allow children to discover relationships through observing the music: "Where is there a change of chords?" "Over what word do we notice a note of longer duration?" Both procedures, *explanation* and *discovery*, can be used in music as well as in other subjects to foster learning.

Evaluation

Evaluation, the third part of the actual lesson, represents a casual assessment of the effectiveness of the lesson. If lesson objectives are clearly stated, evaluation is a matter of the teacher's deciding that the children did indeed what was required.

Enjoyment, participation, smiling faces, and good feelings are no guarantee that the lesson objectives were met, although their presence does not mean the objectives were *not* realized either. These are the fringe benefits of good teaching—and their presence suggests that the aesthetic qualities of music were probably being developed. Fulfillment of the lesson objectives is the tangible evidence, however. Aesthetic fulfillment, the primary value of music education, develops as a result of many successful music experiences.

Follow-up Lessons

A good teacher anticipates what to do next. A song, a recording, or an activity should be chosen because it helps develop one of several specific program objectives. It should also be chosen because it can be used more than once to develop further concepts. Teachers are too busy to plan only activities that can be repeated without variation—or, worse yet, cannot be repeated.

Specific examples will help clarify how old materials can be used to develop new objectives.

Example One (early elementary)

Initial Experience: Rote Singing

F major

Did You Ever See A Lassie
(Ach du lieber Augustin)

Quickly

Germany

Did you ev - er see a las - sie, a las - sie, a las - sie? Did you

ev - er see a las - sie do this way and that? Do

this way and that way, and that way and this way; Did you

ev - er see a las - sie do this way and that?

1. Ach, du lieber Augustin, Augustin, Augustin,
   Ach, du lieber Augustin, Alles ist hin.
   Geld ist hin, Mad'l ist hin, All's ist hin, Augustin,
   Ach, du lieber Augustin, Alles ist hin.

2. Ach, du lieber Augustin, Augustin, Augustin,
   Ach, du lieber Augustin, Alles ist hin.
   Boch ist weg, Stock ist weg, Augh ich bin in dem Dreck;
   Ach, du lieber Augustin, Alles ist hin.

(Translation)

1. O, my dear old Augustin, Augustin. Augustin.
   O, my dear old Augustin, robbed I have been.
   Money's gone, girl is gone, everything else is gone:
   O, my dear old Augustin, robbed I have been.

2. Goat is gone, staff is gone, and I am in a fix:

I = F A C
V7 = C E G B♭

Follow-up Experiences

Singing
Graphing the contour with hand levels while singing.
Singing the German words.

Listening
Identifying the phrase structure AA₁BA₁.

Moving
Tapping the pulse, accent, or melodic rhythm.
Conducting $\frac{3}{4}$ while singing or playing.
Making a singing game. One child does selected motions for "this way and that" as the rest of the class imitates.

Playing Instruments
Playing the pulse, accent, or melodic rhythm on percussion instruments.
Playing the I and V7 chords on the autoharp while singing.

Reading
Identifying the highest and lowest pitches.
Discovering the meaning of $\frac{3}{4}$ meter.

Creating
Creating an ostinato to accompany the song.
Making up new words to the song.
   "Did you ever see a kangaroo . . . do this way and that."
   "Did you ever see a steam engine . . . do this way and that."

Example Two (middle elementary)

Initial Experience: Singing with the Books

I Caught a Rabbit

(Collected by Jean Thomas, The Traipsin' Woman)

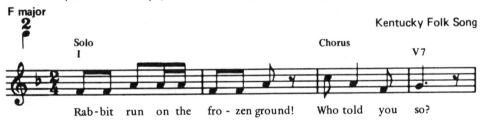

I caught a rab - bit, uh - huh! I caught a rab - bit, oh!

I = F A C
IV = B♭ D F
V7 = C E G B♭

Follow-up Experiences

Singing
Singing as a solo or chorus as indicated in the music.
Singing with hand signals. (five are used: *do, re, mi, fa, sol*)

Listening
Identifying the sequences.
Identifying the phrase length.

Moving
Dramatizing the story according to the solo or chorus parts.

Playing Instruments
Using autoharps to accompany with the I, IV, and V7 chords.
Playing pulse and accent on rhythm instruments.
Playing the *do–mi–sol (F–A–C)* pattern on resonator bells when it occurs in the music.
Playing one instrument on the solo part and a different one for the chorus parts (on the melodic rhythm).

Reading
Identifying patterns.

even   syncopated

Creating
Changing the words to fit other animals.

Example Three (upper elementary)
Initial Experience: Singing While Tapping the Melodic Rhythm

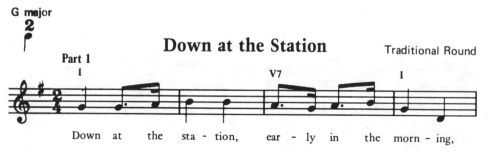

Down at the sta - tion, ear - ly in the morn - ing,

40

Part 2

See the lit - tle puf - fer - bil - lies lined up in a row.

See the en - gine dri - ver pull the lit - tle throt - tle.

Chug! Chug! Poof! Poof! Off we go.

I = G B D
V7 = D F♯ A C

Follow-up Experiences

Singing
Singing a two-part round.
Singing ostinato with the melody.
Singing the ostinato with the round.
Chording vocally on the I and V7 chords.

D → D
B → C
G → F♯

I   V7

Listening
Listening for the contour in each phrase and drawing it on paper.
Identifying the octave jumps in the melody.

Moving
Dramatizing a train with sound effects.

Playing Instruments
Playing the I and V7 chords on the autoharp, piano, guitar, or resonator bells.
Playing an ostinato.

Down at the Station . . .
. . . Off We Go

Chug! Chug!   Chug! Chug! and Poof! Poof!   See the lit - tle train

Easy ⟶ Medium ⟵ ⟶ Difficult

41

Reading
Identifying the patterns.

Creating
Creating an ostinato.
Creating an introduction and coda.

Creating a descant.

The point of departure does not always need to be a song. A teacher can also begin with a listening or reading experience and progress to other activities. Take care in choosing material so that several objectives can be developed and many lessons sequenced.

The following lesson plan incorporates all the points discussed in this chapter.

Lesson Plan

Grade Level
Early elementary

Equipment
A beret, a sombrero, an Alpine hat

Material
Song: "How Would You Say Hello?" from *The Magic of Music Series,* Book I

How Would You Say Hello?

Doris Kellogg

Specific Program Objective
The children will sing unison songs with limited ranges.

Lesson Objectives
The children
    will sing "How Would You Say Hello?"
    will identify the two phrases in the song as a question–answer structure.
    will state three ways of saying hello.

Motivation
Putting the sombrero on, the teacher asks: "If I were wearing this hat, what country might I be from?" (Answers) "What about this hat?" (Beret—answers) "And this?"

(Alpine hat—answers) People from different countries say hello differently. Listen to this song and tell how three different people say hello.

Procedures

The teacher sings the song completely. The children answer question *(Bonjour, Buenos días, Guten Tag).* Then the children are asked to sing just the greeting—the last two notes. Then they are asked to answer the teacher's questions as it is done in the song.

> Teacher: "If you . . . ?"
> Class: "If I were . . ."

The teacher then points out or allows the class to discover that he or she is singing a musical question (antecedent) and they are providing the musical answer (consequent).

Evaluation

Did the children sing the song?
Did they identify the two phrases as a question–answer structure?
Did they state three ways of saying hello?

Follow-Up Lessons

The question is sung by half of the class, the answer given by the other half. Other languages are substituted.
"If you were a little (Italian, Chinese) boy/girl . . .?"

Exercises and Activities

1. Plan a five-minute music lesson using only *one* activity (singing, listening, or moving). Use the form given above and complete it in detail.
2. Observe a thirty-minute lesson in an elementary school and fill in as much of the lesson-plan form as possible from your observation.
3. What five additional activities would you plan as follow-up lessons for the lesson you observed in Exercise 2? Why?

Key Terms and Concepts

Lesson plan   Motivation
Materials   Procedures
Equipment   Explanation
Specific program objective   Discovery
Lesson objective   Follow-up lessons
Pacing   Evaluation

Professional Readings

Cheyette, Irving, and Herbert Cheyette. *Teaching Music Creativity in the Elementary School.* New York: McGraw-Hill, 1969.
Runkle, Aleta, and Mary L. B. Erikson. *Music for Today: Elementary School Methods,* 3rd ed. Boston: Allyn and Bacon, 1976.

Motivating Children 5

Motivation is an inner drive that compels an individual to want to do something—to eat, to move, to reason, to learn. The teacher triggers something in the student that makes him or her want to learn. Initiating this desire is the essence of good teaching.

Schoolchildren are motivated to learn for three reasons: (1) *Intrinsic* motivation prompts learning because of the satisfaction found in the process. People learn to play tennis or soccer because they enjoy sports. (2) *Extrinsic* motivation induces learning because of rewards that come at the end of the learning task. Studying to master a bar exam and become a lawyer or to pass a course to receive a college degree and obtain a good job are both examples of extrinsic motivation. (3) *Extraneous* motivation prompts learning because of the payoff that comes at the end. The grade of *A*, the star on the memorized piano piece, or the material benefits of being a successful and well-paid lawyer are all examples of extraneous motivation.

Children learn for a variety of reasons. Rarely is motivation entirely intrinsic, extrinsic, or extraneous. Within one classroom children do what they do for a variety of reasons. It could be an interest in the process (intrinsic), the product (extrinsic), or the payoff (extraneous). A variety of motivation is necessary if most children are to be reached most of the time.

Music has a natural motivating quality because it deals with sound. Children enjoy music since they can participate through singing, playing instruments, and moving. It provides a welcome relief from those subjects involving only sitting and reading. Music challenges children, while past success and present competence will encourage them. An enthusiastic, well-organized teacher who has a positive attitude will spark children's interest. Although each of these situations may be motivating, there is no guarantee that it necessarily *will* be. Success does cultivate interest; conversely, past failure fosters present lack of interest and apathy. If children have had poor musical experiences, the task of making music exciting is not easy. A teacher may have to counteract negative attitudes established over several years.

Providing Motivation in Lesson Plans

If the teacher exhibits enthusiasm for whatever is to be done, the class usually captures this enthusiasm. Nonetheless, in a specific music lesson it is still imperative that a segment of the lesson plan be devoted to motivation. It is very important for the new teacher to develop this skill, since captivating a young audience and leading them through the learning task is a basic teaching skill.

Although intrinsic motivation is highly desirable, most of the motivation described here is extrinsic. Intrinsic motivation develops through successful, meaningful music experiences—which may never happen if extrinsic motivation is not used first. No teacher should be afraid of using props: there often must be a sense of drama in the classroom. Teachers who can portray moods and stage learning events to achieve worthwhile educational objectives are undoubtedly the most successful.

How is motivation structured for a music lesson? Good extrinsic motivation establishes for the musical task to be achieved a mental set that flows smoothly into the lesson procedure. Several examples will suffice to develop ideas concerning motivation.

Example One

Objective
The children will sing "Bingo."

I = G B D
IV = C E G
V7 = D F♯ A C

Possible Motivation
Five cards or sheets, each with one of the following letters on it: GBNOI.
"What words could be spelled using some or all of the letters on these cards?"
Children may suggest words aloud or write their combinations individually on a
sheet of paper. The teacher says, "In this song, listen to the name of the dog
spelled from these letters." Lesson moves into procedures. Children discover the
name is "Bingo."

Alternative Motivation
The teacher shows a picture of a dog and says his name has five letters in it.
"What might be his name?" Possible suggestions could be Rover or Henry.
"Listen to the song and see what the farmer called his dog." Lesson moves into
procedures.

Example Two

Objective
Children will sing "Sally Go Round the Sun."

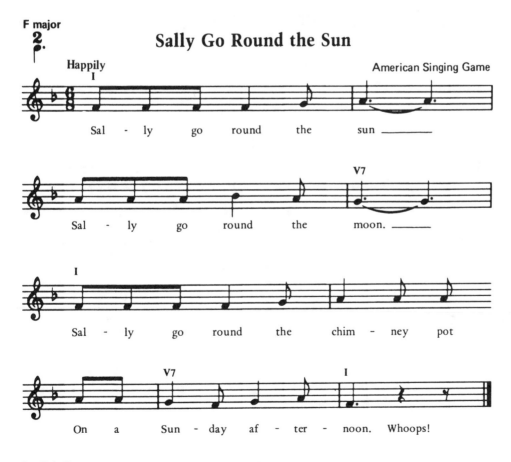

F major
2.

Sally Go Round the Sun

Happily   American Singing Game

Sal - ly go round the sun _____

Sal - ly go round the moon. _____

Sal - ly go round the chim - ney pot

On a Sun - day af - ter - noon. Whoops!

I = F A C
V7 = C E G B♭

Possible Motivation
The teacher holds three pictures—of the sun, moon, and a chimneypot. "What do we have here?" Students respond. Teacher says "Listen to the song and let's place the pictures in the order in which they occur in the song." Lesson moves into procedures.

Example Three

Objective
Children will sing "Make New Friends" and identify the line notation that matches each of four sections in the song.

I = E♭ G B♭

Possible Motivation
Four visuals in line notation are presented in scrambled order to represent part of the melody "Make New Friends" (on chart, transparency, or chalkboard).

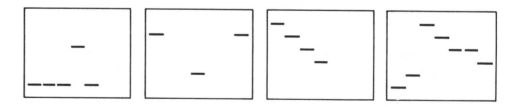

Children are asked to place the four visuals in the proper order as the teacher sings the song. (*Answer: 2–4–1–3.*)

Example Four

Objective
Children will identify three rhythmic patterns used in "Are You Sleeping?"

Are You Sleeping?
(Frère Jacques)

I = G B D

Possible Motivation

The teacher tells the class to echo clap, but to remember one of three patterns that will be repeated several times during the activity. Or students may write these three patterns ⎹⎹⎹⎹ ⎹⎹⎹𝄾 ⊓⊓⎹⎹ on the chalkboard. Using the three patterns, the teacher shows the chart. The children are asked to decipher the "mystery tune." Once the mystery is solved, the lesson procedure continues.

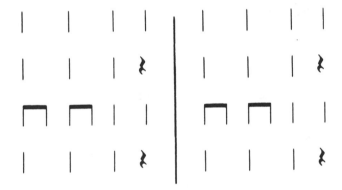

Example Five

Objective
Children will state three ways pitch is controlled on string instruments.

Possible Motivation

The teacher has a guitar and asks children to state from looking at it what is alike and different about the strings. (Alike? Same length and material. Different? Diameter or thickness.) Teacher then asks class to look for differences and similarities on the basis of sound as strings are played. (Differences? Pitch. Similarities? Guitar sound or timbre.) Teacher asks what can be concluded about pitch on a string instrument (Answer? Determined by diameter of strings.)
(NOTE: This example really has no clear dividing line between motivation and procedures, which may be true for many types of lessons of a discovery nature.)

Example Six

Objective
The children will aurally and verbally identify the meaning of piano (*p*) and forte (*f*) in written music.

Possible Motivation

The teacher asks the class to count as the numbers 1 through 10 are written on the chalkboard. The children are told to clap for each number, first loud, then soft. The teacher then says she or he has a way to show that some claps will be loud, others soft. The following diagram is placed on the chalkboard and performed by the teacher:

1   2   3   4   5   6   7   8   9   10

f ——————— *p* ————— *f*   *p*

The children then discuss which symbol means loud (*f*) and which is soft (*p*). Another group of symbols is written and performed by students. Many different patterns can be provided for additional practice.

1   2   3   4   5   6   7   8   9   10

p — *f* — *p*   *f*   *p* ———— *f*

Lesson moves into procedures in which children look at a song in a series book, find the *f*s and *p*s, and then perform the song accordingly.

Example Seven

Objective

Children will aurally identify the sections of a simple rondo form presented in a recording.

Possible Motivation

The teacher asks the children to clap possible rhythm patterns in $\frac{4}{4}$ time; some are placed on the chalkboard at the teacher's suggestion.

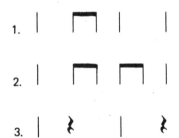

The teacher or students arrange the patterns to create a rondo in ABACA form:
1. repeated four times = A
2. repeated four times = B
3. repeated four times = C

The children perform the rondo, using different timbres for each section. The teacher then tells the class they will listen to a rondo on a recording which has a similar form:

A ? ? ? ? ? ?

Lesson moves into procedures.

Example Eight

Objective

Children will aurally distinguish between monophonic and homophonic textures.

Possible Motivation
The teacher selects several visuals with one person, but some with a background, others with no background at all.
Teacher asks, "What do these pictures have in common?" (Answer—all of people.) "How do they differ?" (Answer—people are young, old, have different facial expressions, some have things in background, others don't.) Pictures are then grouped into those with foreground only, those with a foreground and background. The teacher then explains how music can be all foreground (monophonic) or foreground and background (homophonic) and lesson continues into procedures for listening to several examples.

Example Nine

Objective
The children will state the exact timbres heard in the foreground while listening to a recording (jazz, rock, pop, classical).

Possible Motivation
A variety of visuals is displayed, each representing a musical instrument. Students are asked by teacher to find the ——— (trumpet, bassoon, and so on) and to tell something about it (it has three valves and uses mutes, or it has a double reed and is considered a woodwind). Teacher then asks students to listen to the recording and volunteer to pick out the instruments heard as recording is played. Lesson moves into procedures.

Example Ten

Objective
The students will create a sound picture, working in small groups according to directions on recipe cards.

Possible Motivation
Teacher: "Today I have some recipes on cards. Unlike many recipes, however, these are not for food but for sound pictures or compositions." Reads one.

> "Take two rhythm instruments, one classroom object that is not ordinarily an instrument, and one human voice to create a one-minute composition in which *accelerando* is demonstrated. One person in the group may be chosen to be the conductor."

"Working in groups of four or five, each group will have fifteen minutes to prepare its composition before we perform them for the rest of the class." Cards are then handed out to small groups and the lesson moves into procedures.

The motivation for a lesson can be provided in many ways, through pictures, charts, echo clapping, puzzles, playing instruments, looking for similarities and differences, discovering relationships, arranging and manipulating visuals, or solving musical problems through visual or aural observation. Motivation is created not by *what* is used but *how* it is used. It occurs at the beginning of a lesson but must continue throughout a lesson as well. The extrinsic motivation described here develops eventually into a love of learning music—that is, into intrinsic motivation. The teacher may be able to rely more on intrinsic motivation as the year progresses and the children become comfortable with and competent in music.

Exercises and Activities

1. Observe a thirty-minute music lesson in an elementary school. Was there any extraneous motivation? How effective was it? What devices were used as extrinsic motivation? How effective were they? How could they have been used more effectively? Was there any evidence of intrinsic motivation? How could you tell?

2. Plan the motivation for a music lesson similar to those described in Objectives 1 through 10 in this chapter. Describe or collect the actual materials you would use. List questions and possible responses you might include in your motivation.

Key Terms and Concepts

Intrinsic motivation

Extrinsic motivation

Extraneous motivation

Ostinato

Forte (*f*)

Piano (*p*)

Rondo

Foreground–background

Monophonic texture

Homophonic texture

Accelerando

Professional Reading

Hilgard, Ernest R., ed. *Theories of Learning and Instruction.* Chicago: University of Chicago Press, 1964.

PART THREE

Musical Experiences

Singing in Unison

6

Singing was once considered *the* total elementary music program. It is now seen as one of many vital activities within an ideal music program. The ability to sing and to be comfortable with one's singing voice is as vital a skill as learning to read and write.

Singing is an important activity in elementary school for several reasons. First, the voice is an instrument everyone possesses and is thus a good way for children to experience music. Second, developing the singing voice is as much a physical skill as learning to speak, to walk, or to write, and its neglect is a grave omission. Third, singing is a pleasurable activity that may be done individually or in a group. Finally, singing is a social skill. There are numerous occasions in life when singing is appropriate. It certainly is a skill that should not be neglected in the public schools.

There is no single way to teach singing. Children generally sing quite naturally when given the opportunity and if the teacher does not make them feel uncomfortable about it. Their voices should be light and pleasant, not gravelly and heavy or forcefully loud. The teacher should lead children to see the difference between speaking, in which the vowel is not sustained, and singing, in which the vowel *is* sustained and lengthened by the voice.

When children sing out of tune, it is for various reasons. Children may not have had enough experience singing to match the exact tones in any melody. Possibly they have not heard the song enough to know how it should be. More experience with singing will help get them in tune. Visual reinforcement (such as higher or lower hand levels) of the melody often helps. While the teacher sings "Kum Ba Yah," his or her hands are moving thus:

Kum Ba

Yah, My Lord, Yah.

Ba

Kum

When children respond, their hands should also move to levels that represent the highs and lows of the melody. Line notation is also a good visual reinforcement. Seeing "high" and "low" helps children place their voices.

Criteria for Selecting Songs

The following criteria for selecting songs in the elementary school are important if children are to enjoy singing and to be successful at it.

Subject Matter

The subject matter must be appropriate for the given grade level. First-graders enjoy nursery rhymes and songs about animals; these would be totally inappropriate for fourth- or fifth-graders, where cowboy and work songs have more appeal. Series books generally do a good job of including the appropriate subject matter in songs for each grade.

Vocabulary

The vocabulary should be appropriate for the grade level. If most of the words of a song have to be explained to the children, the vocabulary is obviously beyond them. One or two new words are enough for a valuable language experience.

Musical Interest

The song should have enough musical interest to be a meaningful and worthwhile singing experience: in other words, it should be singable. It should have a melodic quality that lends itself to the singing voice, as well as interesting rhythms. Many traditional folk songs have stood the test of time because they are singable. Use a wide variety of songs—lullabies, chanteys, spirituals, camp songs, singing games—to provide a rich exposure for the children.

Musical Structure

The song's musical structure should be appropriate for the age level. Several factors are important here:

Range and Tessitura *Range* is the difference between the highest and lowest tone. *Tessitura* is the average position of the notes. Generally, children's voices expand from a narrow range of notes in lower elementary to a comfortable range slightly in excess of one octave by the upper years. Since many children in the lower grades can sing the descending minor third between g and e above middle c naturally and comfortably, this is a core range from which songs can be selected. This area also represents a good tessitura for all elementary song choices.

For the lower grades, many of the notes in a chosen song should fall within the range between A and d, although there will be notes in a song that exceed this. Many children in the lower grades can easily sing songs with an octave range. For the middle years, the range can be expanded to an octave, c to c^1, with the infrequent use of higher or lower notes. The tessitura should nevertheless remain around the g or a. By the upper grades, the range will easily exceed the c to c^1 octave, with the tessitura remaining around g or a. In Europe, children's songs are pitched higher, while in the United States there is a general tendency for people to sing lower than necessary. The teacher may find these ranges a bit high, but should use the range given in the songbook rather than lower it constantly.

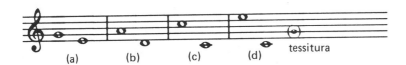

Phrase Length   The *phrase length* should be appropriate for the grade level. Young children need songs with shorter phrases (two to four measures) than those for older children. Phrase length, however, is a function of tempo. If the song has a fast tempo, it is possible to sing a somewhat longer musical phrase.

Conjunct and Disjunct Movement   Melodies that move in stepwise fashion are *conjunct*; those that skip or leap are *disjunct*. It is advisable to use many songs that are mostly conjunct with children who have limited vocal experience. Disjunct melodies are suitable for older or more experienced children.

Syllabic and Melismatic Melodies   *Syllabic* songs are those in which there is one distinct pitch in the melody for each distinct syllable in the text. *Melismatic* songs are those in which there are several pitches for one syllable. Syllabic songs are easier to sing and represent a better choice for inexperienced singers. In the upper grades melismatic songs may be chosen.

Contour   *Contour* is the direction of the melody. Typical and logically direct contours include songs that start high and fall, start low and work to a high point, or combine both qualities, low to high to low, or high to low to high. Another contour is one that circles around a central note. There are other contours that are more intricate than these. For younger children, choose a song with a very direct, logical type of contour that is remembered easily.

Key   The *key* of the song is not a limiting factor in the selection of a song, although some keys are good for the teacher since they are played easily on the piano or guitar. In the selection of songs, however, it is most important to consider how the notes are arranged within the key. Usually, notes are distributed within a key in one of two ways: from low *do* to high *do* or from low *sol* to high *sol* (with *do* in the middle).

The key of C would be a reasonable choice if the range of the notes were like Example A but probably not acceptable if arranged like Example B. Other keys which are appropriate if arranged from *do* to *do'* include D and E♭.

The keys of F and G may be too high for some upper elementary students if arranged this way:

but perfectly acceptable if arranged this way:

Key is not a totally limiting factor since any song can easily be transposed to a suitable key. Many folk, camp, and traditional songs are sung unaccompanied; in this case the tonality may be adjusted for the group if the original key is too high or too low. When an accompaniment is used, chord symbols can be adjusted easily to the desired key and pitch level. Nonetheless, the original key and its arrangement should be a consideration when choosing a song. If transposition is not possible by ear and chord symbol, it can take a great deal of time for the beginner to accomplish.

The Song Index lists many songs which are used throughout this book. It classifies songs suitable for classroom music and gives additional information—key, scale, and meter as well as chords used. It will be valuable in finding appropriate songs as well as for lessons in other musical activities.

To summarize the points above, the following songs are analyzed to see for which level each would be suitable.

Example One
"Shoo, Fly, Don't Bother Me"

F major

Billy Reeves

Shoo, Fly, Don't Bother Me

Frank Campbell

Shoo, fly, don't both - er me, Shoo, fly, don't both - er me,

Shoo, fly, don't both - er me, For I be - long to some - bod - y.

1. I feel, I feel, I feel, I feel like a morn - ing star, I

feel, I feel, I feel, I feel like a morn - ing star.

2. I feel, I feel, I feel, I feel, like my mother said,
   Like angels pouring 'lasses down on my little head.

I = F A C
V7 = C E G Bb

Range   Tessitura

Subject Matter
The nonsense words would appeal to third- or fourth-graders. Since this is a Civil War song, it would also have appeal to grades that study American history, possibly fifth and sixth.

Vocabulary
None of the words would be difficult for the lower grades.

Musical Interest
The use of sequences (bars 1 and 2 are repeated on lower pitches in bars 3 and 4) and the syncopation (♪♩♪) and uneven pattern (♫♩) give this song much rhythmic interest.

Structure
Range
Phrase length: four bars

Generally conjunct except for the jump from middle c to g or a in the verse. There are some half steps.

All syllabic—one note per syllable.

Contour

Chorus: ⌇⌇→ revolves around same notes.

Verse: ⟋⟋→ jumps up and stays around the same level.

Key of F is used as in Example B, low *sol* to high *sol,* with *do* in the middle.

This song has a universal appeal because of its nonsensical nature. The range is not too wide for very young children although the jump from middle C to G or A is wide. It is also appropriate for experienced singers in the middle or upper elementary grades.

Example Two

"Early One Morning"

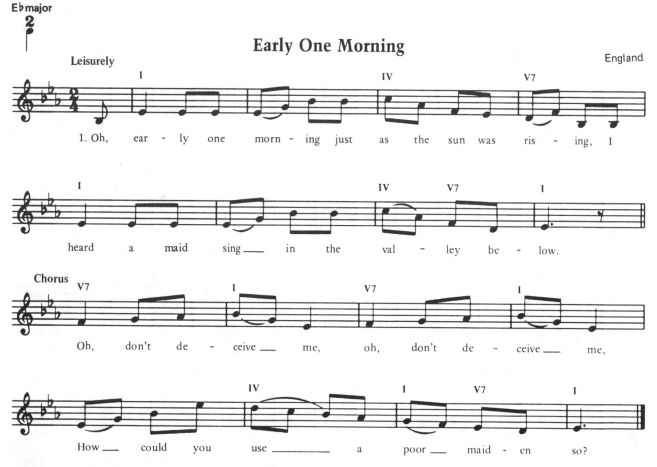

Early One Morning

2. Remember the promise you made to your loved one,
   Remember the place where you promised to be true.

3. Oh, fresh is the garland, and lovely the roses
   I've picked from the garden to lay at your feet.

4. So sang the sweet maiden, her sadness bewailing,
   Thus sang the poor maid in the valley below.

I = Eb G Bb
IV = Ab C Eb
V7 = Bb D F Ab

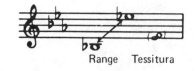

Range   Tessitura

60

Subject Matter

The sentimental references make this suitable for the upper grades.

Vocabulary

A few words might need explanation (*garland, bewailing, use*), but most of the words would present no problem.

Musical Interest

The bell-shaped contour ⌒↘ and occasional melismas give this a satis-fying musical quality.

Structure

Range is wide but the tessitura is in a good position.
Phrases are four bars in length sometimes with a fast pick-up note.
There are many skips in this song, although they are balanced with more conjunct passages.
The text is generally syllabic with an occasional slight melisma on words such as *morning, rising, sing*.
The contour is ⌇ for every phrase or part of the phrase.
Key is E♭ Major, used from low *sol* to high *do*. Because of its vocabulary, subject matter, and complex musical structure, this song is definitely for experienced singers, probably children in the upper elementary grades.

Strategies for Presenting Songs

In singing lessons, the song may be presented entirely by rote, in which the children learn both the words and the notes from listening. In other cases, words may be presented on the chalkboard, a chart, or a transparency. Or the teacher may present the song as the children see the music in a book.

Many songs will be taught by rote, particularly in the lower grades. There are five methods for presenting a rote singing lesson: (1) The *whole-method* and the (2) *part-method* are traditional procedures, which may be combined with the use of a (3) *recording* or a (4) *melody instrument;* (5) the *rote-note* is another strategy.

Whole Method

In the whole method, the entire song is heard several times. Gradually the children sing along. Simple, short and repetitive songs lend themselves nicely to the whole method. "Pawpaw Patch" is such an example.

61

dear lit - tle Ma - ry? Way down yon - der in the paw - paw patch.
(John - ny)

I = F A C
V7 = C E G B♭

Motivation
Pictures of famous people for which children are asked to identify these person's first names.

Procedure
"Listen to this song and see what this person's first name is." (Mary) "Listen again and see whose name I use this time." Teacher sings again using someone's name in the class. Class decides who. "Let's all sing this time. Whose name shall I use?"

Each time the teacher sings the song, there should be a new reason for listening. Difficult songs require several repetitions.

Part Method
The whole method is a logical way to present a rote song, since it moves quickly and easily when the song is simple. When songs have difficult words or phrases, the *part method* is an alternative. The song is first presented in its entirety by the teacher. Each phrase is then sung by the teacher and echoed by the class.

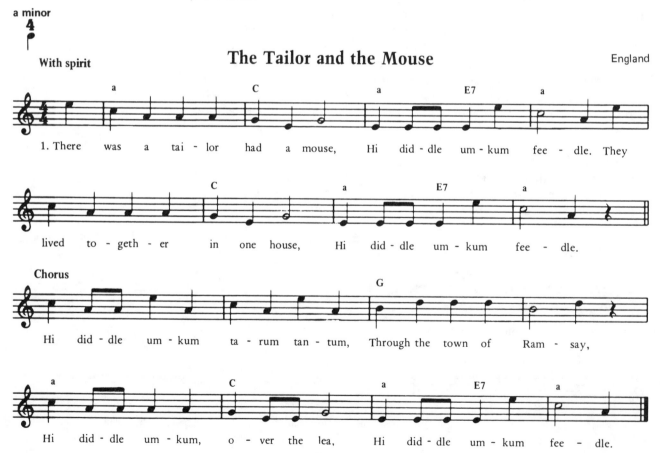

The Tailor and the Mouse

England

a minor

With spirit

1. There was a tai - lor had a mouse, Hi did - dle um - kum fee - dle. They lived to - geth - er in one house, Hi did - dle um - kum fee - dle.

Chorus

Hi did - dle um - kum ta - rum tan - tum, Through the town of Ram - say,

Hi did - dle um - kum, o - ver the lea, Hi did - dle um - kum fee - dle.

2. The tailor thought the mouse was ill,
   Hi diddle umkum feedle,
   Because he took an awful chill,
   Hi diddle umkum feedle.

3. The tailor thought his mouse would die,
   Hi diddle umkum feedle,
   And so he baked him in a pie,
   Hi diddle umkum feedle.

4. He cut the pie, the mouse ran out,
   Hi diddle umkum feedle,
   The mouse was in a terrible pout,
   Hi diddle umkum feedle.

5. The tailor gave him catnip tea,
   Hi diddle umkum feedle,
   Until a healthy mouse was he,
   Hi diddle umkum feedle.

a (i) = A C E
E7 (V7) = E G♯ B D
C = C E G
G = G B D

Motivation

Words that make no sense are presented on board (*tix, pbt, dupd*). Children are asked to write a few more nonsense words.

Procedure

"What are the nonsense words in this song?" Teacher sings entire song and the class answers the question. Then the part method is used. The teacher sings phrase 1; the class echoes without pausing. This procedure for phrase 2, then 1 and 2 combined; 3, 4, and 3 and 4 combined; and then for the entire song.

The part method should move quickly and naturally. Children can be trained to respond immediately after the teacher sings. Once mastered, this procedure is easily assimilated into subsequent rote songs. Children should always hear the *entire* song first before they learn separate phrases. They should always sing the entire song at the *conclusion* of the lesson.

Use of a Recording

A third method employs a recording or tape. Many music series have excellent sound recordings for the songs found in their books. This procedure may be combined effectively with the whole method. There is little change except that the teacher should mouth the words as the children listen to the recording. This provides the same visual-aural reinforcement as when the teacher sings the song.

F major

Hush, Little Baby

Serenely

U.S.

1. Hush, lit - tle ba - by, don't say a word, Dad - dy's gon - na buy you a

mock - ing bird, And if that mock - ing bird won't sing,

Dad - dy's gon - na buy you a dia - mond ring. 2. (And)

2. And if that diamond ring turns to brass,
   Daddy's gonna buy you a looking glass,
   And if that looking glass gets broke,
   Daddy's gonna buy you a billy goat.

3. And if that billy goat won't pull,
   Daddy's gonna buy you a cart and bull,
   And if that cart and bull turn over,
   Daddy's gonna buy you a dog named Rover.

4. And if that dog named Rover won't bark,
   Daddy's gonna buy you a horse and cart.
   And if that horse and cart fall down,
   You'll still be the sweetest little baby in town.

I = F A C
V7 = C E G B♭

Motivation

"If you had a crying baby, what might you give it to quiet it?"
   Children supply various answers.
"Listen to this song. What is the daddy going to give to the baby to hush it? Let's list these as we listen."

Procedure

The teacher draws or writes on the chalkboard as the record plays.

> Mockingbird
> Diamond ring
> Looking glass
> Billy goat
> Cart and bull
> Dog named "Rover"
> Horse and cart

"Let's all sing now that we know."
The record is repeated. The children follow the words or pictures and sing along.

Use of a Melody Instrument

A fourth method is to use a melody instrument. The soprano recorder or song bells are good choices. This method is similar to the part method. The teacher plays one phrase on the recorder after which the children are asked to hum the phrase back. The teacher plays the phrase again and the children are asked to put the words to the melody; this continues for each phrase until the entire song is learned and reassembled.

Motivation

"As I play this song on the recorder, count the number of breaths I take. This will tell us the number of phrases."
The teacher plays. The children identify four phrases.

D major
3

Edwin Star Belknap

Tyrolese Melody

The Hummingbird

Stay, pret - ty hum - ming bird, Whis - per your se - cret;

Say, pret - ty hum - ming bird, Have you no song?

What do you tell to the rose in the dell?_____ Oh,

Say, pret - ty hum - ming bird, Have you no song?

I = D F♯A
IV = G B D
V7 = A C♯E G

Procedure

"As I play again, tell which phrases are alike, similar or different from Phrase 1."
    Answer Phrase 2 is similar, 3 is different, 4 is similar (and like Phrase 2). Hum Phrase 1 as I play and graph it with hand levels. Put these words with Phrase 1 and sing this time: "Stay, pretty hummingbird, Whisper your secret." (This procedure is repeated for the second, third, and fourth phrases until the entire song is learned.)

Rote-Note Method

The rote note method, which involves using a songbook while presenting a rote song, is suitable for children in the middle and upper elementary as well as for mature children in the lower elementary grades. Basically, the children follow the words and melody in their individual books as the teacher sings it. Or it may involve using the whole or part method, a recording, or a melody instrument. The only difference from the other methods is that the children will have the songbook in which to follow the words and music.

Using books provides heightened motivation. Children in the early elementary years are excited by music books. They enjoy looking at the pictures as well as the musical notation and words. Modern series books are very attractive, and the teacher should allow children to explore the book before they must find a specific page and song. The children must have certain basic skills before they use books. Can they read language? Do they understand that English is read left to right? Do they know numbers well enough to find a page? (It is always advisable to write a page number on the chalkboard besides giving it verbally.) Do they understand that the words to a song are under the staff? that in a song with two or more verses you must skip to the appropriate line (second line in each group in the second verse). Do they understand the use of repeats? Time must be taken to develop these skills or both the students and teacher will be frustrated.

The use of books and all equipment in a music lesson requires some type of efficient distribution and collection. Children can assume responsibility for passing out books before the class as well as picking them up afterward. When the books are not being used, they should be placed under the chair or to one side on the desktop.

All five procedures for rote singing have strengths and weaknesses. All may be used with numerous adaptations. The key to effective procedures in singing or any other activity is to provide variety. Variation heightens motivation.

Following are additional points to remember for all types of singing lessons:

1. The children should hear the song several times before they are asked to respond (tap, hum, sing, move) unless the song is extremely simple. Each time they listen to the song, whether sung by the teacher, played on a recorder, or heard on a phonograph, there should be a new reason for listening.
2. The children should be aware of the starting pitch and tempo before they respond. The pitch framework can be sounded by the voice, recorder, or piano. This includes sounding the beginning pitch, the keynote (if different) and the tonic chord. The pulse should be tapped or the teacher may simply say, "One—two—ready, begin." In the event there is a rhythmic pick-up note (anacrusis), counting should reflect the upbeat.
3. Do not play the melody on the piano and sing with it simultaneously. The instrument tends to cover the voice. Use the piano, guitar, ukulele, or autoharp to accompany the song; this provides a harmonic framework to keep the voices in tune. It is much more musically satisfying, thus heightening intrinsic motivation.
4. Avoid drilling on words without music except in those rare cases where the words are extremely difficult to articulate in the song. This separates words from music and the class becomes a lesson in poetic recitation, not singing.
5. Children can respond in various ways as they learn a song, including tapping, humming, graphing with hand levels, or playing rhythm instruments. A variety of techniques should be used by all music educators.

The children may follow the words and music in a songbook.
The children may join in on a repeated passage.
The children may tap the pulse, accents, or melodic rhythm as the teacher sings or plays.
The children may graph the melody with hand levels.
The children may add instruments as the song allows (harmony instruments such as the autoharp).
The children may hum or whistle the melody.

Singing lessons are always fresh and new when the teacher searches for the best motivation and procedure for presenting a song.

CHART 6–1   Objectives for Singing

	Children will
Early elementary (K–2)	sing unison songs with limited ranges sing simple pentatonic songs imitate phrases sing simple rounds and ostinati sing simple partner songs (I chord) sing echo songs sing conjunct intervals (with the exception of the half step) sing chordal patterns (do–mi–sol) match pitches echo tonal patterns
Middle elementary (3–4)	sing songs with wider ranges sing with good tone, diction, and breath support sing in tune and stay in the key sing independently sing advanced rounds sing advanced partner songs sing descants and two-part harmony sing disjunct intervals as well as half steps sing a wide variety of songs
Upper elementary (5–6)	sing songs with expanded ranges in a musically expressive style sing with a great deal of independence, both as a group and individually sing three-part harmony sing harmony by ear chord vocally sing in an appropriate style, including attention to articulation, phrasing, and dynamics

Specific Program Objectives for Singing

Chart 6–1 is a model list of specific program objectives for singing in the elementary school, listed by age levels. This is inclusive for both unison and harmony (Chapter 7) singing. From top to bottom, it represents a rough time line for each objective, not a rigid checklist. Since children's vocal ranges expand as they grow older and develop their singing ability, initial singing experiences should have limited ranges. By the fifth or sixth grade, however, they are able to sing songs with expanded ranges. In the same sense, it is obvious that they should sing unison songs before they sing "descant" or "chord vocally." This list is not a rigid formulation of what *must* occur at any point in the elementary school but what *may* occur with consistent instruction. Achievement depends on the skill level of a class as well as that class's prior experience. Children in the sixth grade who cannot match pitches are obviously not able to sing three-part harmony. The realization of all these objectives by the end of the sixth grade depends upon consistent overall instruction throughout elementary school.

The Problem Singer

Who is the problem singer? Some children do not learn to sing as easily as others. Sometimes they apparently cannot move their voices from one pitch to another. These children are best called *conversational singers*. They stay on one or two pitches and simply "speak" the rhythm of the song.

Other children are *directional singers*. They are able to follow the con-

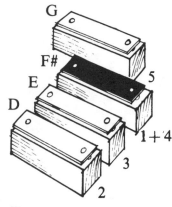

Tum-tum-tum-tum-tum

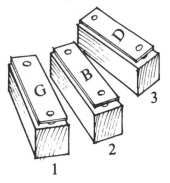

Here we come!

tour of a melody with their voices, moving up or down as needed, but not on the correct pitch nor at the correct interval. Other children sing in tune most of the time but have problems singing certain passages or matching particularly high or low notes. Most of these problems are corrected as the children gain confidence and experience in singing.

Few problems in singing are due to a faulty voice mechanism. When this occurs, the teacher should refer the child to a therapist. If a hearing impairment is suspected, a specialist should also be consulted.

Most problems with singing occur for one of three reasons: (1) The child has a poor sense of pitch. He or she cannot tell high from low, is unable to place his or her voice, or cannot move from note to note correctly. He or she needs help in finding his or her voice and in matching it to pitches in a song. (2) The child has a poor self-concept and will not risk singing for fear of failure. (He or she possibly may have been discouraged earlier by another teacher or a parent.) (3) The child has not been sufficiently motivated to sing.

Many of these problems may be corrected by the teacher with some patience and special techniques, either individually or within the context of the normal class. However, the child should not be identified to the class as a problem singer.

The following techniques are useful:

1. Isolate the parts of a familiar song and repeat them, reinforcing certain tonal patterns with the resonator bells. Encourage the problem singers to play as they sing.

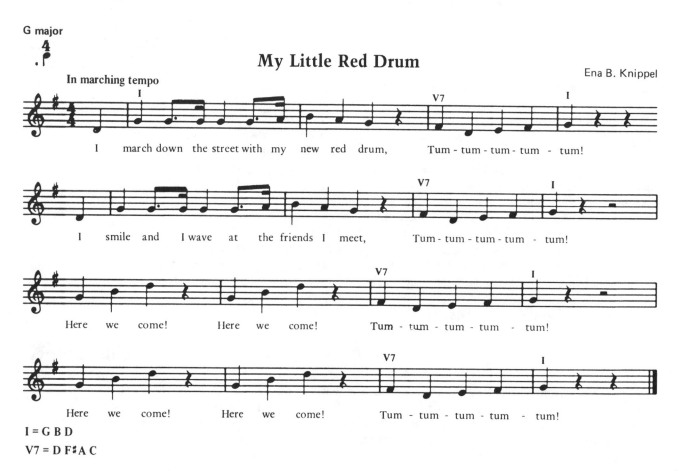

G major

My Little Red Drum

Ena B. Knippel

In marching tempo

I march down the street with my new red drum, Tum - tum - tum - tum - tum!

I smile and I wave at the friends I meet, Tum - tum - tum - tum - tum!

Here we come! Here we come! Tum - tum - tum - tum - tum!

Here we come! Here we come! Tum - tum - tum - tum - tum!

I = G B D

V7 = D F♯ A C

2. Use visual devices and body movement to show the melodic contour and progression of the tonal patterns or of the entire song.

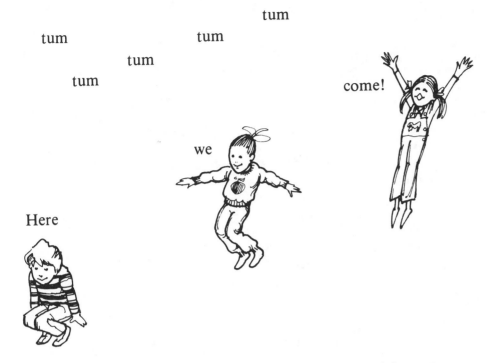

tum

tum   tum

      tum

tum

come!

we

Here

The children can move their hands or their bodies up and down. Patterns may be represented on the chalkboard in line notation.

3. Use songs that have many repeated verses, such as simple ballads, like "Mister Frog Went A Courtin'." Isolate characteristic patterns to chant or to repeat on the resonator bells.

4. Use tone matching in many ways.
   The descending minor third of *sol–mi* (G–E) can be used to improvise a call and response pattern with individuals or small or large groups:

Um-hm!

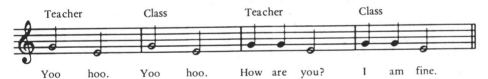

Teacher	Class	Teacher	Class
Yoo hoo.	Yoo hoo.	How are you?	I am fine.

Problem singers must not be singled out for remedial help in front of the entire group. Their needs should be met within the context of the lesson.

5. Echo singing may be incorporated with echo clapping:

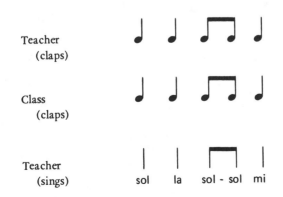

Teacher (claps)

Class (claps)

Teacher (sings)   sol   la   sol - sol   mi

high do¹ or 8¹

ti or 7

la or 6

sol or 5

fa or 4

mi or 3

re or 2

low do or 1

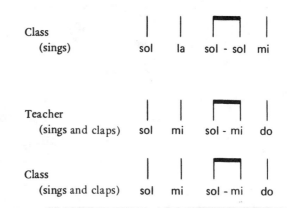

Class (sings)	sol	la	sol - sol	mi
Teacher (sings and claps)	sol	mi	sol - mi	do
Class (sings and claps)	sol	mi	sol - mi	do

6. A nursery rhyme or poem may be sung on *sol–mi* with the pitch indicated by hand levels:

Teacher's hand   *sol*   *sol*

     mi   *mi*
Humpty Dumpty sat on a wall.

sol

   mi   *mi*   *mi*
Humpty Dumpty had a great fall.

     sol   *sol*

mi   *mi*
All the King's horses and all the King's men,

sol   *sol*

     mi   *mi*
Couldn't put Humpty together again!

Additional pitches can be added as the children gain skill. Children can also lead this activity in small groups.

7. Hand signals can be used to designate pitches while a nursery rhyme or poem is sung:

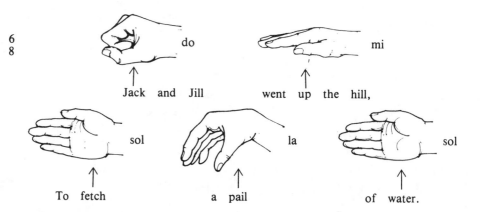

82

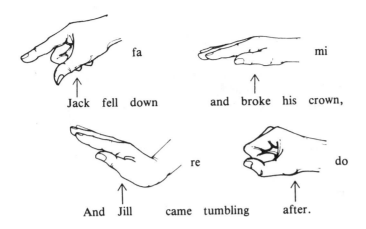

fa   mi

Jack fell down   and broke his crown,

re   do

And Jill came tumbling   after.

8. The children may whistle, hum, or sing on a neutral syllable such as *la* or *loo* instead of singing the words.
9. Tempos may be slowed to facilitate pitch placement and concentration.
10. The teacher, using discretion, may place problem singers next to children who sing well or next to an accompanying instrument such as an autoharp or guitar.
11. The teacher should provide encouragement and many positive activities. Problem singers should never be singled out in front of their peers.

Exercises and Activities

1. With a specific grade level in mind, select a song and justify your choice according to the criteria established in this chapter.
2. Interview a music educator on criteria for selecting a song.
3. Find several songs suitable to use with the whole, part, recording, melody instrument or rote-note method.
4. Plan a specific lesson using one of the songs you chose in Exercise 3, detailing your motivation, objectives, and procedures.

Key Terms and Concepts

Hand levels
Range
Tessitura
Phrase
Conjunct and disjunct movement
Syllabic melody
Melismatic melody
Contour
Key

Rote songs
Whole method
Part method
Method using a recording
Method using a melody instrument
Rote-note method
Problem singer
Conversational singer
Directional singer

Professional Readings*

Dallin, Leon, and Lynn Dallin. *Heritage Songster*. Dubuque, Iowa: Wm. C. Brown, 1966.

Haines, B. Joan E., and Linda L. Gerber. *Leading Young Children to Music: A Resource Book for Teachers*. Columbus, Ohio: Charles E. Merrill, 1980.

Kodály, Zoltán. *Fifty Nursery Songs Within the Range of Five Notes; 333 Elementary Exercises* (tr. by Percy M. Young). Oceanside, N.Y.: Boosey & Hawkes, 1964 (English edition).

Metz, Donald. *Teaching General Music in Grades 6–9*. Columbus, Ohio: Charles E. Merrill, 1980.

Nye, Robert Evans, and Vernice Trousdale Nye. *Music in the Elementary School*, 4th ed. Englewood Cliffs, N.J.: Prentice-Hall, 1979.

Nye, Vernice. *Music for Young Children*, 2nd ed. Dubuque, Iowa: William C. Brown, 1979.

RCA Victor Basic Record Library for Elementary Schools. The Singing Program (one album each for primary, fourth, fifth, and sixth grades). N.Y.: RCA Victor Educational Sales.

Smith, Robert B. *Music in the Child's Education*. New York: The Ronald Press, 1970.

*For Chapters 6 and 7.

Experiences with Harmony

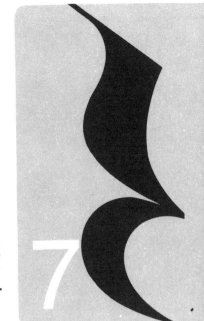

7

Singing in harmony is an exciting extension of singing and should occur soon after children are able to sing well in unison. Harmony singing was once reserved for the upper grades, but simple arrangements can be devised to provide the experience for younger children as well.

Normally, Western music has a homophonic texture, with one melody supported by an accompaniment:

Polyphonic textures, the use of two or more simultaneous melodies, can also be produced in the classroom through rounds and canons:

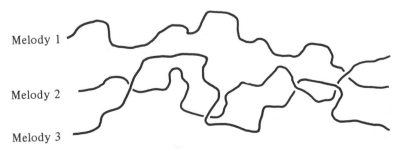

These two textures predominate in music of our culture. The added dimension of sound that results from harmony contributes to an overall aesthetic experience.

Harmony experiences suitable for classroom use include rounds and canons, chordal accompaniments and vocal chording, echo songs, partner songs, ostinati, and descants. Songs written in two-part or three-part harmony are excellent experiences for mature middle elementary and upper elementary children.

Rounds and Canons

A *canon* is a composition in which one melody is sung or played by different people or instruments at different times. If each group's melody is identical to those of the others, it is called a strict canon or a *round*. If the melody has been altered but is similar each time, it is termed an *imitative canon*. How-

ever, most early experiences in polyphony should be with rounds or strict canons.

Some rounds are entirely harmonized by one chord, the tonic of the key. Each part of the round is in harmony with the other parts at any point in time. "The Donkey," which is in the key of F major, is a good example. Since the

majority of notes in each measure are either F, A, or C, each bar can be harmonized with the I (F-A-C) chord. If the song is sung as a round at a two-measure interval, each part will be in harmony with the other parts.

F major

Round
Germany

Music Alone Shall Live

Moderately

Part 1

I   V7   I

All things shall per - ish un - der the sky;

Part 2

I   V7   I

Mu - sic a - lone shall live, Mu - sic a - lone shall live,

Part 3

V7   I

Mu - sic a - lone shall live, nev - er to die.

Himmel und Erde müssen vergehn:
Aber die Musica, aber die Musica,
Aber die Musica, bleiben bestehn.

I = F A C
V7 = C E G B♭

"Music Alone Shall Live" has a more complicated harmonic structure. The harmony is constructed in four-measure phrases. Therefore, the parts can enter only at four-measure intervals if the harmony is to remain clear. This song, which is in F Major, uses the I (F-A-C) and V7 (C-E-G-B♭) chords:

Line 1   I   V7   V7   I
Line 2   the same
Line 3   the same

Some guidelines for singing rounds are listed below:

1. Children should not be asked to sing any song as a round before they know it very well in unison. A round should seldom be attempted in the same lesson in which children learn it as a unison song; it should be used in the third or fourth lesson as a follow-up.

2. Use two parts in rounds at first and then gradually include three and four parts as the round allows. Definite cues such as an arm or head gesture should be given by the teacher to start each group.

3. Do not allow the singing of a round to become a contest between groups. Each part should listen to and enjoy the harmonic effect being created by the others, rather than try to sing louder.

4. Rounds collapse for two reasons. Either the children do not know it well enough in unison or a strict tempo is not maintained. If tempo is a problem, the children can clap lightly or tap their feet to maintain the beat as they sing.

5. Not every song can be sung as a round. A song's suitability depends on its harmonic structure. Most rounds are identified as such in the series books but teachers should understand how rounds work so that many strategies can be used in presentation.

Chordal Accompaniments and Vocal Chording

Another valid harmony lesson for all grades is to experience melody against its harmonic background. This results in a homophonic texture. Most simple melodies are harmonized with three chords: I, IV, and V7 (see Appendix I).

	syllables	numbers	in C Major
I (tonic chord)	*do–mi–sol'*	1–3–5	C–E–G
IV (subdominant chord)	*fa–la–do'*	4–6–8	F–A–C
V7 (dominant seventh chord)	*sol–ti–re–fa'*	5–7–2–4	G–B–D–F

These three chords may be sung or played on the autoharp, guitar, ukelele, piano, or resonator bells.

In the early elementary grades, this type of harmony lesson can be used with songs that are harmonized with one chord. "Little Tom Tinker" uses only the I chord (D–F♯–A). The song moves in ⁶⁄₈, so the chord could be played once or twice in a bar. The concepts of pulse and tempo are also reinforced in such an experience.

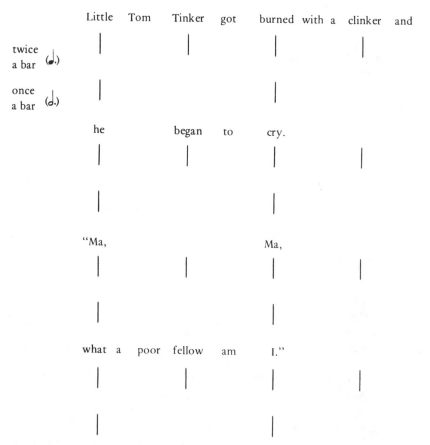

Resonator bells (D–F♯–A) may be passed out and some children can be chosen to play them. Other children might be able to play the chord on the autoharp. The piano can be used too, by having several children play one of the notes or assigning the entire chord to one child who has the coordination. This simple harmony experience can be used effectively in the early elementary grades as well as in the middle and upper grades. An experience of this complexity would obviously occur after the children had worked with the song in unison several times, not while they are learning it.

For additional experiences of this nature, particularly in the middle and upper elementary years, songs with two or three chords are appropriate. "He's Got the Whole World in His Hands" uses the I (F–A–C) and V7 (C–E–G–B♭) chords. Since the meter is $\frac{4}{4}$, the harmony can occur on each beat, every other beat, or possibly once in a measure.

F major
$\frac{4}{4}$

He's Got the Whole World in His Hands

Afro-American Spiritual

With conviction

(musical notation — verse 1)

1. He's got the whole world ___ in His hands,_ He's got the

possibilities (♩)

(♩)

(o)

whole world ___ in His hands,_ He's got the whole world ___

in His hands,_ He's got the whole world in His hands.

2. He's got the wind and rain in His hands.

3. He's got that little baby in His hands.

4. He's got you and me in His hands.

5. He's got everybody in His hands.

6. He's got the whole world in His hands.

I = F A C
V7 = C E G B♭

77

When autoharps are used, some children can be assigned the I chord, others the V7. They can be grouped on opposite sides of the room. Individual resonator bells can be assigned to students in a I or V7 group as well. The teacher can let children discover that the C bell plays in both chords. Children with particularly good coordination can play both chords on the autoharp or the piano. Guitars can be integrated in the same manner. This method accommodates individual differences.

Advanced experiences for upper grades include using songs with three chords (I, IV, and V7) or combining round singing with a chordal accompaniment. Vocal chording, singing the tones the resonator bells are playing, is another method. This is an advanced skill but provides an excellent harmony experience for older children. One group of children sings the melody while four additional groups provide the harmony, each group singing one note from the I, IV, and V7 chords. The I chord is used in root position while the other chords are used in inversion, enabling each harmony group to move to the closest chord tone in changes. Each group is responsible for only two or three tones but must know when to change as well as to what tones. Resonator bells can be given to each group to reinforce the harmony until the children can accomplish this independently.

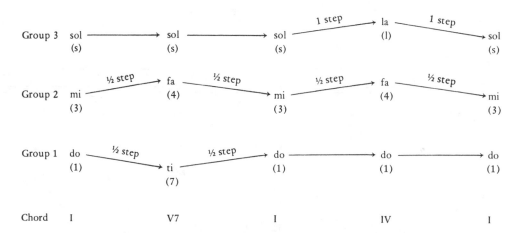

The following general guidelines for harmonic accompaniments and vocal chording, are important: (1) The tempo and harmonic rhythm should be strictly maintained. Children must understand how often each chord is to be played (every beat, every other beat) as well as when changes occur. (2) Children who play instruments should also sing. Singing the melody while providing the harmony is part of the experience.

Echo Songs

Echo songs are those in which the same melody is sung by two groups in call-response (antiphonal) fashion. Harmony is generated by the overlapping of the two parts.

"Old Texas" is a good example. As a general procedure, the song should first be learned well in unison. In a later lesson, the teacher can sing the "call" with the entire class "responding." Then the class can be divided into two parts. As with rounds, the beat must remain steady and consistent. Echo songs are good harmony experiences for all elementary levels.

F major

Old Texas
(Bury Me Not on the Lone Prairie)

Cowboy

2. I'll take my horse, and I'll take my rope,
   I'll hit the trail upon a lope;
   Say *adiós* to the Alamo,
   And turn my face towards Mexico.

I = F A C
V7 = C E G B♭

Partner Songs

Partner songs are two songs (or two parts of one song) that can be sung together because they have identical harmonic structures, the same length, and compatible meters. Sometimes one song has a verse and chorus which are sung together, like "Rocka My Soul." Or, two different songs can be put together.

Some rounds can be combined as partner songs. Since many rounds are harmonically based on the I chord, two rounds in the same key with compatible

Rocka My Soul

Afro-American Spiritual

F major

Part 1 — Lively

Rock-a my soul _ in the bos-om of A - bra-ham; Rock-a my soul _ in the

bos-om of A - bra-ham; Rock-a my soul _ in the bos-om of A - bra-ham;

Oh, rock-a my soul. So high you can't get o - ver it,

So low you can't get un - der it, So wide you

can't get a - round _ it, You must go in at the door.

I = F A C
V7 = C E G B♭

meters and identical lengths (or one twice as long as the other) become partner songs when sung simultaneously. "Row, Row, Row Your Boat" and "Little

There's Work to Be Done

Words and music by Richard C. Berg

C major

In Calypso rhythm

Part I — mf

1. Hur - ry, hur - ry, hur - ry, hur - ry, come on the run; Hur - ry, hur - ry, hur - ry, hur - ry,
2. Get a - long, you sleep - y head, and come on the run; Must you be so slow and la - zy?

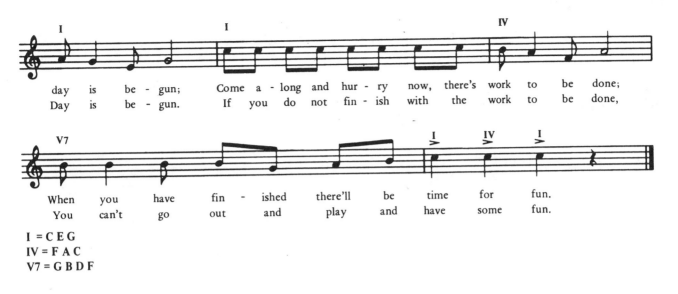

day is be - gun; Come a - long and hur - ry now, there's work to be done;
Day is be - gun. If you do not fin - ish with the work to be done,

When you have fin - ished there'll be time for fun.
You can't go out and play and have some fun.

I = C E G
IV = F A C
V7 = G B D F

C major
4

No Need to Hurry

Words and music by Richard C. Berg

In Calypso rhythm

Part II

1. All right, I come now; all right, I come; No need to hur - ry,
2. Don't be so nois - y, my lit - tle one, You'll wake the town be -

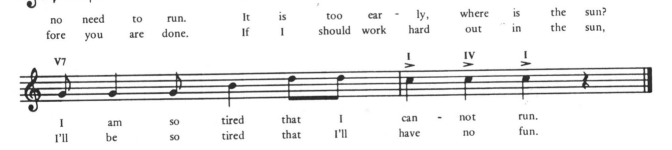

no need to run. It is too ear - ly, where is the sun?
fore you are done. If I should work hard out in the sun,

I am so tired that I can - not run.
I'll be so tired that I'll have no fun.

I = C E G
IV = F A C
V7 = G B D F

Tom Tinker'' are typical examples. As with all harmony songs, children should know the entire song or songs well in unison before groups attempt combining them into partner experiences. This often provides a better harmony experience more quickly for some groups of children than singing rounds.

81

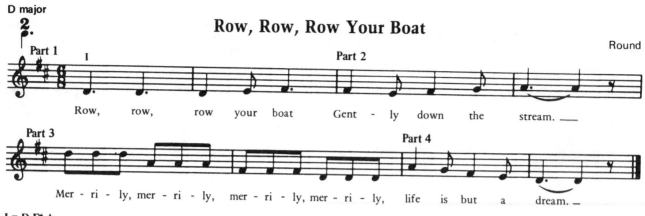

Ostinati

Ostinati are repeated patterns in music. Although they can be rhythmic patterns or chords, the typical ostinato used for harmonic experience in the elementary school is the pitch or melody ostinato. Ostinati represent a type of chanting when sung, but may be played effectively on melody instruments. Ostinati must be in the same key and meter as the original song. They may be created when a song is pentatonic, is accompanied by a I chord, or is accompanied by alternating I and V7 chords.

Pentatonic songs are those built on a five-tone scale. There are many pentatonic scales, but the one most commonly used in elementary school music is

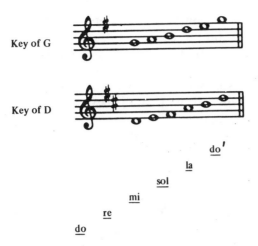

Key of G

Key of D

do'
la
sol
mi
re
do

This type consists of *do–re–mi–sol–la* and high *do*. It is like an incomplete major scale since it has no *fa* or *ti*—that is, no intervals smaller than a whole step. For this reason, any of the five tones are consonant when sounded with the others. Any one of them can be used to create an ostinato.

Star Light, Star Bright

Mother Goose

J. O'B.

Star light, star bright, first star I see to-night,

Wish I may, wish I might have the wish I wish to-night.

Ostinati

s   m   s   r

Star light, star bright.

d   r   m   d   r   m

Pret - ty star, pret - ty star.

d   s   m

See the star.

"Star Light, Star Bright" is D pentatonic. Ostinati can be created from D–E–F♯–A or B as long as the pattern is compatible in $\frac{4}{4}$. They are usually one or two measures long. Words are often derived from the song if the ostinato is to be sung. They may be made as simple or as difficult as necessary. Using them is a good way to accommodate individual differences and to make each child, from the EMR child to the gifted, feel competent in music.

Adding ostinati gradually once the song has been learned in unison is a good procedure.

Ostinati are also possible in nonpentatonic songs. Songs like "Little Tom Tinker" which are built on the I chord also may be accompanied by vocal or instrumental ostinati. However, the ostinato must be based on tones of the I chord (*do–mi–sol*). The following ostinati can be used to harmonize with "Little Tom Tinker."

I = D F# A

Songs harmonized with the I and V7 chords are also suitable for ostinati. Here the ostinato must be built on the tone the two chords have in common, which is always *sol,* the dominant tone; therefore, it is called a *dominant ostinato.* It must conform to the key and meter of the song. "Hush, Little Baby" is accompanied by the I (F–A–C) and V7 (C–E–G–B♭) chords. Analysis shows that the common tone is *sol* or C. The core of each ostinato must then be C, the dominant tone.

2. And if that diamond ring turns to brass,
   Daddy's gonna buy you a looking glass,
   And if that looking glass gets broke,
   Daddy's gonna buy you a billy goat.

3. And if that billy goat won't pull,
   Daddy's gonna buy you a cart and bull,
   And if that cart and bull turn over,
   Daddy's gonna buy you a dog named Rover.

4. And if that dog named Rover won't bark,
   Daddy's gonna buy you a horse and cart,
   And if that horse and cart fall down,
   You'll still be the sweetest little baby in town.

I = F A C
V7 = C E G B♭
Dominant tone (sol) = C

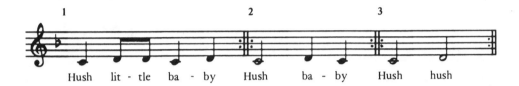

In addition to their use as accompaniments, ostinati may be used as introductions to and codas for songs. This may be combined with instruments to provide a varied musical experience. In "Hush, Little Baby," the three ostinati can serve as both introduction and coda.

There are a few guidelines for using all ostinati:

1. The song must be known well in unison first.
2. Ostinati may be added one at a time as follow-up lessons, moving from the simple to the complex.
3. Three or four children on an ostinato with one set of resonator bells provides a good balance. The foreground melody is the most important element of the song. The ostinati are background accompaniment and should not overshadow the melody.
4. Using many ostinati of varying difficulty accommodates diverse skills in the classroom, particularly with mainstreamed children. Instruction is thus individualized within the group setting.
5. The beat and tempo should be kept consistent.
6. Children should be allowed to write and adapt their own ostinati, including the notes, rhythms, words, introductions, and codas. This allows for creativity.

Descants

A descant is a countermelody that is usually sung higher than the original melody. Sometimes descants are provided in songs; at other times the teacher or students can write an appropriate one based on the harmony of the song.

"The Ash Grove" is an appropriate song for the upper elementary grades. The descant should be learned as a separate tune and then sung with the main melody. Descants are a particular challenge for students who are musically advanced. They also may be played on resonator bells, recorders, or the piano.

The Ash Grove

Adapted from traditional Welsh song

I = G B D
IV = C E G
V7 = D F♯ A C

86

How is a descant written when none is provided in the music? An analysis of the song's harmony is first necessary: "Springfield Mountain" is accom-

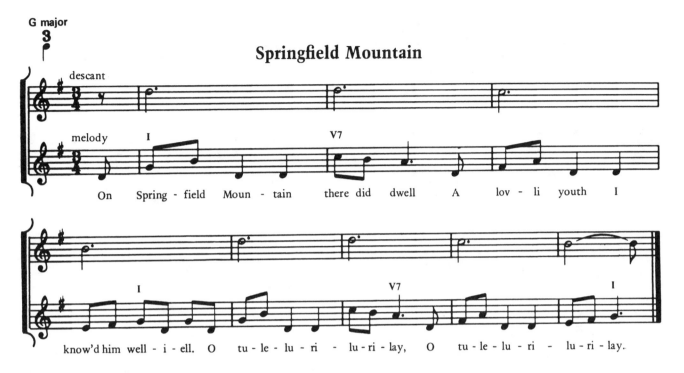

Springfield Mountain

G major

descant

melody   I   V7

On Spring - field Moun - tain there did dwell A lov - li youth I

I   V7   I

know'd him well - i - ell. O tu - le - lu - ri - lu - ri - lay, O tu - le - lu - ri - lu - ri - lay.

2. One Friday morning he did go
   Down to the meadow for to mow.

I = G B D
V7 = D F♯ A C

panied entirely by the I (G–B–D) and V7 (D–F♯–A–C) chords. A countermelody can be added above by using other tones from the same chords. The finished descant can be sung on *loo*, or appropriate words may be added. Like ostinati, descants can be simple or difficult to fit the needs of a class or an individual.

Two- and Three-Part Harmony

A harmony song has a given melody and one or more dependent parts. All upper and many middle elementary children can learn these. The songs may be taught either by a rote or rote-note method. The melody and the second harmony part should first be learned by all the students. The class then may be split and the two parts put together, although this does not always mean an even division of the class. Sometimes a smaller number of singers on the harmony part will provide a good balance. The teacher must listen carefully to determine what type of division sounds best. All divisions should be flexible so that all the children gain experience in singing both the melody and the harmony. If a third part is to be added, it should be learned by all the children and added to the successful singing of the melody and the second part. This should occur over two or three lessons, with the harmony experiences as follow-ups to the initial presentation of the song.

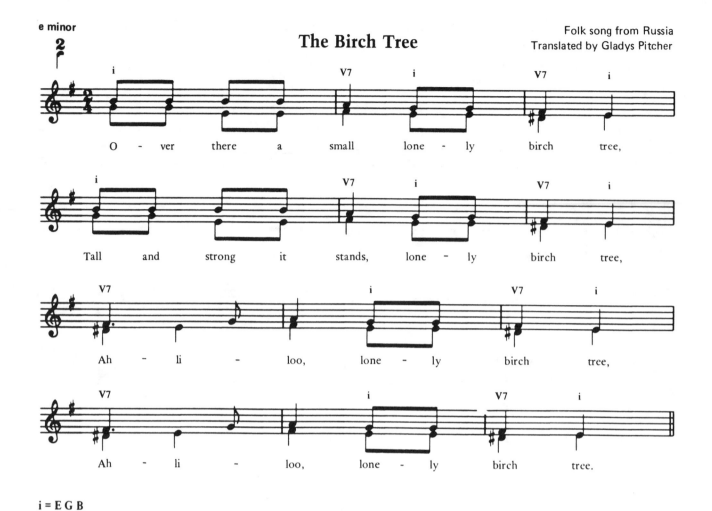

The Birch Tree

Folk song from Russia
Translated by Gladys Pitcher

e minor

O - ver there a small lone - ly birch tree,

Tall and strong it stands, lone - ly birch tree,

Ah - li - loo, lone - ly birch tree,

Ah - li - loo, lone - ly birch tree.

i = E G B
V7 = B D♯ F♯ A

Harmony experiences enhance normal classroom singing. Since the basic textures in Western music are homophonic and polyphonic, experiencing them through singing is an essential part of elementary school music. Children should sing harmony as soon as they are able to sing well in unison.

Exercises and Activities

1. Select a round and analyze its chordal structure.
2. Plan a harmony lesson for a chordal accompaniment or vocal chording to a song that uses the I, IV, and V7 chords.
3. Select echo songs or partner songs.
4. Select a suitable song and write several ostinati (simple to complex) for it. Remember that your song must be pentatonic, built on the I chord, or built on I and V7 chord. The ostinati must also agree wth the song in key and meter.
5. Select a song with a descant and show how the harmony works together, or write a simple descant for a song that has none.

Key Terms and Concepts

Round (strict canon)

Imitative canon

Chordal accompaniments

Vocal chording

Root position

Inversion

Echo songs

Call-response (antiphonal) songs

Partner songs

Ostinato

Dominant ostinato

Descant

Two-part harmony

Three-part harmony

How Children Develop Listening Skills

All facets of music education require listening skills. Children must listen in order to learn a song, tap a pattern, or play an instrument. They also listen when they move to music or when they create an accompaniment to a song. In all of these examples, however, listening serves another purpose. This chapter describes how to encourage children to listen to music as an end in itself, to hear and enjoy it as an aural experience without singing, moving, or playing instruments.

Listening skills can be developed in many ways. In the classroom, this is accomplished most typically through the use of recordings with an occasional live performance. To understand how listening lessons should be planned, it is necessary first to consider the different ways people listen.

Types of Listeners

There are four types of listener: the sensuous, the associative, the critical, and the aesthetic.

Sensuous listeners bathe in sound. Music makes them feel good if they are depressed or calms them if they are excited. Sensuous listeners like an environment in which sound, not silence, is present. When a record is played while children do another task, such as reading or drawing pictures for art, the listening is sensuous. Although there is nothing wrong with this, it does not constitute a valid *listening* experience for children. Music in the background while children paint pictures may assist the art lesson, but it does not

90

develop musical discrimination. Using soft music after recess to quiet the children is little more than listening at a sensuous level.

Another type of listening perception is termed *associative*. Music is heard and then associated with something that is basically nonmusical. Associative listeners see pictures as they listen to music, or they imagine a story. Or perhaps the music suggests something from their past associations. There is nothing wrong with making associations with a piece of music. However, seeing pictures is a visual art experience; creating stories is a literary experience. Both can be accomplished without music. It is true that programmatic music, which is based on a story or visual image, has extramusical references and associations. But the *music* is still the most important ingredient, since this was the medium the composer chose to tell the story. Music best communicates music, not extramusical associations.

A third type of listening perception is termed *critical*. It occurs in two ways. First, it means listening and determining what is good or bad about the performance. Were the notes correct? Was the interpretation valid? This type of listening is the province of the trained critic. Children may become aware of what constitutes a good performance, but this is not a prime objective for music education in the elementary school. Secondly, critical listening is knowing everything about a piece of music before hearing it. Who was the composer? When did he or she live? When did he or she write the piece? Why? Giving children this type of information before they hear a composition is of little value. It is doubtful that this enhances initial enjoyment or appreciation of a piece or even develops good listening skills. Many times it bores the children. If they are interested in the music, they will want to know these things later. The music should be allowed to speak to them as music before other considerations are allowed to enter.

What alternatives are left to the teacher if children should not bathe in sound, create stories or draw pictures, or criticize the performance? What is left is listening aesthetically. *Aesthetic* listeners process musical information and derive meaning from this information. Composers have always wanted their audiences to enjoy the music—but they have wanted to convey music, not pictures, stories, or words. If music could be expressed in another medium, there would be no reason for its existence. In the elementary school, the teacher can help children develop a framework for perceiving music aesthetically.

Aesthetic Listening

Aesthetic listening strives to develop two aspects:

1. What is the character or nature of the music? (What is its mood, overall feeling, and so on?)
2. What is happening in the music to create this character or nature? (Is it fast, slow, loud, soft? Does it repeat? What instruments are used?)

Children do not need to react to both facets in *each* listening lesson, but over a school year both should be developed.

What is the character or nature of the music? Understanding this is really the basis of music listening. "What is the mood of the music? Is it energetic and forceful? Is it melancholy and languid? Does it seem to change? Is the change gradual or sudden, slight or considerable?" These questions focus directly on the music and lead children to hear music as music. There is a difference between these questions and those that depend on the taste and opinion of the individual child. "What do you think about the music? What does the music make you feel? What kind of mood does the music put you in? Do you like the music?" These questions should be avoided. Unlike the first set of questions, which are based on observation and from which there should be some homogeneity among the answers, the latter group provides no common set of answers since they are based largely on opinion, not observation. They concentrate on individual reaction to the music rather than on the nature of the music itself.

Discussing the character or nature of the music should probably receive some attention in every listening lesson. Children should be encouraged to develop a rich, colorful vocabulary to describe music they hear. Children's responses should progress beyond the notion that music is either beautiful or not beautiful, good or bad, pleasant or unpleasant.

What is happening in the music to create this character or nature?   The second facet of aesthetic listening is equally important. A framework should be established for processing music. This framework, of course, takes many listening lessons to develop, but should include the following:

Tempo and Rhythm
1. What is the tempo (fast, moderate, slow, changeable)?
2. Is there a beat? (Can you tap to it?) Does the beat ever stop? Does it change?
3. How are the beats grouped? (accent groupings) In twos, threes, fours? Are they asymmetrical? changeable?
4. Are there predominant rhythm patterns? How do they affect the music?
5. How does the tempo or rhythm contribute to the overall character of the music?

Pitch (Melody and Harmony) and Texture
1. Is there a melody you can remember? several melodies? How are they alike? How are they different?
2. Is the melody singable? Is it better suited to an instrument? Is the range wide or narrow?
3. Is the melody played alone (monophonic)? With an accompaniment (homophonic)? With other melodies at the same time (polyphonic)?
4. Is the accompaniment tense-sounding (dissonant)? relaxed-sounding (consonant)? Does it ever change?
5. How does the melody (or harmony or texture) contribute to the overall character or nature of the music?

Timbre (Instruments)
1. What are some of the predominant timbres heard in the foreground? background? Do these change?
2. Are there special effects from some timbres? Are the violins plucked (played *pizzicato*) instead of bowed (*arco*)?
3. How does the timbre contribute to the overall character or nature of the music?

Intensity (Dynamics)
1. Is the music generally loud or soft?
2. Does it change from loud to soft? How? Suddenly or gradually?
3. How does the intensity contribute to the overall character or nature of the music?

Form (Design)

1. How is the music designed? Does it ever repeat? Is one idea repeated again and again (A A A A—strophic)? Is one idea presented with slight variations (A A$_1$ A$_2$ A$_3$—processive)? Are two or more ideas repeated in rotation (ABA, ABABA, ABACABA—return)? Or are new ideas continually presented (ABCDE—additive) without repeating the old?
2. Is it possible to identify the form by specific letters (ABA, AB)?
3. Is it possible to identify the form by a specific name (theme and variations, rondo, song form, binary and ternary, strophic)?
4. How does the form or design contribute to the overall character or nature of the music?

These points are not definitive nor are they a checklist of questions to be used in each listening lesson. However, these types of questions do lead to an aesthetic understanding of the music. At the end of a year of meaningful listening experiences, it is reasonable to expect that children can both describe the character of the music in words at their level of understanding and comment on what is happening in the music to give it a unique character.

Specific Program Objectives for Listening

Specific program objectives for listening may also be outlined for each level in the elementary school (Chart 8–1, p. 94). These objectives represent aural recognition of concepts from a generalized notion (early elementary) to a specific refinement (upper elementary). In the first grade, children may discern a difference between fast and slow tempos. By the sixth grade, however, this concept should include recognition of many levels of slow (*largo* to *andante*) and fast (*allegretto* to *prestissimo*) as well as the subtleties of *accelerando* and *ritardando*. Similarly, second-grade children may hear the difference between strings and winds, but by the fourth grade their listening should be refined so they can identify the difference between violin and cello, flute and oboe. By the end of the sixth grade, they will recognize specific timbres of individual instruments, such as the pizzicato technique of string players or the muting effect used on brass instruments. By the end of their elementary-school music experiences, *all* objectives on Chart 8–1 should ideally be realized.

Criteria for Selecting Listening Materials and Equipment

The *RCA Adventures in Listening* series and the *Bowmar Orchestral Library*, the contents of which are included in the Appendix, are excellent sources for listening lessons. Both compilations include profuse notes on the selected works, composers, styles and characteristic musical elements, with teaching strategies for presenting them.

Many music-series texts have listening experiences correlated to songs as well as to other classroom subjects. The songs are usually available in the recordings that accompany the textbooks.

Such a profusion of material and ideas can be very helpful to a teacher but it can also be confusing and overwhelming. It is important that a listening selection be chosen because it fits into the overall program objectives for a particular classroom, not merely because it is suggested for a given grade level.

The same composition can be used again and again to develop further concepts. If tempo is emphasized in the initial listening lesson, the piece may

CHART 8–1   Objectives for Listening

	Children through listening will
Early elementary (K–2)	identify repeated or contrasting phrases in a composition
	discuss the mood of a selection
	identify the predominant foreground timbres in a general way
	identify musical elements heard, including a. gross dynamic changes (loud to soft) b. high and low sounds (register) c. fast or slow tempos d. beat and accent groupings (2, 3, 4) e. phrases and cadences in the melody
	identify certain timbres as being high or low (flute vs. tuba)
Middle elementary (3–4)	identify orchestral families and common instruments by sound (including those in both the foreground and background)
	identify major, minor, and pentatonic sounds, tonality, and modulation
	identify AB, ABA, and variation form
	relate musical elements to the mood of the piece and to extramusical associations
	graph melodic contour
	recognize melodic quality conjunct-disjunct simple-ornamented narrow-wide
	recognize consonance and dissonance
	identify texture (monophonic, homophonic, polyphonic)
	identify finer dynamic changes as well as transitions (*pp, p, mp, mf, f, ff, crescendo, decrescendo, subito, sforzando*)
	identify specific forms and styles, such as binary, ternary, rondo, fugue
Upper elementary (5–6)	identify select musical styles, such as classical, folk, jazz, rock
	identify all orchestral timbres as well as how they are being used (*pizzicato*, muted, etc.)
	identify asymmetrical meters and tempo deviations (fives, sevens, *accelerando, ritardando, rubato, a tempo*)
	recognize select genres, such as symphony, concerto, suite, opera, lied
	identify select works by name, composer, and historical style
	identify whole-tone, chromatic, twelve-tone, and modal sounds
	use musical vocabulary to describe a listening experience

be repeated later for identifying instrument names, accent groupings, or form. Ten to twenty pieces that are tastefully and logically presented to children during the course of one year become a listening repertoire. The children may even enjoy listening to these selections individually at a listening post equipped with headsets and a record or cassette player. This provides another avenue for individualizing instruction.

Children may be interested in sharing their own recordings with the class in a musical show and tell (or hear and tell). These selections may be of a popular nature but can provide a valuable learning experience if balanced with recordings of the masterworks. Of course, a lesson must be structured even when children provide the recordings. Such an experience should never be merely a chance for children to listen to "their" kind of music as a kind of reward or diversion. They can do this outside the classroom and should not substitute for planned instruction. Allowing this suggests to children that listening to "their" music is "fun and relaxation" whereas listening to "school" music is "work" and tedious.

When popular selections are provided by the children, the objectives of Chart 8–1 must still be considered. The teacher might take the recording and plan a lesson which is compatible with the ongoing objectives. The children might also plan such lessons, individually or as a group. Such coherence in listening will provide reinforcement for *all* listening experiences and give children more insight into listening to popular music as well as to the classics.

All records selected for listening lessons should be of good quality. A scratched record does not enhance the development of sensitive listeners. Similarly, playback equipment should be the best the school can afford. Poor equipment and damaged records in the school do not enhance motivation to learn about music. The teacher should strive to purchase the best equipment and recordings possible and to maintain these in peak condition.

Lesson Plans

The components of lesson planning discussed in Chapter 4 should be included in listening lessons. The teacher should plan a captivating motivation before intense listening is required. Listening lessons should be scheduled at appropriate times within the music period, preferably after the group has sung, moved, or played as a whole. Listening should take place in a quiet classroom with equipment that allows the children to concentrate.

Lesson objectives in listening are sometimes difficult for teachers to state. "The children will listen to . . ." is not sufficient since the lesson objective must include evaluation. Listening is difficult to observe; objectives for listening are therefore better structured using musical elements which can be measured. For example, children might be asked to identify:

the tempo as fast, moderate, or slow
the accent groupings as 2, 3, or 4
the texture as monophonic, homophonic, or polyphonic
three of the four instruments heard in foreground
crescendo (soft to loud) used in the composition

Sample Lesson Plans

Experiencing Environmental Sounds (any level)

Motivation
The classroom teacher has made a cassette tape of some environmental sounds. They may be randomly grouped, or the teacher may categorize them as:
1. Sounds made by people
   a. The crunch of someone eating a carrot

   b. Footsteps in an empty room
   c. Someone breathing
   d. Tapping various parts of the body with the hand
2. Machine sounds
   a. A power lawnmower
   b. The static on a radio (between stations)
   c. A car on a gravel road
   d. A jet plane taking off or landing
3. Sounds of nature
   a. Water in a flowing stream
   b. The sound of thunder and rain during a storm
   c. A coyote howling
   d. The sound of the wind in a forest

Procedure

The children are asked to
1. Identify the sound as specifically as possible and
2. Describe the sound as best they can in musical terms as the tape is played. Footsteps in an empty room might be described as "a regular, hollow sound that grows louder as the person comes closer." "Hollow" describes the timbre, "regular" describes the rhythm, and "gets louder" describes the intensity.

Follow-up Experiences

1. The children may use graphic notation to picture what they heard in a musical way.

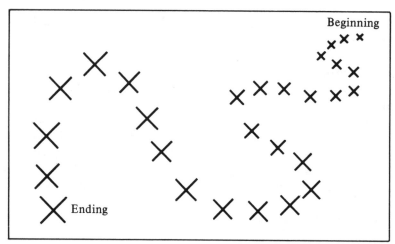

x = footsteps (size of x indicates intensity)

2. These graphic compositions may be interpreted with classroom instruments. The entire composition may be dramatized.
3. The children may gather their own environmental sounds to be used in the classroom in a similar manner, working individually or in small groups.

Experiencing Timbre in a Composition
(early elementary level)

Recording
RCA Adventures in Listening (Grade 5–2)
Bartok, "An Evening in the Village"

Motivation

The teacher has five blank areas on the chalkboard with several pictures of orchestral instruments on the chalktray. "This composition, as we will hear, has five sections. Some of the instruments pictured here are used in some of the sections. As you listen, try to determine which instruments are used in each section." (Answer: Sections 1, 3, and 5 use strings, 2 and 4 use woodwinds.)

Procedure

The recording is played and the children place the pictures of the instruments in the appropriate sections on the chalkboard. (Violins, violas, cellos in sections 1, 3, and 5; flutes, oboes, and so on in sections 2 and 4)

Follow-up Experiences

1. The children listen to other examples of rondo in an ABABA form.
2. The children create their own composition in five sections using only two timbres (see Chart 8–2).

CHART 8–2   Timbre Identification

Early elementary	Middle elementary	Upper elementary	
Voices	High voices	soprano alto	coloratura soprano mezzo-soprano
	Low voices	tenor bass	baritone
Strings (Chordophones)	High strings	violin viola	*pizzacato* muting *col legno*
	Low strings	cello bass	*sul ponticello* harmonics double stops
Winds (Aerophones)	Woodwinds		
	No reed	flute	piccolo
	Double reed	oboe bassoon	English horn contrabassoon
	Single reed	clarinet saxophone	soprano, alto alto, tenor
	Brass	cornet trumpet French horn trombone tuba	muting stopping Sousaphone
Percussion (Membranophones and Idiophones)	Drums	snare bass tympani	
	Unpitched	triangles maracas gongs, etc.	
	Pitched	xylophone marimba celesta vibraphone	
	Miscellaneous	guitar piano organ harp	harpsichord clavichord
Electronic (Electrophones)		musique concréte synthesized	
Environmental Sounds			

Experiencing Melody in a Composition
(middle elementary level)

Recording
RCA Adventures in Listening (Grade 4–2)
Schumann, "Träumerei" (a live performance could be substituted)

Motivation
The teacher has a set of resonator bells arranged c to c^1 plus four visuals, each with a characteristic contour. "I'm going to improvise on these bells a melody that is represented by one of these contours. Which is it?" The melody is played and the problem is solved. Some students are also given the opportunity to improvise a short melody represented by one of the four contours.

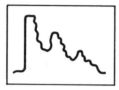 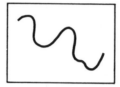 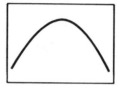 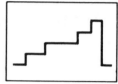

Procedure
"The following listening selection has a melody that is similar to one of these contours. Which is it?" (Answer: 3)

Follow-up Experiences
1. The children use the form of "Träumerei" to create their own composition (AABA or song form).
2. Other selections that fit contours shown in the visuals are used for listening or singing.

Experiencing Form in a Composition
(upper level elementary)

Recording
RCA Adventures in Listening (Grade 4–1)
Caillet, "Variations on 'Pop! Goes the Weasel' "

Motivation
The teacher has written this statement on the chalkboard: The dog walked across the street. "How could we express this thought in a similar manner? What other way might we say it?"
> *Answers:* The canine ran across the alley. The mutt sauntered across the avenue. The domestic pet scrambled across the road. "We've made variations on the original statement. This is often done in music. Let's take the theme 'Pop! Goes the Weasel' [teacher plays it on piano] and see what we could do in music to vary this."
> *Answers:* "Play it higher or lower, faster or slower, legato or staccato, change the harmony, make it minor, play it softer or louder." (The teacher may demonstrate some of these at the piano.)

Procedure
"Listen to the recording and write down which ways the composer does vary the tune of 'Pop! Goes the Weasel.' "

Follow-up Experiences

1. In small groups, children create variations on a folk tune. All variations are then played for the class and taped to create a set of variations on the folk tune.
2. The children listen to other examples of a theme and variations.

Summary

The following points apply to lessons designed to develop aesthetic listening:

1. A variety of music should be used, including popular, rock, jazz, ethnic, and classical. Use music children know well to expose them to the aesthetic way of listening so that introducing new types of music will serve to broaden their tastes and tolerances. They will see that all music shares common characteristics and that one type is not the province of any special age group.

2. Listening lessons should be short, initially five to ten minutes at the most. Teachers may use short excerpts of longer compositions. After several lessons on one work, the entire movement or symphony can be played.

3. The general procedure is to pose a listening question, play a short segment, stop, and answer the question. A new question is posed, the same or another segment is played, and so on until the lesson objective is reached.

4. In all cases, the teacher should have listened to the selection several times *before* the lesson. This preview can provide the material for structuring both the motivation and the procedure.

Exercise and Activities

1. Ask several people: "When you listen to music, what do you give your attention to first? What else do you listen for?" Can you draw any conclusions?
2. Ask several elementary school youngsters the questions listed in Exercise 1. What conclusions can you draw?
3. Find a recording (five to ten minutes long) you particularly enjoy. Plan a detailed listening lesson in which you state objectives, motivation, and procedures.
4. Find several recordings of all types of music (popular, rock, jazz, ethnic, and classical) which demonstrate one of the elements shown in Chart 8–1.

Key Terms and Concepts

Sensuous listening
Associative listening
Program music
Critical listening
Aesthetic listening
Duration (Rhythm)
Tempo
Beat (Pulse)
Accented beat
Pitch
Melody
Harmony
Monophonic texture
Homophonic texture

Polyphonic texture
Consonance—Dissonance
Timbre
Pizzicato
Arco
Strophic form
Processive form
Return form
Additive form
Theme and variations
Rondo
Song form (ternary)
Binary form

Professional Readings

Copland, Aaron. *What to Listen for in Music,* rev. ed. New York: Mentor Books, 1964.

Smith, Charlene W. *The Listening Activity Book: Teaching Literal, Evaluative and Critical Listening in the Elementary School.* Belmont, CA: Fearon Publishers, 1975.

Swanson, Bessie R. *Music in the Education of Children.* 3rd ed. Belmont, Calif.: Wadsworth, 1969.

Tipton, Gladys, and Eleanor Tipton. *Teachers' Guides for Adventures in Music Recordings.* New York: RCA Victor.

Playing Classroom Instruments

The use of instruments provides added motivation in the music classroom since everyone is attracted to them. Children want to handle instruments and to experiment with their sounds; often they wish to become competent in using them, too. Playing classroom instruments is thus an important component of a well-balanced elementary music program. Instruments may be used as an experience in themselves, for example, in composing. They also enhance all other activities, whether singing, listening to, reading, or making music.

Specific Program Objectives for Playing Classroom Instruments

Chart 9–1 suggests objectives for playing instruments in the classroom. Generally, large muscle development and gross distinctions must be learned before small-muscle movements and refined distinctions can be developed, and allowances must be made for individual differences. A sensitive and alert teacher can quickly assess the motor development of each child and provide a playing task at which he or she will be successful. The specific program objectives suggested in Chart 9–1 must be fluid possibilities, not rigid guidelines, allowing instruction to be individualized whenever possible..

The variety of instruments available for classroom use can be grouped in three categories: (1) rhythm instruments, such as drums, woodblocks, sticks, maracas, sandblocks, cymbals, and triangles; (2) melody instruments, such as the recorder, resonator and melody bells, xylophones, metallophones, and keyboards as well as band instruments in those schools where such instruction

CHART 9–1 Objectives for Playing Instruments

	Children will
Early elementary (K–2)	play the basic beat on percussion instruments
	play simple melodies and tonal patterns on resonator bells
	play the accent groupings (meter) on percussion instruments
	play simple, even rhythmic patterns as ostinati
	maintain a steady tempo while playing
Middle elementary (3–4)	play simple chordal accompaniments (two or three chords) on the autoharp
	play tunes and phrases on the bells and piano
	play simple chords (I, IV, and V7) on the piano
	play simple melodies on the recorder
	play uneven rhythmic patterns as ostinati
Upper elementary (5–6)	expand their skill on all classroom instruments
	play both chords and melodies on the piano
	play select chords on the ukulele or guitar
	play syncopated rhythmic patterns as ostinati
	play melodies and chords by ear and by notation
	play a variety of patterns while maintaining the beat and tempo
	play in an appropriate style, including attention to articulation, phrasing, dynamics

is available; and (3) harmony instruments, such as autoharps, guitars, and ukuleles. Some simple instruments can always be constructed as part of a classroom project when they are not otherwise available.

Rhythm Instruments

Rhythm refers to the time element of music. In classroom music, this means the (1) *tempo*, the speed of the music; (2) *pulse*, the regularly recurring, underlying beat of the music; (3) *accent grouping*, the regular accenting of certain beats; (4) *melodic rhythm*, the durations (long and short) of notes in the melody; and (5) *characteristic patterns*, the recurring patterns in the melodic rhythm. Rhythm instruments of all types can be used to develop each of these concepts.

Rhythm instruments: tambourines and snares

Tempo and Pulse

Tempo and pulse are closely related. Pulses that are less frequent produce slower tempos, whereas pulses that occur close together result in faster tempos. Experiences with both concepts include having children tapping rhythm instruments (sticks, drums, tambourines) to the pulse of a well-known song; a recording; a metronome; a favorite poem, chant, or jingle; or as echos. Experience with tempo and pulse is basic for the lower grades. It must also be emphasized with the upper grades if the concepts have not been formed already.

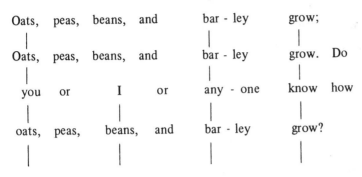

Oats, peas, beans, and bar - ley grow;

Oats, peas, beans, and bar - ley grow. Do

you or I or any - one know how

oats, peas, beans, and bar - ley grow?

G major

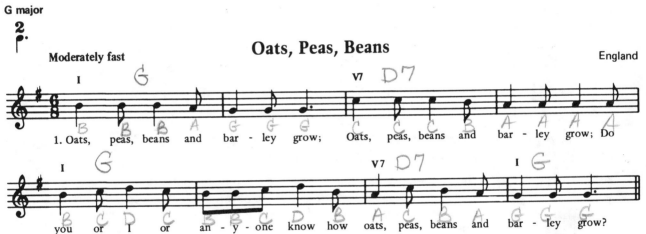

Oats, Peas, Beans

England

Moderately fast

1. Oats, peas, beans and bar - ley grow; Oats, peas, beans and bar - ley grow; Do you or I or an - y - one know how oats, peas, beans and bar - ley grow?

2. First the farmer sows his seed,
   Then he stands and takes his ease;
   He stamps his foot and claps his hands,
   And turns around to view his lands.

3. Waiting for a partner,
   Waiting for a partner,
   Open the ring and take one in
   While we all gaily dance and sing.

I = G B D
V7 = D F♯ A C

Experiencing Pulse and Tempo with a Metronome
(early elementary)

The teacher sets a metronome to 100. "Listen to the metronome. How is it moving?" (Children respond "fast" or "quickly.") "Let's play our rhythm sticks with it on the beat."
"Watch how I change it." Tempo is changed to 60. "What happens to the sound?" (It gets slower.) "Let's play our rhythm sticks with it now."
The teacher then lets children change the speed on the metronome by moving the weight on the pendulum. Each change is then played with rhythm sticks. If a metronome is not available, a pulse can be set from the second hand of a watch. Seconds = 60, half-seconds = 120, and so on.)

103

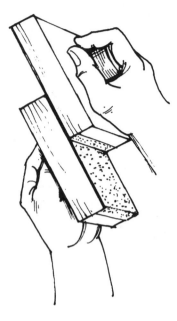

Experiencing Pulse in a Poem (middle or upper elementary)

The teacher presents a poem, saying, "As you listen to this rhyme, decide how many pulses are used in it." The children identify sixteen pulses in the poem and then accompany the reading of the limerick with various rhythm instruments.

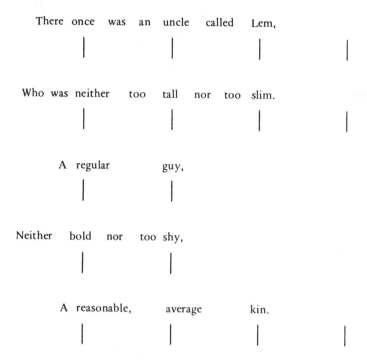

There once was an uncle called Lem,

| | | | |

Who was neither too tall nor too slim.

| | | | |

A regular guy,

| | |

Neither bold nor too shy,

| | |

A reasonable, average kin.

| | | | |

Experiencing Pulse and Tempo with a Recording
(early and middle elementary)

The children will play selected rhythm instruments to the steady pulse of a recorded selection. The selection should be relatively free of tempo deviations such as *accelerando*, *ritardando*, and *rubato*. Recordings for this experience are listed in Chart 9–2.

CHART 9–2   Selected Recordings for Tempo

		Bowmar Orchestral Library		RCA Adventures in Listening
Slow Tempos	#58	*Arabian Dance* Tchaikovsky	1-1	*Berceuse* Stravinsky
	#59	*Morning* Grieg	1-1	*Walking Song* (middle section) Thomson
	#62	*Third Movement, Symphony #1* Mahler	1-2	*The Elephant* Saint-Saëns
	#63	*Jimbo's Lullaby* Debussy	2-1	*Bydlo* Moussorgsky
	#63	*Sarabande* Corelli	2-2	*Sehr langsam* Webern
	#63	*Träumerei* Schumann		
Moderate Tempos	#51	*Royal March of the Lion* (with accelerando) Saint Saëns	1-1	*Gigue* J. S. Bach
	#54	*Cortège of the Sardar* Ippolitov-Ivanov	1-1	*Walking Song* (first and third sections Thomson

CHART 9–2 *(continued)*

	Bowmar Orchestral Library		RCA Adventures in Listening
	#54 *March of the Siamese Children* Rodgers	1-2	*Dance of the Sugar-Plum Fairy* Tchaikovsky
	#59 *In the Hall of the Mountain King* (with *accelerando*) Grieg	2-1	*Viennese Muscial Clock* Kodály
		2-2	*The Twittering Machine* (with *accelerando* and *ritardando*) Schuller
Fast Tempos	#52 *Flight of the Bumble Bee* Rimsky-Korsakov	2-2	*Dance of the Buffoons* Rimsky-Korsakov
	#58 *Trepak* Tchaikovsky	2-2	*Sun Dance* Elgar
	#63 *Doctor Gradus ad Parnassum* Debussy	3-1	*Finale (William Tell Overture)* Rossini
	#63 *Badinèrie* Corelli	3-2	*Bear Dance* Bartók
	#64 *Gypsy Rondo* Haydn	3-2	*Tarantella* Rossini

Accents and Meter

Playing on the accented beat is a concept that logically follows experience with tempo and pulse. Beats are usually grouped as twos, threes, or fours in the following meters.

S= Strong beat

w= weak beat

$$\text{Duple} \quad \begin{matrix} S & w \\ 1 & 2 \end{matrix} \quad \left(\mathbf{\frac{2}{4}, \frac{4}{4}, \frac{6}{8}, \frac{6}{4}}\right)$$

$$\text{Triple} \quad \begin{matrix} S & w & w \\ 1 & 2 & 3 \end{matrix} \quad \left(\mathbf{\frac{3}{4}, \frac{3}{8}, \frac{9}{8}, \frac{9}{4}}\right)$$

$$\text{Quadruple} \quad \begin{matrix} S & w & w & w \\ 1 & 2 & 3 & 4 \end{matrix} \quad \left(\mathbf{\frac{4}{4}, \frac{12}{8}}\right)$$

Meter is the written manifestation of such accent groupings. There are also asymmetrical accent groupings. Children should have the experience of working with these as an extension of the more traditional duple and triple meters.

$$\text{Fives} \quad \begin{matrix} S & w & S & w & w \\ 1 & 2 & 3 & 4 & 5 \end{matrix} \quad (2+3)$$
or
$$\begin{matrix} S & w & w & S & w \\ 1 & 2 & 3 & 4 & 5 \end{matrix} \quad (3+2)$$

$$\text{Sevens} \quad \begin{matrix} S & w & S & w & w & S & w \\ 1 & 2 & 3 & 4 & 5 & 6 & 7 \end{matrix} \quad (2+3+2)$$
or
$$\begin{matrix} S & w & S & w & S & w & w \\ 1 & 2 & 3 & 4 & 5 & 6 & 7 \end{matrix} \quad (2+2+3)$$
or
$$\begin{matrix} S & w & w & S & w & S & w \\ 1 & 2 & 3 & 4 & 5 & 6 & 7 \end{matrix} \quad (3+2+2)$$

The concept of accent grouping can also be experienced through singing a song, with a recording, or with a poem or rhyme. This concept can be developed with any grade level, particularly the early elementary, after pulse is understood.

Experiencing Accent with a Metronome (all grade levels)

The teacher uses a metronome as described above but the children play in a set: accent grouping. Tempo can be varied as before:

Metronome	| | | | | | | |	(wood block)
Duple time	| | | |	(finger cymbal)

Metronome	| | | | | | | |	(castanet)
Triple time	| | |	(tambourine)

Metronome	| | | | | | | | | | | |	(bongo)
Quadruple time	| | |	(conga)

Metronome	| | | | | | | | | | | | | | | |	(maracas)
Asymmetrical 5 (3+2)	| | | | | |	(guiro)

Experiencing Accent in a Poem or Song (all levels)

This is similar to the activity described above for pulse. Each poem has a distinct accent grouping which can be discovered by reading it in unison. Most English poems with a set rhythmic scheme are in duple meter:

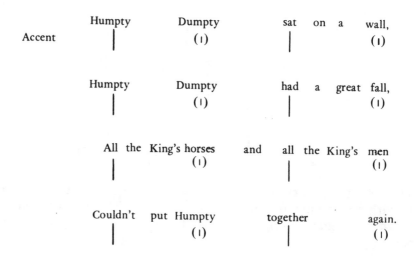

The pulse may then be played by one instrument, the accent by another as the poem is read:

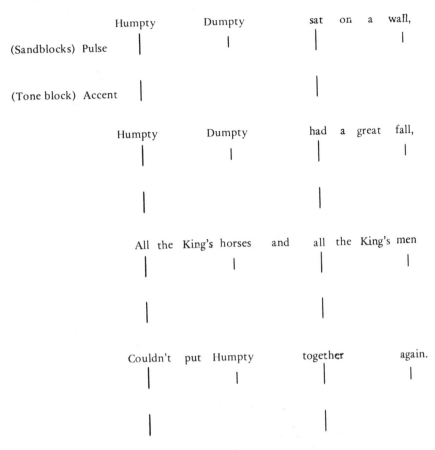

Experiencing Accent and Meter with a Recording

The children will play selected instruments in unison with the accent grouping and the pulse of a recorded selection. The selection should be relatively free of tempo deviations such as *accelerando, ritardando,* and *rubato* (Chart 9–3).

CHART 9–3   Selected Recordings for Accent and Meter

	Bowmar Orchestral Library		RCA Adventures in Listening	
Duple Meter	#53	*March of the Dwarfs* Grieg	1-1	*Air Gai* Gluck
	#58	*Overture Miniature* Tchaikovsky	1-2	*Dance of the Reed Pipes* Tchaikovsky
	#62	*Theme and Variations* Haydn	2-2	*Dragoons of Alcala* Bizet
	#62	*Bourrée* Handel	4-2	*Entrance of the Emperor and His Court* Kodály
			5-1	*Allegro (Symphony #5)* Schubert
Triple Meter	#53	*Minuet* Mozart	1-2	*Anitra's Dance* Grieg
	#53	*A Ground* Handel	2-1	*Hornpipe* Handel
	#55	*Skaters' Waltzes* Waldteufel	2-2	*Bolero* Rossini–Britten
	#56	*España Waltzes* Waldteufel	3-1	*Circus Music* Copland

CHART 9–3 *(continued)*

		Bowmar Orchestral Library		RCA Adventures in Listening
	#58	*Waltz of the Flowers* Tchaikovsky	4-1	*Waltz* Tchaikovsky
	#62	*Minuet* Mozart	4-2	*Minuetto* Bizet
			5-1	*Jesu, Joy of Man's Desiring* Bach
Quadruple Meter	#54	*March from the Love of Three Oranges* Prokofieff	1-2	*March of the Kings* Menotti
	#57	*Pavane of the Sleeping Beauty* Ravel	2-1	*March of the Toys* Herbert
	#60	*Londonderry Air* Grainger (arr.)	2-2	*Troika* Prokofieff
	#62	*Third Movement (Symphony #1)* Mahler	4-1	*Bridal Procession* Rimsky-Korsakov
Asymmetrical Meter			1-2	*Promenade* ($\frac{5}{4}$ and $\frac{6}{4}$) Moussorgsky
			6-1	*Street in a Frontier Town* ($\frac{4}{8}$ and $\frac{5}{8}$) Copland

Melodic Rhythm

The melodic rhythm is the arrangement of long and short sounds in the actual melody. Usually certain notes of longer duration emphasize key words of the text.

Like pulse-tempo and accent groupings, melodic rhythm can be developed through the use of a song, a recording, or a rhymed chant. It is best introduced after pulse and accent have been explored.

Characteristic Patterns

Characteristic patterns are those which occur several times in the melodic rhythm, often enough to be considered a motive or basic unit. In "Oats, Peas, Beans," (page 103) the ♩ ♪♩ ♪ pattern is heard several times.

Characteristic patterns are termed either even, uneven, or syncopated. Even patterns generally have notes of equal duration (or divisions of two notes in pairs) over the basic pulse:

Uneven patterns in simple meters frequently utilize dotted rhythms, which provide a long-short or uneven pattern over the pulse:

Uneven patterns in compound meters, however, will have notes of unequal duration in sequence, long followed by short. These will not necessarily be dotted:

Syncopated patterns typically have a note of longer duration where it is unexpected, for example on an accented beat (or fraction of a beat) resulting in a short-long pattern over the beat:

Experiencing Pattern in Songs

Example One (all levels)

A single song may be used to summarize pulse, accent, melodic rhythm, and characteristic pattern. "Oats, Peas, Beans" is a typical example:

A culminating lesson could include all of these simultaneously, allowing for individual differences through the assigning of parts.

Example Two (upper elementary)

Rhythm patterns are added to a song ("Mary Ann") to provide a calypso accompaniment.

F major

Words by Kathy Alexander

Calypso song

Mary Ann

Not too fast, but rhythmically

1. All day____ all night,__ Miss Mar - y Ann,_____
2. If you____ come to____ this is - land fine,_____

Down by____ the sea - side____ sift - ing sand,_____
You'll love____ the sea and____ bright sun - shine,_____

All the lit - tle chil - dren__ love Mar - y Ann,_____
You will be____ en - chant - ed____ with this fair land,_____

You, too,__ will love her,__ Miss Mar - y Ann._____
You'll be__ be - witched by__ Miss Mar - y Ann._____

I = F A C
V7 = C E G B♭

Conga

Maracas

Claves

Bongos

Guiro

110

An introduction, coda, and interlude (between verses) may be added to enhance the musical effect.

Experiencing Patterns in Poems (all levels)

The format shown in Example One above is applied to a rhyme or poem:

Jack be nimble, Jack be quick,
Jack jump over the candlestick.

Experiencing Pattern through Echo-Clapping (all levels)

The pulse, accent grouping, and a pattern provide the background for echo-clapping:

Experiencing Patterns in Recordings
(middle and upper elementary)

Even, uneven, and syncopated patterns may also be played with a recording, using a variety of percussion instruments.

CHART 9–4   Selected Recordings for Pattern

	Bowmar Orchestral Library		RCA Adventures in Listening	
Even	#53	*Gavotte* Lecocq ♩ ♫♪ ♫♪ ♩	1-2	*Morris Dance* German ♩ ♫
	#54	*Marche Militaire* Schubert ♩ ♫♪ ♫ ♩	1-2	*Russian Dance* Stravinsky ♫♪ ♫♪♪
	#62	*Theme and Variations* Haydn ♩ ♩ ♩ ♩	2-2	*Entrance of the Little Fauns* Pierné ♫♪ ♫♪
	#63	*Minuet* Haydn ♩ ♩ ♩ ∣ ♩ ♫♪ ♫♪	3-1	*Badinèrie* J. S. Bach ♫♪ ♫♪
Uneven	#54	*March of the Little Lead Soldiers* Pierné	2-1	*Waltz* Meyerbeer
	#60	*The Moldau* (first theme) Smetana ♩ ♪♩ ♪	2-2	*Non troppo mosso* Cimarosa–Malipiero ♩ ♪♩ ♪
	#61	*On the Trail* Grofé ♩ ♪♩ ♪	3-1	*Barcarolle* Offenbach ♩ ♪♩ ♪
	#63	*Anvil Chorus* Verdi ♩. ♪♩. ♪	4-2	*Copacabana* Milhaud ♩. ♫♪
Syncopated	#56	*Jamaican Rumba* Benjamin ♫♪ ♩	4-1	*Romanze* Mozart ♪♩ ♪∣♪♩ ♪
	#61	*Mardi Gras* Grofé ♫♪	4-2	*Copacabana* (second theme) Milhaud ♩. ♫♪
	#64	*Little Train of the Caipira* Villa-Lobos ♩. ♪∣♪. ♫♪ ∣ ♩	5-1	*Grand Walkaround* Gottschalk ♪♩ ♪♩ ♩
	#63	*Golliwog's Cakewalk* Debussy ♫♪♩ ♫		

To summarize:

1. Rhythm concepts develop through experience. The teacher leads children to categorize this experience and to label rhythmic components as tempo, pulse, accent, melodic rhythm, and pattern.

2. A variety of experiences should be provided in rhythm. If the concept of accent is being developed, for example, it should be done through a wide variety of songs, recordings, chants, and instruments in a variety of tempos throughout the entire year.

3. Children should have creative input when it comes to selecting instruments to play various rhythmic components. The pulse does not always have to be played by the drum or the melodic rhythm by the sticks. Students can provide many ingenious alternatives when given this option.

Melody Instruments

Melody instruments are those with which several pitches may be played. The recorder, piano, resonator and song bells, and xylophones and metallophones are all in this group. Traditional band instruments such as the trumpet, clarinet, and flute are sometimes available too.

A melody instrument: two-octave pianica

Melodee bells

Melody instruments are used in three ways: (1) to create simple pitch ostinati, (2) to play descants or countermelodies, and (3) to duplicate a melody being sung.

Pitch Ostinati

Pitch ostinati, discussed in Chapter 7, are appropriate when the song either is pentatonic or can be harmonized entirely by the I chord *or* by the I and V7 chords. Special ostinati can be created with instruments or voices to meet the individual needs, skills, and interests of the students.

"Hey, Ho, Nobody Home" is a round in F minor. It can be accompanied

Round

England

Hey, Ho, Anybody Home

f minor

Stoically

Part I

Part II

Hey, ho, an - y - bod - y home? meat and drink and

Part 3

mon - ey have I none, Yet I will be mer - ry!

I = F A♭ C

entirely by the I chord, F–A♭–C. Individual ostinati that could be devised and included are presented here in order of difficulty:

Ostinati are also devised for pentatonic melodies. "Turn the Glasses Over" is built on the F pentatonic scale. Ostinati may be created using these pitches:

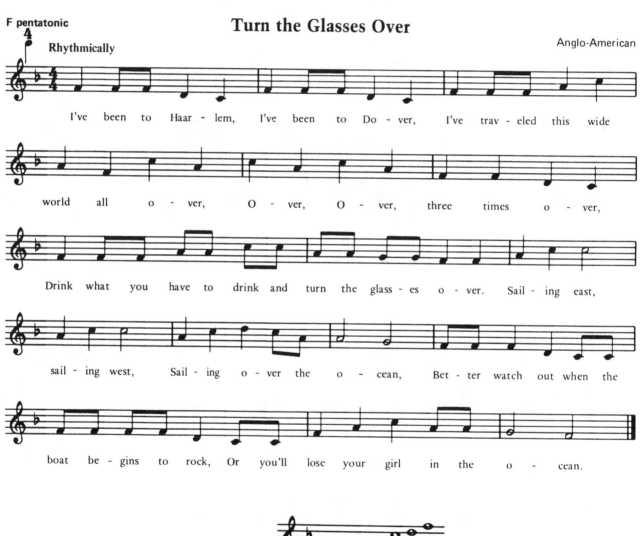

Turn the Glasses Over

Anglo-American

I've been to Haar - lem, I've been to Do - ver, I've trav - eled this wide world all o - ver, O - ver, O - ver, three times o - ver, Drink what you have to drink and turn the glass - es o - ver. Sail - ing east, sail - ing west, Sail - ing o - ver the o - cean, Bet - ter watch out when the boat be - gins to rock, Or you'll lose your girl in the o - cean.

Any melody instrument with these pitches could play the given ostinato. For students in the early elementary grades, it is better to use an instrument in which individual pitches for the ostinato can be isolated, such as resonator bells or xylophones with movable bars.

Middle and upper elementary students will be able to use such instruments as the recorder, piano, or song bells to play their ostinati. Ostinati should also include the addition of words for singing, as described in Chapter 7.

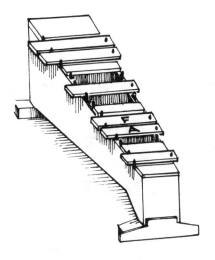

Descants

Descants or countermelodies offer another opportunity for playing melodies on a simple melody instrument. They appear in varying degrees of difficulty. "Hey Diddle Diddle" has a descant with only four notes which could easily be played on the recorder.

J.W. Elliott

Hey Diddle Diddle

Mother Goose Rhyme
F major

Hey did-dle did-dle, the cat and the fid-dle, The cow jumped o-ver the moon,— The

lit-tle dog laughed to see such sport, And the dish ran a-way with the spoon.—

I = F A C
IV = B♭ D F
V7 = C E G B♭

The Entire Melody

A final melody experience includes using instruments to play the entire melody, a skill usually achieved by the upper elementary grades. Some children might play the melody on the recorder while others sing. A third group could provide harmony on autoharps. The melody might be played as one part in a round while the other parts are sung. In all of these experiences each child should be allowed to have the opportunity of singing as well as playing an instrument. The teacher can allow for individual differences by tailoring a musical part for each child.

Harmony Instruments

Harmony instruments are those on which entire chords can be produced by one person (autoharp, guitar, piano) or by a group of people (resonator bells). The autoharp is an excellent instrument for early experiences in playing harmony since chords are set by simply depressing a button and strumming. The guitar and the piano are more appropriate for mature middle and especially upper elementary students. These instruments are an excellent application for the learning of music theory. Resonator bells used by several students at any age level can provide harmony too.

Many elementary songs are accompanied by one, two, or three chords and should be the core experience for these instruments.

"Three Blind Mice," a well-known round, can be accompanied entirely by the I chord of C major. Harmony instruments could play either once or twice a bar. "The Old Gray Goose" uses the I and V7 chords of F major. Chords could be played once, twice, or four times per bar. It is good to experiment with all possible ways of chording to see which is most suitable as a harmonic accompaniment, depending upon the tempo chosen and the mood desired. This is an important aesthetic choice for children. They may even decide to play the chords on a pattern of their own invention instead of the pulse or accent.

A harmony instrument with fifteen chords: the ChromAharp

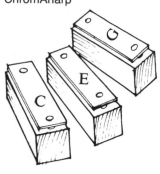

"Old Folks at Home" uses the I, V7, and IV chords in the key of D major. Since chord changes often occur on the third beat of a measure, the strumming pattern must be either twice or four times per measure.

As described in Chapter 7, different groups can be assigned the responsibility of the I, IV, or V7 cords. Later, individual children can play all chords on appropriate instruments, including the guitar and ukulele.

Success in harmony playing depends upon the children's knowing *when* chords change as well as to *what* they change. In addition, singing while playing provides a total musical involvement and keeps students interested. Children should always have flexible involvement in these experiences; they should never be locked into rigid roles.

D major
4/4

With feeling

Old Folks at Home

Words and music by Stephen C. Foster

'Way down up - on the Swa - nee riv - er, Far, far a - way,
All up and down the whole cre - a - tion, Sad - ly I roam,

There's where my heart is turn - ing ev - er, There's where the old folks __ stay.
Still long - ing for the old plan - ta - tion, And for the old folks at home.

Chorus

All the world is sad and drear-y, Eve-ry where I roam;

Oh, dear ones, how my heart grows wear-y, Far from the old folks at home.

I = D F#A
IV = G B D
V7 = A C#E G

C major

Three Blind Mice

Mother Goose Rhyme

Round

Zestfully

1. Three blind mice, —— Three blind mice, ——

2. See how they run, —— see how they run, —— They

3. all run af-ter the farm-er's wife, who

4. cut off their tails with a carv-ing knife. Did you

ev-er see such a sight in your life as three blind mice.——

I = C E G

F major

The Old Gray Goose
(Go Tell Aunt Rhody)

Moderately

1. Go tell aunt Rho - dy Go tell aunt Rho - dy,

117

Go   tell   aunt   Rho - dy,   the   old   gray   goose   is   dead.

2. The one she was saving
   To make a feather bed

3. She died in the mill pond
   Standing on her head.

4. The goslings are crying
   Because the goose is dead.

5. The gander is weeping
   Because the goose is dead.

I = F A C
V7 = C E G Bᵇ

Special Effects

Instruments can also be used to enhance the overall effect of a song, poem, or story through a creative interpretation of the words. The rhyme about Jack and Jill might be performed this way:
Wood block begins to tap x x x x x at a walking tempo and continues throughout the rhyme.

> Jack (triangle)
> and
> Jill (sand blocks)
> went up (*glissando* up song bells)
> the hill to fetch a pail of water.
> Jack (triangle)
> fell down (thump on drum)
> and broke (clash of cymbals)
> his crown,
> And Jill (sand blocks)
> came tumbling after (*glissando* down song bells).
> Wood block fades out x x x x x

A logical extension would be to include all types of instruments—rhythm, melody, and harmony—in an extended story read by the teacher or invented by the children. In all cases, the selection of instruments should be an *aesthetic* accompaniment to whatever activity is selected.

Experiencing a Sound Story (all levels)

A RAINY NIGHT

TEACHER: As I read this short story, decide what sounds we might add to enhance its effect. These might be made with instruments or with your body.

Story	Children's Suggestions
One night, Rob and Tom found themselves without a ride home after a scary movie. It was very stormy, with rain falling and thunder clapping.	*oo-oo-oo* sounds with voices tapping on wood block boom on bass drum
Rob and Tom decided to take a short cut across the railroad track and barely missed being hit by a freight train.	train whistle (voice) clack sound with jingle sticks

They walked past old houses and heard some doors being slammed as well as some weird laughing.

They heard an owl in the distance so they decided to run.

The rain continued to fall harder. They ran faster and faster until they had to stop and catch their breath. Just then, they heard the engine of Tom's father's sports car in the distance, gradually coming closer. "Whew!" they both sighed in relief.

bang on wood block
laughter with voices
hooting with voices
running sound on guiro
more tapping
gasping sounds
RRRRRR with voices
big sigh

Constructing Simple Instruments

Most schools have a basic supply of rhythm instruments. Melody and harmony instruments are usually rarer. For schools that have nothing the teacher can plan a classroom project to make a few simple instruments. Constructing and decorating instruments is a craft lesson, but their use in ways described above is music education.

The following instruments are suggested:

1. *Rhythm sticks.* Cut doweling, broomsticks, or bamboo to convenient lengths.
2. *Sand blocks.* Use small blocks of wood, 2 × 4 × ¾", with spool handles glued on. Fold sandpaper (varying grains) over ends and attach it with thumbtacks on sides or top.
3. *Shakers.* Use small cardboard or plastic containers (or inside rolls from paper towels or toilet tissue) with a few seeds, beads, beans, peas, or pebbles sealed in.
4. *Tambourine.* Use jingle bells sewed around a piece of material held by an embroidery hoop, or bottle caps attached to the edge of an aluminum or cardboard plate.
5. *Jingle sticks.* Nail two or three bottle caps to a slender piece of wood. (Make a hole in each cap, then attach them to the wood with a nail with a head larger than the hole.)
6. *Drums.* Use plastic containers, barrels, oatmeal boxes, or cardboard tubes (from inside rolled carpeting) as shells and cover either or both ends with cut old inner tubes, stretched chamois, muslin, down ticking, or old drumheads.
7. *Flowerpot chimes.* Suspend a variety of clean flowerpots (preferably pottery) from a frame with twine. Smaller pots are higher in pitch.
8. *Tuned nails.* Suspend nails of varying sizes from a frame with string. Smaller nails sound higher. Another nail may be used as the striker.
9. *Glass-jar scale.* Use eight jars of identical size and shape and tune with different amounts of water in each. (The more water, the lower the sound.)
10. *Mallets (Beaters).* Use doweling or pencils covered at one end with cork, rubber balls, balls of yarn, or the like.

This list is only a beginning. When instruments of a special type are needed, specific directions on how the instrument is to be made can be given. Children may even "invent" instruments when provided with materials.

It is important to remember that *using* the instruments through playing and creating is the musical endeavor and experience, not the *making* or *decorating* of the instruments. Such activities provide ongoing motivation in the classroom through individual and group participation.

119

Exercises and Activities

1. Find a song for a given grade level and analyze it for tempo, pulse, accent grouping, melodic rhythm, and characteristic pattern.
2. Find a pentatonic song or a song that can be accompanied by the I chord or by the I and V7 chords. Create six ostinati, ranging from easy to difficult, which could be used to accompany it with melody instruments.
3. Make a chart showing what changes occur and when for a simple song using I, IV, and V7 chords.
4. Find or write a song or poem which would allow many creative sounds to be added as special effects with various instruments.

Key Terms and Concepts

Rhythm instruments
Melody instruments
Harmony instruments
Tempo
Pulse (Beat)
Accent (Accent grouping)
Duple meter
Triple meter
Quadruple meter
Meter (Time signature)
Simple meter
Compound meter

Asymmetrical accent grouping
Melodic rhythm
Characteristic pattern (motive)
Even pattern
Uneven pattern
Syncopated pattern
Descant
Transposition
Tonic (I) chord
Dominant seventh (V7) chord
Subdominant (IV) chord
Glissando

Professional Readings

Autoharp

The Many Ways to Play the Autoharp, Vols. 1 and 2. Union, N.J.: Oscar Schmidt International.
Null, Cecil. *Autoharp Instruction*. Miami Beach, Fla.: Charles Hansen Publishers, 1969.
Nye, Robert, and Margaret Peterson. *Teaching Music with the Autoharp*. Union, N.J.: Music Education Group, 1973.

Guitar

Bay, Mel. *Mel Bay Guitar Series*. Kirkwood, Mo.: Mel Bay Publishing Co. (elementary level; fourth grade and up).
Noad, Frederick M. *Playing the Guitar*, 2nd ed. New York: Schirmer, 1972.
Silverman, Jerry. *Beginning the Folk Guitar*. New York: Oak Publishing Co., 1964.
Timmerman, Maurine, and Celeste Griffith. *Guitar in the Classroom*, 2nd ed. Dubuque, Iowa: William C. Brown, 1976.

Recorder

Allen, Stacey, and Saul Feldstein. *Creating Music with Melody Instruments*. Port Washington, N.Y.: Alfred Music Company, 1970 (may be used with companion books for guitar and rhythm instruments).
Brimhall, John. *Fun-Way Pre-Band Instrument Method*. Miami Beach, Fla.: Charles Hansen Publishers, 1966 (contains many recent popular tunes).

Buchtel, Forrest L. *Buchtel Recorder Method,* Book 1. Park Ridge, Ill.: Neil A. Kjos Music Co. (Baroque system for C recorders—soprano and tenor).

Earle, Frederick. *Trophy Elementary Recorder Method, Baroque System.* Cleveland, Ohio: Trophy Music Co.

Trapp Family. *Enjoy Your Recorder.* Storrs, Conn.: Magnamusic Distributors, 1964.

Constructing Instruments

Coleman, Satis. *The Drum Book.* New York: John Day, 1931.

10 Moving to Music

Movement is a vital activity for developing musicianship and understanding of musical concepts. There is something basically therapeutic about moving to music that children enjoy when it is used with singing, listening, and playing instruments in the music classroom.

Traditionally, finger plays, action songs, singing games, folk and social dances, and dramatizations generally have been the total experience in music and movement for most children. The goals of these types of activities are: development of large and small muscles; awareness of body parts and laterality and directionality; socialization; and experience with folk dances of our own and other cultures. Pure recreation and diversion may be the entire objective in some cases. However important these goals may be in the general school environment, they are of secondary value in the music program. In the music classroom, movement is neither physical education nor an outlet for emotional release.

There are two fundamental types of movement. *Axial* movement, when the child moves in place, includes bending, swaying, and shaking. *Locomotive* movement is movement from one place to another and includes walking, running, skipping, and jumping. Both types need to be developed in the classroom, depending upon available space and physical resources. These types of experience are the core of *eurhythmics*, a system refined by the Swiss educator Emile Jacques-Dalcroze early in this century.

Reinforcing Concepts through Movement

How can movement be used in the classroom to reinforce musical concepts? A first step is to examine selected concepts that lend themselves to movement. Below are a few examples; this list can be expanded by adding others from those listed in Chapter 2.

Rhythm

Tempo: Children move in the room to the tempo set by a drum beat, piano, recording, or the like (locomotion).

Beat: Children move a body part (bend fingers, wiggle shoulders, nod head, bend knees, tap feet) to the pulse set by a drum beat.

Accent Grouping: Children sway or bend in place to the accented beat of a recording or drum.
　　　Children create and repeat a body ostinato for a set accent grouping.

For triple groupings:
　　　Nod head on 1
　　　Wiggle left shoulder on 2
　　　Wiggle right shoulder on 3

For quadruple groupings:
　　　Jump on 1
　　　Clap on 2 and 3
　　　Bend down on 4 (to prepare for next jump)

　　　Children conduct meter patterns to various accent groupings they hear.

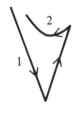
Duple

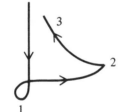
Triple

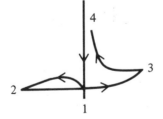
Quadruple

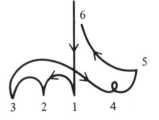
Sextuple

Pitch
High–Low: Children assume a low or high body position (crouching versus walking on tiptoe) to show when a low or high pitch is played on the piano, resonator bells, or wood block.

Articulation
Legato–Staccato: Children make smooth arm movements when they hear a legato passage and jerky movements when they hear a staccato passage.

Texture
One group of children moves to the melodic rhythm of each part in a round to show how two or more melodies interweave in polyphony.

Intensity

Children demonstrate a crescendo or decrescendo by open or closed body gestures as they listen to a recording.

Timbre

One group of children moves at the sound of the trumpet, another at the sound of the clarinet in a given recording.

Form

In an ABA form, each section has its distinct gesture.

A = slow movements in a circle
B = faster in any direction
A = repeat of slow movements in a circle

These activities can be combined so that children respond to more than one musical element. It is certainly possible for children to walk to the pulse as well as respond to the legato or staccato quality of the melody heard over the pulse. This is part of the essence of interpretive dance and movement. It is an activity that logically follows time spent with individual musical elements, particularly in the upper grades where concepts are less isolated than they are in the early elementary years.

Specific Program Objectives for Movement

The objectives listed in Chart 10–1 provide a model for movement. As was mentioned in the discussion of objectives, for playing instruments, children will not all achieve a selected objective at a given time or year. However, consistent music instruction will help each child achieve most of these program objectives by the end of the elementary-school experience.

CHART 10–1   Objectives for Moving

	Children will
Early elementary (K–2)	echo clap
	tap, clap, walk, and run to the basic pulse
	move in place through swinging, swaying, and so on to show the mood of the music
	move their bodies to show loud and soft, fast and slow, high and low
	participate in action songs, finger plays and singing games
	participate in interpretive movement such as dramatizations
Middle elementary (3–4)	move to even patterns
	skip and gallop to music
	participate in more involved singing games and folk dances
	improvise movements and dances
	show understanding of musical elements through movement, including attention to phrasing, dynamics, articulation, and so on

CHART 10–1 *(continued)* Objectives for Moving

Upper elementary (5–6)	participate in more involved folk dances
	use conducting patterns (2, 3, 4, 6)
	perform stylized period dances
	use movement to show deviations in tempo and dynamics, such as *accelerando*, etc.
	use movement to show the mood and style of the music

Recordings or songs for movement are chosen because they are suitable for a concept and objective. Physical coordination, relaxation, diversion, socialization, or just fun should be the byproducts of movement through music, not its *primary* goal.

Experiencing Musical Concepts through Movement

Example One (early elementary)

Objective

The children will demonstrate a crescendo with their bodies.

Motivation

"Listen, class, and tell me how my voice changes as I say hello". Teacher says hello five times, saying it louder each time. Children state the voice was louder each time.

Procedure

The children are asked to listen as the teacher plays a series of chords on the piano, louder each time they are repeated.

1st time - *pp*
2nd time - *p*
3rd time - *mf*
4th time - *f*
5th time - *ff*

Discussion follows on what happens to the dynamics and how this was related to the teacher's saying hello. The children are then asked to crouch on the floor and gradually open their bodies and rise as the music crescendos (or suggest motions that show this difference).

Example Two (middle elementary)

Material

Recording of "In the Hall of the Mountain King" (Grieg, BOL #59)

Objective

The children will demonstrate both a *crescendo* and an *accelerando* with their bodies.

Motivation

A series of graphs on construction paper are shown, representing respectively *crescendo, accelerando, decrescendo,* and *ritardando.*

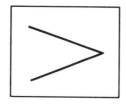  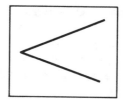 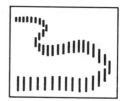

"Some of these graphs give us a picture of what is happening in the music to which we'll listen. You decide which graphs apply as well as why." (Answers: 2 and 3)

Procedure
The recording is played. The children discuss it with the teacher who leads them to discover the music may be represented by both Graph 2 (*accelerando*) and Graph 3 (*crescendo*). The children are asked to tell how they could move their bodies to show a crescendo (possibility: from closed to open position). Many children demonstrate this in place as the record is played again. The children then discuss how to show the *accelerando* (possibility: by walking and increasing the pace to a fast run). Many children demonstrate this by moving around the room as the record is repeated. The children may now try moving both ways, using a closed position in a walk and gradually opening as the music speeds up and they begin to run.

Example Three (upper elementary)

Material
Recording of "An Evening in the Village" (Bartok, RCA 5-2; form: ABABA)

Objective
The children will demonstrate an ABABA form with their bodies in movement.

Motivation
The teacher asks the children to arrange three blue and two red cards in many possible ways.

Possibilities

B	R	B	B	R
B	B	R	R	B
B	R	B	R	B
B	R	R	B	B

Procedure
"The blue and red represent sections in the composition to which we are going to listen. One of the combinations we placed on the chalkboard is the way the music is organized. Listen to see which combination it is and be able to give musical reasons why."

The children listen and discover the form is blue–red–blue–red–blue (ABABA). A discussion follows in which it is pointed out that the A sections all use string instruments and are legato, while the B sections use woodwinds and are staccato. The children are now divided into A or B groups and move to a space in the classroom. They then move to the appropriate portion of the recording, using legato motions if they are As, staccato motions if they are Bs.

When recordings are used to stimulate movement, allow the children to listen carefully before they are asked to respond in movement. As children become more confident with movement, their suggestions for gestures and patterns should be incorporated as much as possible.

Example Four (early and middle elementary)

Objective
The children will dramatize a selected object, event, or phenomenon.

Motivation
These ideas may be written on note cards that are given to individual students or to small groups to act out. They may also be whispered in the child's ear. When one child moves, the others may tell what they think it is, always giving musical reasons. For example, "He's a toy that is winding down because he's going *slower* and *lower*."

Procedure
The following directions are written or whispered for children to act out. The teacher leads them to verbalize how they move (fast–slow, heavily–lightly, and so on) so the experience is related to musical elements:
You

    grow like a flower
    melt like a snowman
    move like an elephant, deer, kangaroo, cat, mouse, turtle, tugboat, jet plane,
     bicycle, leaf, ball
    are jumping rope
    are a windmill
    are sweeping
    are a boxer
    are climbing a ladder, a wall, a hill
    are a toy soldier who has a wind-up spring
    are having a tug-of-war

You are a balloon. Someone is blowing you up. Then you

    fly away
    pop
    gradually lose your air

You are walking barefoot over
    sand
    sharp stones
    fire
    glue
    ice

You have jumping beans inside you.

You are a special machine:
    a dishwasher
    a washing machine
    a lawn mower
    a jet engine

You

move as leader does in mirror imitation.

are balancing a heavy load on your head as you walk/run/jump.

are walking twenty feet above the ground on a tightrope with a balancing pole.

are a jumping jack. Someone keeps opening the box you are in.

Example Five (any level)

Objective

The children will move in the ways described in one or more of the following lists.

Motivation

These lists may be kept on a bulletin board. The children may take turns selecting a movement on one or two lists for the class to do. It may also be a guessing game, with one child doing the movement and letting the class figure out what and why. (The children should be encouraged to be individual in their interpretations. Not everybody should do exactly what the teacher or leader does.)

Procedure

One movement at a time should be tried. Gradually two, three, or four may be combined.

Type of Movement		Direction to Move		Quality		Variation
Axial						
bend		up		slowly		with repetition
spin		down		quietly		with contrast
swing		back		quickly		at a high level
clap		forth		loudly		at a low level
stretch		sideways		heavily		in an open
tap	+	over	+	sadly	+	position
rock		under		smoothly		in a closed
snap		above		bumpily		position
twist		below		gradually		
pat		in a circle		suddenly		
push		in a square				
pull		in a triangle				
hit						
shake						
stamp						
shrink						
rub						
squeeze						
bounce						

Locomotive	
walk	shuffle
run	spin
jump	wriggle
hop	crawl
gallop	creep
lunge	slide
skip	skate
limp	

Traditional Movement

Many elementary series and resource books include traditional material in movement—finger plays, action songs, singing games, folk and social dances, and dramatizations. These may be used to develop musical concepts as well as to provide a motivating experience for children.

Finger Plays

Finger plays are used almost entirely with early elementary children. These songs or rhymes suggest movement for the hands, fingers, or feet. They are usually done in place and therefore are axial. They help the children develop small muscle coordination. Children learn to follow the instructions in these finger plays. They are best done to a steady pulse.

Jack-in-the-box
Sits so still,
Won't you come out?
Yes, I will
    (bury thumbs in fist—then
    pop them out) or (child
    crouches on floor and then
    jumps up)

Here's the church,
    (fingers interlocked fingers
    inside)
And here's the steeple,
    (index fingers rise to a point)
Open the door
    (keep fingers interlocked but
    turn palms up)
And see all the people
    (wiggle fingers)

I'll touch my chin,
My cheek
My chair,
I'll touch my head,
My heels,
My hair.
I'll touch my knees,
My neck,
My nose,
Then I'll dip down and touch
    my toes.

A little ball, A bigger ball,
A great big ball I see.
    (Shape hands to make each ball.)
Now let us count the balls we've made,
One, two, three
    (To count, point with one hand.)

Here's a bunny,
    (raise two fingers)
With ears so funny,
    (wiggle fingers)
And here's a hole in the ground.
    (Make hole with fingers of other hand.)
At the first sound he hears,
    (straighten fingers)
He wiggles his ears,
    (wiggle fingers)
And pops right into the ground.
    (put fingers into hole)

These finger plays are used by permission of Shirley J. O'Brien, Cooperative Extension Service, University of Arizona, Tucson.

The Wiggle Song

Kansas singing game

1. My thumbs are start-ing to wig-gle, My thumbs are start-ing to wig-gle,

My thumbs are start-ing to wig-gle A-round, a-round, a-round. __

2. My thumbs and fingers are wiggling, etc.

3. My hand is starting to wiggle, etc.

4. My arms are starting to wiggle, etc.

5. My head is starting to wiggle, etc.

6. Now all of me is a-wiggling, etc.

I = G B D
IV = C E G
V7 = D F♯ A C

Action Songs

Action songs, also used in the early elementary grades, are similar to finger plays except that children may move out of place.

Tune: *Little Brown Jug*

Clap my hands and make a fist,
Tap my-self up-on the wrist,
Wig-gle my fin-gers and wig-gle my toes,
Feel the ma-te-ri-al in my clothes.
Point straight up and then point down,
Pull your mouth in-to a frown,
Slap your arm and tap the chair,
Pull ver-y soft-ly on your hair.
Snap your fin-gers if you can,
Then walk a-way like a lit-tle man.

Example One

G major

Raindrops

L. W.

1. One lit - tle rain - drop rid - ing on a cloud, Rid - ing on a cloud,
2. Two lit - tle rain - drops fall - ing from the sky, Fall - ing from the sky,

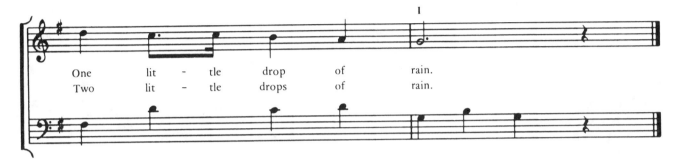

rid - ing on a cloud. One lit - tle rain - drop rid - ing on a cloud,
fall - ing from the sky. Two lit - tle rain - drops fall - ing from the sky, -

One lit - tle drop of rain.
Two lit - tle drops of rain.

3. Three little raindrops knocking on the roof, etc.

4. Four little raindrops dancing up and down, etc.

5. Five little raindrops sliding down the pane, etc.

6. Six little raindrops sleeping in the sun, etc.

7. Seven little raindrops run away and hide, etc.

I = G B D
V7 = D F♯ A C

Riding on a cloud

Falling
from
the
sky

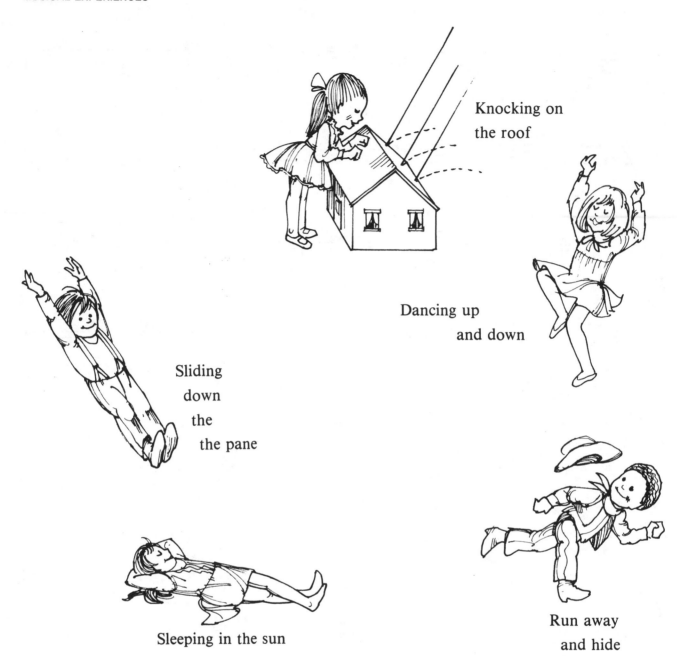

Knocking on
the roof

Dancing up
and down

Sliding
down
the
the pane

Run away
and hide

Sleeping in the sun

Procedure

The song should be introduced as a rote experience. Actions may then be done as the words suggest, the children giving ideas on what action would be appropriate.

A small group of children may do the movements as others sing or play instruments. These roles can be interchangeable, with everyone being able to sing, play, and move within one or over several lessons.

Example Two

Procedure

The children follow the directions given in each verse of the song. New verses may be made up by the teacher or the children.

Put Your Finger in the Air

Words and music by Woody Guthrie

D major

Lightly, humorously

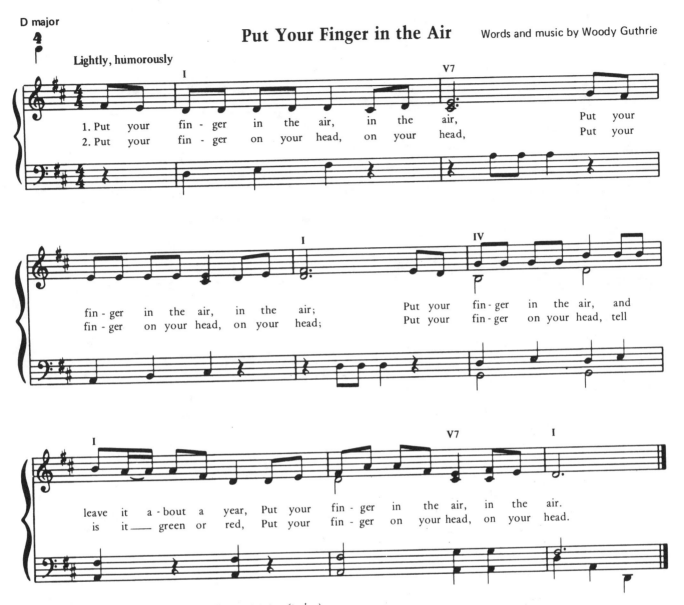

1. Put your fin-ger in the air, in the air, Put your finger in the air, in the air; Put your finger in the air, and leave it a-bout a year, Put your fin-ger in the air, in the air.

2. Put your fin-ger on your head, on your head, Put your finger on your head, on your head; Put your finger on your head, tell is it green or red, Put your fin-ger on your head, on your head.

3. Put your finger on your nose, on your nose *(twice)*
Put your finger on your nose And let the cold wind blow.
Put your finger on your nose, on your nose.

4. Put your finger on your shoe, on your shoe *(twice)*
. . . And leave it a day or two, *etc.*

I = D F♯ A
IV = G B D
V7 = A C♯ E G

Singing Games

Singing games are usually used in the early or middle elementary grades. They are very similar to action songs except there is a patterned way of moving (often in a circle). Many of these singing games reflect traditional movements of earlier generations or of different cultures.

F major
2

Chair, Chair, Chair
(Chaise, chaise, chaise)

Creole folk song

Not too fast

French Dialect:

Oh, sit in - side the ring up - on the chair, chair, chair,
As - si - sez vous, ma soeur des - sus la chais', chais', chais',

We cir - cle a - round, cir - cle a - round, cir - cle . a - round you ___ there,
Vous a - vez per - du ça q'vous a - viez, ça q'vous ai - miez hier au soir.

Now you stand up on your feet, bow to the one you greet,
Le - vez - vous des - sus vos pieds, et le pre - mier q'vous sa - lue - rez

And the one you choose will sit up - on the chair, chair, chair.
S'ra ce lui qui s'as - si - ra des - sus la chais', chais', chais'.

I = F A C
V7 = C E G B♭

Example One

Procedure

One child, who is "it," sits in a circle. The children sing and circle the child inside. On the appropriate line, the child bows to someone else, who then becomes "it."

Example Two

Procedure

The children do these actions as they sing the refrain:

First measure: Tap knees rapidly. (Ho-li-ah)
Remaining measures: Beat 1 Slap knees.
                                  Beat 2 Clap hands.
                                  Beat 3 Snap fingers.

G major
3

The Cuckoo

Austrian folk song

Lively

1. Oh I went to Pe - ter's flow - ing spring Where the wa - ter's so
2. Aft - er East - er come ___ sun - ny days That will melt all the
3. When I've mar - ried my ___ maid - en fair, What then can I de -

good, And   I heard there   the   cuck - oo   as she sang from   the   wood.
snow; Then   I'll mar - ry   my   maid-en fair, We'll be hap - py,   I   know.
sire? Oh,   a   home for   her   tend - ing And some wood for   the   fire.

Ho - li - ah,   ho - le - rah - hi - hi - ah, Ho - le - rah cuck - oo! Ho - le - rah - hi - hi - ah,

Ho - le - rah cuck - oo! Ho - le - rah - hi - hi - ah, Ho - le - rah cuck - oo Ho - le - rah - hi - hi - ah - ho!

From *Songs of Many Nations*, Cooperative Recreation Service, Inc., Delaware, Ohio.

I = G B D
V7 = D F♯ A C

On the 2nd singing of the refrain an extra "cuckoo" (and fingersnap) is added (*) each time.

On the 3rd singing of the refrain one more "cuckoo" is added (*). The tempo is also increased.

Folk and Social Dances

Folk and social dances represent the strictest organization in movement. Traditional floor patterns and body gestures are present in these dances, which are usually appropriate for the middle and upper elementary grades. Unlike singing games, folk and social dances are usually accompanied by a piano or a recording without any singing involved.

Example One

Procedure

Formation   Partners in single circle, all hands joined, with girl on right of partner.

Shoo, Fly, Don't Bother Me

U.S.

Shoo, fly, don't bother me,
Shoo, fly, don't bother me,
Shoo, fly, don't bother me,
For I belong to somebody
I feel, I feel,
I feel like a morning star.
I feel, I feel,
I feel like a morning star.

Measures

1–2	Move forward toward center of circle with 4 walking steps, swinging joined hands forward and up.
3–4	Move backward to place in circle with 4 walking steps, swinging joined hands downward and backward.
5–8	Repeat movements in Meas. 1–4.
9–14	Partners join both hands and turn clockwise in place two times with 12 walking steps.

15–16   Boy drops right hand as he passes girl under his left arm so that she moves clockwise to next boy in circle. She is now on the left of her original partner who has a new girl on his right as his new partner for repetition of dance.

                    Repeat dance as many times as desired.

Dramatization

Dramatization is acting out a story, a song, or a recording through movement.

Example One (all levels)

Procedure

A story is told. The children then move or play instruments which reinforce this story. Such stories may be invented, orchestrated and choreographed by the children.

     There is an old cat who is lost, cold, and hungry on Halloween. He is frightened by the children who wear weird costumes. There are many other sights and sounds that scare him. He hears the wind, pumpkins, ghosts, witches on broomsticks, and doorbells ringing. He also hears children running and shouting "Trick or Treat." He finally decides to crawl into an old barn where there are only bats flying around. Finally the old cat falls asleep as the sun comes up on a new day.

Example Two (early elementary)

The following story is dramatized as the words suggest:

Percussion Walk

One day I went for a walk. As I walked along on the sidewalk, I could hear my footsteps going WALK, WALK, WALK. Some other people came by. . . . Their footsteps went WALK, WALK, WALK. . . . I passed a new house. . . . Some men were fixing the roof. I could hear their hammers going TAP, TAP, TAP. . . . I heard a train coming, so I

went down to the corner to watch it. My feet went RUN, RUN, RUN. . . . Oh, it was a long train. The wheels going 'round and 'round went CLICK-CLICK-CLACK. . . . Then I saw a man riding in a wagon which was being pulled by a horse. The horse's hoofs went CLIP-CLOP, CLIP-CLOP. . . . It was getting very late. My watch said TICK, TICK, TICK. . . . It was very late for my dinner. I ran all the way home. My feet went RUN, RUN, RUN. . . . I came to my house and knocked on the door. KNOCK, KNOCK, KNOCK. . . . My mother came to the door. I washed my hands and sat down to eat. Everyone was talking. It sounded like a broken television. . . . NOISE.

Example Three (early elementary)

The words of a poem may suggest movement:

I live in a forest
Where animals be.

I often can hear
The bumblebee

And there are also
Deer that leap,

Bunnies that hop,
And mice that creep.

The other night
I heard a frog,

Two wild pigs,
And an old lost dog.

Close to the ground
I can see a worm,

A snake that crawls,
And a bug that squirms.

To live in the woods
Is a real-life zoo—

Monkeys and lions,
And me and you.

All the traditional movements have great appeal for youngsters. They are fun and provide motivation because of the participation. All should be used as musical learning as well as experience in movement. A game or dance should never be learned before the music is sung or heard. The music is the initial experience from which the motions logically follow. A good music program cannot rely on doing clever motions to the instructions on a recording or in a song. Movement must develop solid musical concepts if primary values are being developed. A sense of laterality and directionality, social awareness, some knowledge of tradition, and coordination are all byproducts of the musical experience.

Exercises and Activities

1. Find a recording that can be used to develop a concept similar to ones listed in this chapter or Chapter 2. Plan a lesson using this recording.
2. Plan a lesson that develops a musical concept from a finger play, action song, singing game, or folk dance.
3. Create a dramatization and provide movement and instrumental accompaniment for it.

Key Terms and Concepts

Axial movement
Locomotive movement

138

Eurhythmics
Legato
Staccato
Finger plays
Action songs
Singing games
Folk and social dances
Dramatizations

Professional Readings

Birkenshaw, Lois. *Music for Fun/Music for Learning*, 2nd ed. Toronto: Holt, Rinehart and Winston of Canada, 1978.

Cherry, Clare. *Creative Movement for the Developing Child*, 2nd ed. Belmont, Calif.: Fearon Publishers, 1971.

Dorian, Margery, and Frances Gulland. *Telling Stories Through Movement*. Belmont, Calif.: Fearon Publishers, 1974.

Eaton, Janet P. *The Discipline of Movement*. Fairfax, Calif.: Janet P. Eaton, 1978.

Findlay, Elsa. *Rhythm and Movement: Applications of Dalcroze Eurhythmics*, Evanston, Ill.: Summy-Birchard, 1971.

Gray, Vera, and Rachel Percival. *Music, Movement and Mime for Children*. London: Oxford University Press, 1962.

Hood, Marguerite V., and E. J. Schultz. *Learning Music Through Rhythm*. Boston: Ginn, 1949.

Nash, Grace C. *Creative Approaches to Child Development with Music, Language and Movement*. New York: Alfred Publishing, 1974.

Selected Recordings for Movement and Dramatization

Bowmar Orchestral Library (Excerpts)

BOL #51 ANIMALS AND CIRCUS
Saint-Saëns, CARNIVAL OF THE ANIMALS
    Royal March of the Lion, Hens and Cocks, Turtles, The Elephant, Kangaroos
BOL #52 NATURE AND MAKE-BELIEVE
Grieg, MARCH OF THE DWARFS
Donaldson, ONCE UPON A TIME SUITE
    Three Billy Goats Gruff, Little Train
Rimsky-Korsakoff, FLIGHT OF THE BUMBLEBEE
BOL #53 PICTURES AND PATTERNS
Liadov, VILLAGE DANCE
Debussy, EN BATEAU (IN A BOAT) (Petite Suite)
BOL #54 MARCHES
Pierné, MARCH OF THE LITTLE LEAD SOLDIERS
Rodgers, MARCH OF THE SIAMESE CHILDREN (The King and I)
BOL #55 DANCES, Part I
Copland, HOE-DOWN (Rodeo)
Walton, POLKA (Facade Suite)
Waldteufel, SKATERS' WALTZ
Khatchaturian, MASQUERADE SUITE
    Mazurka, Galop
BOL #56 DANCES, Part II
Lecocq, CAN-CAN (Mlle. Angot Suite)
Rossini-Respighi, TARANTELLA (Fantastic Toyshop)
BOL #57 FAIRY TALES IN MUSIC

Ravel, MOTHER GOOSE SUITE
  Pavane of the Sleeping Beauty, Hop o' My Thumb, Laideronette, Empress of the Pagodas, The Conversations of Beauty and the Beast, The Fairy Garden
Coates, CINDERELLA
BOL #58 STORIES IN BALLET AND OPERA
Tchaikovsky, NUTCRACKER SUITE
  Dance of the Sugar-Plum Fairy, Trepak, Waltz of the Flowers
BOL #59 LEGENDS IN MUSIC
Saint-Saëns, DANSE MACABRE
BOL #61 AMERICAN SCENES
Grofé, GRAND CANYON SUITE
  Sunrise, On the Trail, Cloudburst
BOL #62 MASTERS OF MUSIC
Wagner, RIDE OF THE VALKYRIES
BOL #63 CONCERT MATINEE
Debussy, CHILDREN'S CORNER SUITE
  Serenade for the Doll, The Snow is Dancing
BOL #64 MINIATURES IN MUSIC
Schubert, THE BEE
Schumann, WILD HORSEMEN (Album for the Young)
Liadov, MUSIC BOX
Gounod, FUNERAL MARCH OF THE MARIONETTE
Villa-Lobos, LITTLE TRAIN OF THE CAIPIRA (Bachianas Brasilieras No. 2)
BOL #65 MUSIC, USA
Caillet, VARIATIONS ON "POP! GOES THE WEASEL"
BOL #67 FANTASY IN MUSIC
Coates, THE THREE BEARS
BOL #68 CLASSROOM CONCERT
Pinto, MEMORIES OF CHILDHOOD
  Running, Marching, Hobby Horse, Devil's Dance
BOL #70 MUSIC OF THE SEA AND SKY
Debussy, CLOUDS (Nocturnes for Orchestra)
Debussy, DIALOGUE OF THE WIND AND THE SEA (La Mer)
BOL #78 MUSICAL KALEIDOSCOPE
Glière, RUSSIAN SAILORS' DANCE (The Red Poppy)
Bizet, MINUET (L'Arlèsienne Suite No. 1)
BOL #85 MUSICAL IMPRESSIONS
Respighi, FOUNTAINS OF ROME

Adventures in Listening (RCA) (Excerpts)

Grade 1, Vol. 1
Moussorgsky, BALLET OF THE UNHATCHED CHICKS (Pictures at an Exhibition)
Tchaikovsky, DANCE OF THE LITTLE SWANS (Swan Lake)
Bizet, LEAP FROG (Children's Games)
Ibert, PARADE (Divertissement)
Delibes, WALTZ OF THE DOLL (Coppélia)

Grade 1, Vol. 2
Saint-Saëns, THE ELEPHANT (Carnival of the Animals)
Bartók, FROM THE DIARY OF A FLY (Mikrokosmos Suite for Orchestra)
Menotti, MARCH OF THE KINGS (Amahl and the Night Visitors)
McBride, PONY EXPRESS (Punch and Judy)

Grade 2, Vol. 1
Prokofieff, DEPARTURE (Winter Holiday)
Bartók, JACK-IN-THE-BOX (Mikrokosmos Suite No. 2)
Ibert, THE LITTLE WHITE DONKEY (Histoires No. 2)
Herbert, MARCH OF THE TOYS (Babes in Toyland)
Kodály, VIENNESE MUSICAL CLOCK (Háry János Suite)

Grade 2, Vol. 2
Rimsky-Korsakoff, DANCE OF THE BUFFOONS (The Snow Maiden)
Pierné, ENTRANCE OF THE LITTLE FAUNS (Cydalise Suite No. 1)
Schuller, THE TWITTERING MACHINE (Seven Studies on Themes of Paul Klee)

Grade 3, Vol. 1
Copland, CIRCUS MUSIC (The Red Pony)
Elgar, FAIRIES AND GIANTS (Wand of Youth Suite No. 1)
Vaughan Williams, MARCH PAST OF THE KITCHEN UTENSILS (The Wasps)

Grade 3, Vol. 2
Thomson, THE ALLIGATOR AND THE 'COON (Acadian Songs and Dances)
Bartók, BEAR DANCE (Hungarian Sketches)
Saint-Saëns, THE SWAN (Carnival of the Animals)

Grade 4, Vol. 1
Rimsky-Korsakoff, BRIDAL PROCESSION (Le Coq d'Or Suite)
Ginastera, WHEAT DANCE (Estancia)

Grade 4, Vol. 2
Menotti, SHEPHERDS' DANCE (Amahl and the Night Visitors)
Khatchaturian, WALTZ (Masquerade Suite)

Grade 5, Vol. 1
Ravel, THE CONVERSATIONS OF BEAUTY AND THE BEAST (Mother Goose Suite)
Charpentier, ON MULEBACK (Impressions of Italy)

Grade 5, Vol. 2
Copland, HOE-DOWN (Rodeo)
Brahms, HUNGARIAN DANCE #1
Carpenter, THE HURDY-GURDY (Adventures in a Perambulator)

Grade 6, Vol. 1
Falla, SPANISH DANCE #1 (La Vida Breve)
Griffes, THE WHITE PEACOCK

Grade 6, Vol. 2
Guarneri, BRAZILIAN DANCE (Three Dances for Orchestra)
Smetana, DANCE OF THE COMEDIANS (The Bartered Bride)

Other Movement Recordings from Bowmar

Bowmar Singing Games and Folk Dances Six albums which include singing games,
American dances, world dances, and Latin American dances (Records B201, B202,
B203, B204, B205, B206). Directions included on record jackets.
Dances of Hawaii (B217)
Mexican Folk Dances (B211)
Canadian Folk Dances (B213)
Rounds and Mixers, 1 and 2 (B214)
Singing Square Dances (B215)
Rhythm Time 1 (B301) and *2* (B303)
Small Singer Series
  The Small Dancer (B550)
  The Small Player (B551)
  The Small Listener (B561)

Records from Folkways/Scholastic Records

American Games and Activity Songs for Children (FC 7674)
Call and Response (Ellen Jenkins) (SC 7638)
Dance-a-Long (SC 7651)
Learning as We Play (FC 7659B)
More Learning as We Play (7658)

Records from Activity Records

Hap Palmer

Getting to Know Myself (AR 543)
Homemade Band (AR 545)
Movin' (AR 546)
Pretend (AR 563)
Mod Marches (AR 527)
Modern Tunes for Rhythms and Instruments (AR 523)
Folk Song Carnival (AR 524)

Learning to Read Music

Reading Music

Reading music is as important in music education as singing, listening, playing instruments, and moving to music. If basic concepts have been formulated through these four activities, reading music is the next step in developing and refining these concepts.

We saw in Chapter 2 that concepts develop through three steps. First, experience with an object or idea is necessary (enactive stage). Children must experience many songs before high and low, for example, have meaning for them. Second, after many experiences, they mentally sort objects and ideas into appropriate categories (iconic stage). Some tones are low, others high; some sounds are loud, others soft. After many experiences that have been categorized correctly, children are ready to deal with the concept mentally at the third step of development, the symbolic stage. This is when reading, whether of language, music, or mathematical symbols, begins to make sense in the child's world.

Very young children have a limited ability to operate at the iconic or symbolic level. By the end of the early elementary grades, however, children do have the mental capacity to read music, although there is no definitive rule for when this should occur. If children have had sufficient experience in an area and have properly categorized this experience, music reading is appropriate, whether the children are first- or sixth-graders.

The purpose of reading music is rarely to make the individual child an independent music reader. This is the province of the private music teacher, not the classroom teacher or music specialist. Music reading in the classroom can enable children to decipher and understand the principles of pitch, rhythm, and intensity.

Reading Pitch

A direct symbol is one that looks the way it sounds. A high pitch is placed high on a staff, a low one is placed low. Pitch notation is a graph of the highness or lowness of a note on a staff. This is known as *diastematic* notation and has been used in the Western world for nearly a thousand years. Our graph is a staff of five lines and four spaces that are used to represent seven recurring pitch names: A, B, C, D, E, F, and G. Reference points determine which lines are designated as certain pitches. These references are called *clefs*. The 𝄞 (G or treble clef) tells where G above middle C is located. Tradition has placed it on the second line from the bottom of the staff, with other pitches following in pattern by line or space.

The 𝄢 (F or bass clef) tells where F below middle C is located, on the second line from the top, all other notes following in pattern by line or space.

When placed in proximity, the F and G staffs form the grand staff, with middle C on the ledger line between the two:

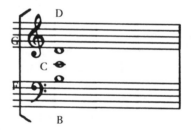

Teaching pitch reading makes children aware of the highness or lowness of points on this graph. This is a gradual development leading from gross awareness of high and low to specific identification of pitches. Children are ready to respond to pitch notation when:

1. They aurally recognize the difference between high and low pitches.
2. They graph melodic contours with hand levels.
3. They aurally discriminate between stepwise (conjunct) and skipwise (disjunct) motion.
4. They aurally identify specific tonal patterns.

The earliest music-reading activities related to these include:

Line Notation Line notation is the use of lines (Figure 11-3) to represent pitches. It is appropriate for use with young children or older ones with no notational experience.

Characteristic intervals that occur in songs may be isolated and put onto paper in line notation. The descending minor third and ascending perfect fourth would be:

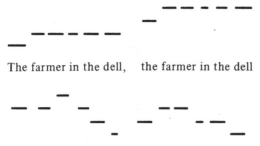

An entire song, such as "Farmer in the Dell," may be noted this way:

The farmer in the dell,   the farmer in the dell

Heigh ho the merry-o,   the farmer in the dell.

Children do not learn to read music from line notation as such, but it does remind them of the direction of pitches and makes them aware of the direct correlation between highness or lowness of sound.

(Kum ba yah, my Lord)

(Twinkle, twinkle, little star)

Line notation is also effective when used to display a mystery song (one the class has heard already) on the chalkboard or as part of a bulletin board.

Line Notation with Letters, Numbers, or Syllables Using letters (A, B, C), numbers (1, 2, 3), or syllables (*do, re, mi*) with line notation is a good way to identify pitch more specifically. There is nothing inherently sacred about using letters to designate scale tones, numbers, or syllables.

g   5   sol

or   or

e   3   mi

Each system has advantages as well as disadvantages. Consistency by the teacher and within the school system is the most important consideration. Children should be able to use the same system as they progress through the elementary grades.

F major

Lovely Evening

Round

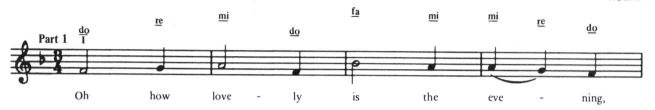

Oh how love - ly is the eve - ning,

is the eve - ning, When the bells are

sweet - ly ring - ing, sweet - ly ring - ing,

Ding, dong, ding, dong, ding, dong.

I = F A C

Line notation with consistent use of one system allows children to see a written reminder of a song they know as well as to play or sing these pitches on a melody istrument. "Little Tom Tinker" becomes

sol __ _ __ _ __

mi __ _ __ _ __ _

do __ _ _ __ _ __

Letters, numbers, or syllables alone do not allow children to decipher *new* material. They do, however, refine pitch placement from the gross level of line notation and make children aware of specific narrow or wide intervals in melodies.

146

Limited Staff Using lines and spaces to represent specific pitch placement is a refinement of line notation, with or without a supporting system. It would be deceptively easy to assume that one could introduce the *entire* staff all at once and expect children to grasp what it took music educators many years to comprehend fully. A partial staff may be used for music-reading activities after the children have used line notation. Since G is the fundamental reference in the treble staff, initial experiences might be to use

to show the descending minor third seen earlier. Lines and spaces are extended upward or downward as needed. Complete songs may be written with the limited staff, too.

Limited Staff

France

Full Staff

G major

Au clair de la lune

1. Au   clair   de   la   lu   —   ne,   Mon   a – mi   Pier – rot,
2. Au   clair   de   la   lu   —   ne,   Pier – rot   ré – pon – dit,

Prê – te – moi   ta   plu – me,   Pour   é – crire   un   mot.
"Je   n'ai   pas   de   plu – me,   Je   suis   dans   mon   lit.

147

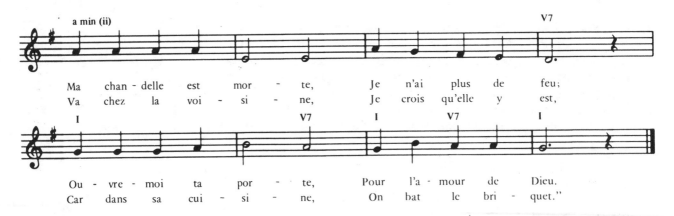

a min (ii)　　　　　　　　　　　　　　　　　　　　　V7

Ma chan - delle est mor - te,　Je n'ai plus de feu;
Va chez la voi - si - ne,　Je crois qu'elle y est,

I　　　　　　　　　　　　V7　　　I　　　V7　　　I

Ou - vre - moi ta por - te,　Pour l'a - mour de Dieu.
Car dans sa cui - si - ne,　On bat le bri - quet."

I = G B D
V7 = D F♯ A C
ii (a min) = A C E

Full Staff   A full staff can be realized as upper or lower pitches are needed as they occur in songs or to accompany ostinati.

Moving gradually from line notation to a full staff allows pitch reading and literacy to develop without having to *unlearn* anything. The child moves from gross visual discrimination to precise placement. This may occur by the upper elementary grades. Do not use the full staff to teach a new song, but rather to follow melodies and intervals already known in a song. This includes all of the following in an example such as the *Caisson Song.*

1. Finding tonal patterns, such as *sol-mi* and *sol-fa-re-do*

sol   mi   sol   fa   re   do   sol   do'

2. Tracing the melodic contour while singing the song

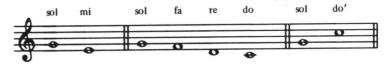

3. Identifying stepwise or skipwise motion in a song
4. Finding phrases which are repeated ("Over hill . . ." and "In and . . .")

C major

Words and music by Edmund L. Gruber

The Caisson Song

Marked rhythm

(sol   mi)   I   (sol   mi)   (sol   mi)

O - ver hill,　o - ver dale,　we have hit the dust - y

I = C E G
IV = F A C
V7 = G B D F
vi (a min) = A C E

All of these skills represent a level of music literacy that is sufficient for elementary school children. As music readers they function primarily as a group, not as individuals. This is a practical and reasonable expectation for all youngsters. Refinement of pitch reading can easily be achieved at a later age, if needed.

Reading Rhythm

Unlike pitch reading, rhythm reading deals with indirect symbols. In pitch, a high sound looks high, but in rhythm, a long sound does not necessarily look long. A "fast" musical composition does not necessarily look any different from a "slow" one. In spite of this, children respond easily and naturally to rhythm reading.

Rhythm reading involves all the components discussed in Chapter 9: tempo, pulse, accent groupings, melodic rhythm, and characteristic patterns. Rhythm in our notational system is based on the premise of an underlying and usually inaudible pulse. This pulse or beat is the basis for determining what occurs in the other components of music, including melody and harmony.

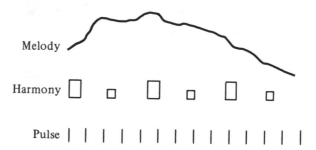

Reading tempo is accomplished two ways. Italian tempo markings can be placed as a general guide to tempo as well as to style:

Slow tempo ———— Medium tempo ———— Fast tempo
Lento——Adagio——Andante——Moderato——Allegro——Vivace——Presto

These are indirect symbols, since there is no way to determine *Allegro* or *Andante* from looking at the words. One simply has to know the general tempo indicated by the word. A second indication of tempo is a metronome marking. M.M. ♩ = 120 means the quarter note is the basic pulse and 120 of them occur in one minute. This gives the musician much more precision than merely seeing an *Allegro* or *Moderato* in the music.

Pulse *reading* does not really occur. However, in any piece a pulse must be assumed. Accent groupings, characteristic patterns, and the melodic rhythm are measured against it. Frequently the pulse is assigned to the quarter note. The other components are measured against a steady flow of inaudible quarter notes, each receiving one beat. However, the pulse may be eighth notes or even half notes. A quarter note, thus, does not always receive one beat, depending upon what type of note is being counted as the basic pulse.

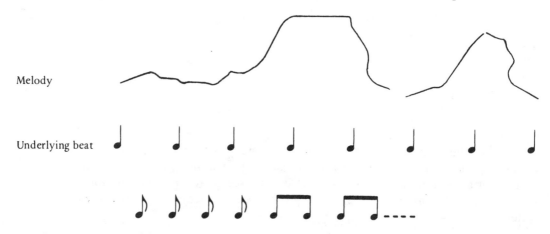

Accent groupings are reflected in the time signature. In simple meters, the signature tells two things: (1) how the accents are grouped (upper number) and (2) what type of note is being counted as the pulse (bottom number):

$$\frac{3}{4} = \frac{\text{accent groupings of 3}}{(\ \text{♩}\ )\ \text{note is the pulse}}$$

$$\frac{2}{8} = \frac{\text{accent groupings of 2}}{(\ \text{♪}\ )\ \text{note is the pulse}}$$

$$\frac{4}{2} = \frac{\text{accent groupings of 4}}{(\ \text{♩}\ )\ \text{note is the pulse}}$$

Some textbooks have adopted a more graphic system for meter signatures:

$\frac{3}{4}$ is written as $\frac{3}{♩}$

$\frac{2}{8}$ is written as $\frac{2}{♪}$

$\frac{4}{2}$ is written as $\frac{4}{♩}$

Compound meters are somewhat different. Any meter with *other* than a 2, 3, or 4 as the top number is probably a compound meter, including all of the following:

6	9	12	6	9	12	6*	9	12
8*	8*	8*	16	16	16	4	4	4

*most common

Compound meters divisible by three allow composers to split the division over the pulse into three equal parts instead of the traditional two. Each represents a simple meter in disguise. The simple meter is found by dividing the top number by three:

$\frac{6}{8}$ 6 ÷ 3 = groupings of 2

The basic beat is no longer the bottom number. However, it is found by multiplying the bottom number by 3.

♪ x 3 = ♪ ♪ ♪ = ♩ ♪ or ♩.

Thus, in the most common compound meters, the basic division is

$\frac{6}{8} = \frac{2}{♩.}$ $\frac{12}{8} = \frac{4}{♩.}$

$\frac{9}{8} = \frac{3}{♩.}$ $\frac{6}{4} = \frac{2}{♩.}$

(Composers use this way of notating simple meters as well as compound meters in which the basic pulse is always a dotted note.)

Reading characteristic patterns and melodic rhythm against a steady pulse is really the core of rhythm reading. These are always measured against the basic pulse in the following proportion:

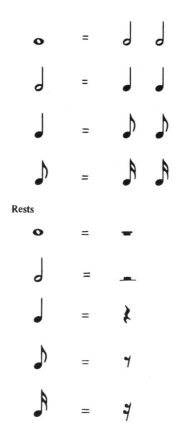

Rests

In compound meters, the proportion is:

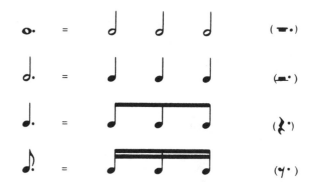

A look at the following songs will serve to clarify the relationship of melodic rhythm and pattern to the underlying pulse and accent groupings:

"All Night, All Day"

All Night, All Day

Spiritual

With conviction

152

All night, all _____ day, An-gels watch-ing o-ver me.

Verse

1. Now I lay me down ___ to sleep,
2. If I die be-fore ___ I wake,

An-gels watch-ing o-ver me, my Lord.___

Pray the Lord my soul ___ to

1. keep,
2. take,

An-gels watch-ing o-ver me.

I = G B D
IV = C E G
V7 = D F♯ A C

"Row, Row Your Boat" $\frac{6}{8}$ 2

C major

Row, Row, Row Your Boat

Round

Steadily

Part 1   **Part 2**

Row, row, row your boat gent-ly down the stream,

Pulse

Part 3   **Part 4.**

Mer-ri-ly, mer-ri-ly, mer-ri-ly, mer-ri-ly, Life is but a dream.

I = C E G

As with pitch reading, the rhythm system should not be presented in one or two lessons. It should be be introduced in many experiences over the years after the children have developed the following rhythmic concepts through aural experience:

1. The ability to discern tempos (slow, moderate, fast) aurally and perform music in these tempos
2. The ability to maintain a steady pulse while singing, moving, or playing instruments
3. The ability to perceive aurally and perform basic accent groupings of 2, 3, and 4 in simple and compound meters

4. The ability to duplicate all types of characteristic patterns (even, uneven, syncopated) through echo clapping, singing, moving, playing, and listening

Notation is best introduced with even patterns that are echo clapped and then notated without noteheads.

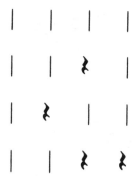

Eighth notes are introduced later as a third variable:

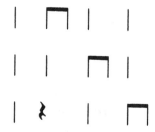

Children should be given the opportunity to identify visually a pattern they listen to as well as to write down patterns dictated to them. Patterns can also be identified in known songs such as "A-Hunting We Will Go."

A-Hunting We Will Go

England

F major

Briskly

Oh, a - hunt - ing we will go, a - hunt - ing we will go. We'll

catch a lit - tle fox and put him in a box and nev - er let him go.

I = F A C
IV = B♭ D F
V7 = C E G B♭

"Which of the following occur in *A Hunting We Will Go?*"

Where?

Children can set even patterns to their names, cities, states, names of famous people, or makes of automobiles in a variety of accent groupings:

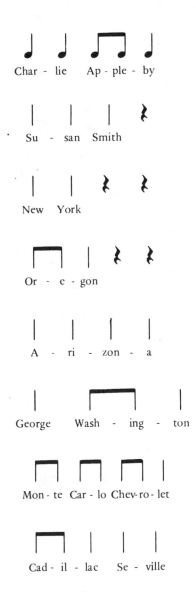

Char - lie   Ap - ple - by

Su - san   Smith

New   York

Or - e - gon

A - ri - zon - a

George   Wash - ing - ton

Mon - te Car - lo Chev-ro- let

Cad - il - lac   Se - ville

Patterns can be grouped together to form rhythmic rondos that are then performed by body sounds (stamping, clapping, and so on) or with rhythm instruments.

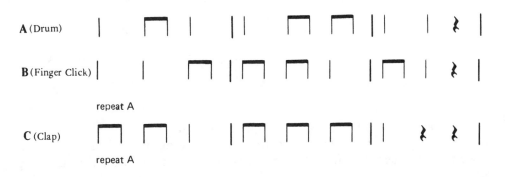

A (Drum)

B (Finger Click)

repeat A

C (Clap)

repeat A

Longer note values are built up through the use of ties:

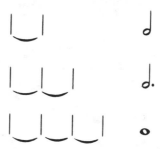

A transfer is later made to the actual note values.

Ties are also an excellent way to introduce the concept of uneven patterns, especially those using dots:

Transfer to the actual notation may occur after experience with the ties in uneven patterns:

Syncopated patterns may be introduced in the same manner:

When patterns are grouped a quasi-meter signature may be used:

$$\frac{4}{|} \left(\frac{4}{\rho} \text{ or } \frac{4}{4}\right)$$

$$\frac{3}{\flat} \left(\frac{3}{\rho} \text{ or } \frac{3}{8}\right)$$

A transfer can later be made to the actual signature when note heads are added. Devices that are used to facilitate the reading of rhythm should not have to be "unlearned" when a transfer is made to the traditional form.

Tempo markings are assimilated easily when the teacher reinforces the Italian terms as appropriate. "Let's repeat this at a fast, *allegro* tempo" or "Try it with an *adagio* or slow tempo." Rote memorization should be avoided. These tempos will be experienced constantly and the proper label can be attached through consistent use.

After sequential experiences in rhythm, children should be able to:

1. Take simple rhythmic dictation
2. Write simple rhythmic compositions
3. Write rhythms to known words (names, states, and so on)
4. Clap or play the simple rhythmic notation of a song (melodic rhythm)
5. Create rhythmic ostinati to fit a selected song
6. Identify aurally and visually select patterns in a song
7. Respond to meter signatures correctly
8. Interpret Italian tempo and metronome markings correctly

Rhythmic reading should pervade all of the elementary school teaching of music.

Reading Dynamics

Reading dynamics means responding to symbols that describe the loudness or softness of music. Like rhythmic notation, the notation of dynamics or intensity is generally indirect. Loud sounds are called *forte* or *f*, soft ones are *piano* or *p*. This is best perceived on a continuum ranging from very soft to very loud:

pp—— *p* ——*mp* ——*mf* ——*f* ——*ff*

pp = pianissimo	very soft
p = piano	soft
mp = mezzo piano	medium soft
mf = mezzo forte	medium loud
f = forte	loud
ff = fortissimo	very loud

Gradual transitions from soft to loud or vice versa are indicated in music with the *crescendo* and *decrescendo*.

Sudden transitions are indicated by *sfz* (*sforzando*), meaning suddenly louder (for one note or chord) or by placing *subito* (meaning "suddenly") in front of *p* or *f* (suddenly soft or suddenly loud).

Children are ready to respond to the notation of dynamics when they:

1. Aurally discern the difference between loud and soft
2. Can perform songs, accompaniments, and ostinati in an expressive manner using louds and softs

Rote memorization of dynamics does not foster retention. The music educator should reinforce concepts by using both the English and Italian designations. "Let's sing that again loud or *forte!*" "Remember to get louder—to crescendo—in the last section."

The meaning of the terms can be absorbed by actual practice. "We usually sing the first part of 'The Battle Hymn of the Republic' softly, the last

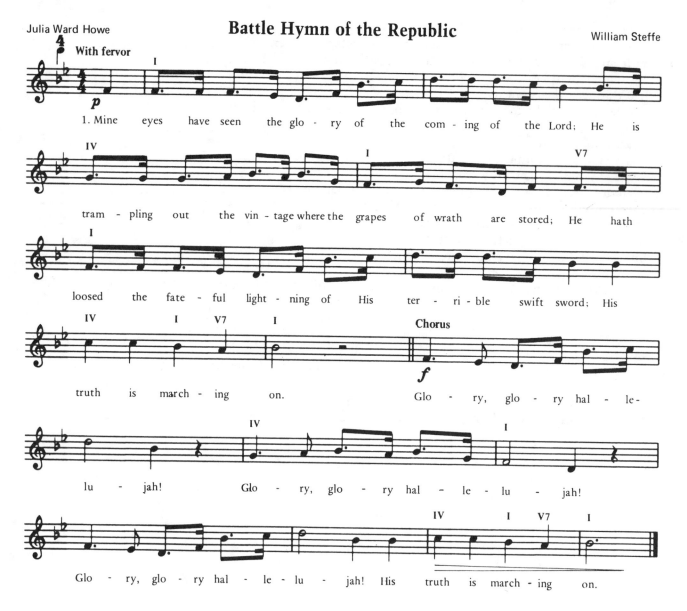

Battle Hymn of the Republic

Julia Ward Howe

William Steffe

I = B♭ D F
IV = E♭ G B♭
V7 = F A C E♭

part loud. What do you see in the written music that might be the direction for doing this? Why do we gradually get softer at the end?"

Children need to have the opportunity to see these symbols in many songs and to incorporate them in their other musical activities, such as playing accompaniments and ostinati.

Application of Music Reading

Songs are the core experience for introducing and reinforcing music-reading skills. One song can serve to develop many aspects of music reading, as the following examples demonstrate.

158

C major

Taffy

Taf - fy was a Welsh - man,

Taf - fy was a thief,

Taf - fy came to our house and

Stole a leg of beef.

I went to Taf - fy's house,

Taf - fy was in bed.

I took a mar - row bone and

Hit him on the head.

I = C E G
IV = F A C
V7 = G B D F

Melody
1. Upward contour in 1st half (4 measures) for syllables
2. Downward contour of 2nd half (4 measures)
3. Stepwise motion
4. Key of C major

Rhythm
1. Even patterns throughout
2. Basic use of ♩, ♪ and ♫
3. ⁴⁄₄ meter

F major

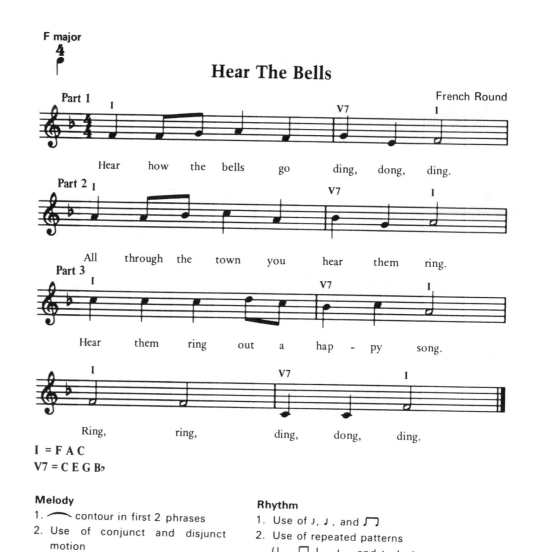

Hear The Bells

French Round

Part 1

Hear how the bells go ding, dong, ding.

Part 2

All through the town you hear them ring.

Part 3

Hear them ring out a hap - py song.

Ring, ring, ding, dong, ding.

I = F A C
V7 = C E G B♭

Melody
1. ⌒ contour in first 2 phrases
2. Use of conjunct and disjunct motion
3. Key of F major

Rhythm
1. Use of ♩, ♪, and ♫
2. Use of repeated patterns (♩ ♫ ♩ ♩ and ♩ ♩ ♩)
3. ¾ meter

F major

The More We Get Together

Old German Melody

The more we get to - geth - er, to - geth - er, to - geth - er,

The more we get to - geth - er, the hap - pi - er we'll be.

For your friends are my friends, and my friends are your friends.

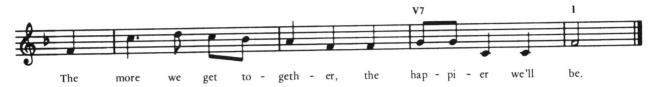

The   more   we   get   to - geth - er,   the   hap - pi - er   we'll   be.

I = F A C
V7 = C E G B♭

Melody
1. Use of repeated or similar phrases
2. Key of F major
3. Use of conjunct and disjunct motion
4. Repeated use of do-sol interval

Rhythm
1. Use of even (♩ ♩ ♩)
   and uneven pattern (♩. ♪ ♫)
2. Use of ¾ meter
3. Use of the dot
4. Use of anacrusis beat (pick-up)

Specific Program Objectives for Music Reading

It is suitable to introduce notation as soon as children have a clear understanding of musical concepts. This may occur as early as Grades 1 or 2. Chart 11-1 is a model list of specific program objectives. These should be adapted for the specific system the teacher is using in the classroom, whether numbers, syllables, or pitches, full or partial staff. Undoubtedly, children would become better music readers if one system were applied uniformly throughout a school system. This list reflects what should normally occur by the end of the sixth grade.

CHART 11-1

	Children will
Early elementary (K–2)	use line notation to represent high and lows
	read melodies by numbers, pitch names, or syllables
	use hand levels or hand signals to represent high and low pitches and tonal patterns.*
	use ❘ . ⊓ . and 𝄼 to represent even patterns
	become aware how pitch and duration are notated
	scan music pages for melodic level and rhythmic value
Middle elementary (3–4)	notate word rhythms — but ter fly — Tex as — huc kle ber ry
	know rhythm names: o = whole note (𝄻), ♩ = half note (𝄼), ♩ = quarter note (𝄽), ♪ = eighth note (𝄾)
	know pitch names on the treble clef

*See page 70.

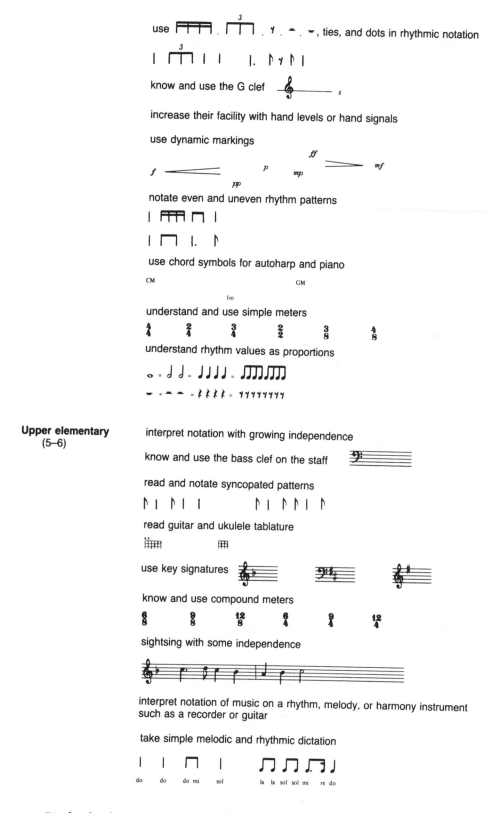

use ⌐⌐⌐ , ⌐⌐³ , ♩ ♪ ♪ , ties, and dots in rhythmic notation

know and use the G clef

increase their facility with hand levels or hand signals

use dynamic markings

notate even and uneven rhythm patterns

use chord symbols for autoharp and piano

understand and use simple meters

understand rhythm values as proportions

Upper elementary
(5–6)

interpret notation with growing independence

know and use the bass clef on the staff

read and notate syncopated patterns

read guitar and ukulele tablature

use key signatures

know and use compound meters

sightsing with some independence

interpret notation of music on a rhythm, melody, or harmony instrument such as a recorder or guitar

take simple melodic and rhythmic dictation

Pitch, rhythm, and dynamic notation do not represent discrete skills for the trained musician who reads rapidly at sight. They have been treated as separate variables here, however, since the premise behind each is slightly different. To the classroom teacher or music specialist who is an adequate music reader, it might not be obvious how difficult it is to integrate each into the whole system of music notation. These types of notation must be isolated initially in the classroom, but as skills and abilities develop be reincorporated into total music reading. Thus, culminating lessons for upper grades might include work on rhythm, pitch, and intensity simultaneously. In no case, though, should music reading be a verbal explanation of how the pitch, rhythm, or intensity system works. Music reading develops from experience and categorization of that experience to a written symbol or system to represent the experience. The process takes several years. Each reading experience in the elementary classroom helps develop musical literacy.

Exercises and Activities

1. Develop a lesson plan for music reading of either pitch, rhythm, or dynamics notation as outlined in this chapter. (You may wish to use one of the systems described at the end of the chapter.)
2. Develop a brief, aural pretest to determine if children are ready to begin one of the reading activities described.
3. Devise a "ŋew" system to facilitate music reading (in pitch, rhythm, or dynamics) that will transfer smoothly into traditional notation.

Key Terms and Concepts

Conceptual
   development
    Enactive phase
    Iconic phase
    Symbolic phase
Direct symbol
Diastematic notation
Staff
G clef (staff)
F clef (staff)
Grand staff
Line notation
Italian tempo markings
   Lento
   Adagio
   Andante
   Moderato
   Allegro
   Vivace
   Presto
Metronome
M.M. ♩ =
Simple meter
Compound meter

Note values
(proportional)
Ties
Dots
Dynamic markngs
   pp
   p
   mp
   mf
   f
   ff
Crescendo
Decrescendo
sfz (sforzando)
subito

Professional Readings

Bruner, Jerome S. *The Process of Education.* Cambridge, Mass.: Harvard University Press, 1961.

———. *Toward a Theory of Instruction.* Cambridge, Mass.: Harvard University Press, 1968.

Erdei, Peter, and Katalin Komlos. *150 American Folk Songs to Sing, Read and Play.* Oceanside, N.Y.: Boosey & Hawkes, 1974.

Gagne, Robert. *The Conditions of Learning,* 3rd ed. New York: Holt, Rinehart and Winston, 1977.

Heffernan, Charles W. *Teaching Children to Read Music.* New York: Appleton-Century-Crofts, 1968.

Kidd, Eleanor. *Threshold to Music,* 2d ed. Belmont, Calif.: Fearon Publishers, 1974. Three volumes: early childhood, level 1, and level 2.

How Children Can Create Their Own Music

12

Creative Activities

All musical activities should be creative. But there are times when a lesson objective is "The children will create . . . ." What *can* children create in music? Can children be composers? Indeed, they can and should be. They can create many types of musical composition. The art educator could not conduct an art program if children did not paint, draw, mold, and weave. Neither can the teacher develop a music program unless children create and compose.

Children should be able to experience the elements of music in other than the traditional ways. Pitch, for example, is undoubtedly experienced through singing and playing someone else's songs but the concept is enhanced when children invent their own tunes and notation. The same may be said for any musical element: timbre, rhythm, intensity, or harmony. Creative activities prepare children to understand the workings of a composer's mind and to appreciate the effort involved in composing music. They also allow children to expand their talents in individualized ways. From the teacher's standpoint, creative endeavors can reinforce and expand the development of musical concepts, objectives, and skills in particularly motivating ways.

Specific Program Objectives for Creating Music

Specific program objectives may be outlined for each level in the elementary school. Some children may be capable of achieving at an upper grade level

165

while only in the first or second grade. Chart 12-1 may be considered as a list of possibilities rather than as rigid guidelines.

CHART 12-1   Objectives for Creating Music

	Children will
Early elementary (K–2)	make up rhythmic and melodic patterns, including simple ostinati
	suggest instruments to interpret the words or mood of a song
	make up phrases and set them to music on a pentatonic scale
	set nursery rhymes or poems on pentatonic instruments
	create and interpret sound pictures
	improvise phrases, patterns, ostinati
	discover new ways to play instruments
Middle elementary (3–4)	create and interpret sound pictures
	make up words and notes for ostinati for older songs
	create new verses to songs
	make up tunes in various scales, including the diatonic, pentatonic, and whole-tone
	invent musical notation (graphic) to represent a sound picture
	transpose songs to new keys
Upper elementary (5–6)	create their own songs and/or lyrics
	notate their own songs, traditionally or graphically
	compose electronically
	invent musical games
	notate electronic compositions
	write in twelve tones
	compose palindromes

Some creative endeavors can be accomplished in one music lesson. These include finding new ways to play instruments, creating new echo patterns and ostinati, adding classroom instruments to a song or recording to enhance its overall effect or to reinforce one of its elements (such as pulse or accent), writing new words to a song, or improvising phrases. Others are longer projects which take several music lessons and include writing and interpreting sound pictures, devising graphic notation to represent sounds, composing with *musique concrète*, writing haiku and traditional songs, transposing a song by numbers to a new pitch system, writing in twelve tones, and composing palindromes.

New Ways to Play Instruments
Children see the teacher play classroom instruments and they soon develop the appropriate technique for playing a drum, a woodblock, etc. A creative experience may be simply to explore new ways to make sound on these.

Example (all levels)
TEACHER (holding a hand drum): We always play this instrument by tapping its head with our hand. What other ways could I play it and still have a *musical* sound?

The children suggest using fingers, a mallet, a pencil, tapping on the side instead of the head, placing it on various surfaces, and so on.

Additional experiences include giving a small class committee an instrument and letting its members discover five new ways to play the instrument. The teacher should always specify that a musical sound is desired. This type of experience can be followed with a listening lesson in which traditional instruments are used in new ways (such as BOL #69—*Tango, Waltz* and *Ragtime;* BOL #83—*Theme and Variations for Percussion Quartet;* RCA 2-2—*The Twittering Machine;* and RCA 6-1—*Street in a Frontier Town* as well as selected works by modern composers such as Varèse, Stockhausen, or Cage).

Creating New Echo Patterns and Ostinati

Ostinati have already been discussed in Chapters 7 and 9. Children can create both rhythm patterns and ostinati.

Example one (middle–upper elementary)

Children who have mastered the notation described in Chapter 11 can create patterns over two-, three-, or four-beat units:

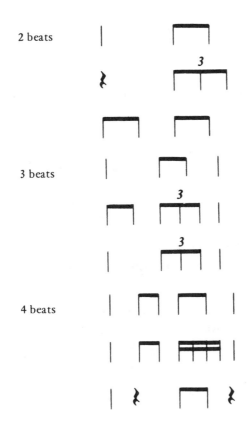

These patterns may be used to accompany a song in the appropriate meter.

Example two (middle–upper elementary)

Ostinati may be created similarly, beginning first with a rhythm pattern compatible with the song. The ostinato must also fit with the scale and harmony structure of the song.

167

Song built on the I chord (I-*do–mi–sol*):

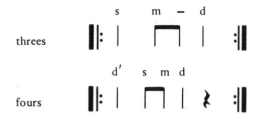

Song built on the I and V7 chords (dominant ostinato):

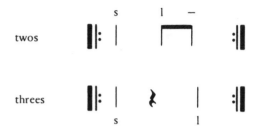

Song built on the pentatonic scale (*do–re–mi–sol–la*):

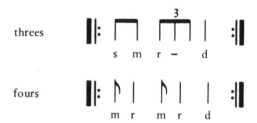

Adding Classroom Instruments to a Song or Recording

This creative activity was discussed in Chapter 9. Instruments are best added after the song or recording has been enjoyed first as a singing or listening experience. Then special effects are appropriate.

Example One (early elementary)

TEACHER: What instruments might be added to "My Little Red Drum" to make it more interesting?
Suggestions:
a drum to tap: "Tum-tum-tum-tum-tum"
resonator bells on "Here we come!" (G–B–D)
woodblocks on the steady pulse, four to a bar
cymbals on the accented first beat of each bar

Example Two (lower elementary)

TEACHER: What instruments might be added to "Viennese Musical Clock" (RCA 2-1) to sound like clocks?
Suggestions: Triangles and cymbals play as they wish when leader points to them to "ring" the clock.

As stated in Chapter 9, the end effect when instruments are added to a song, poem, or recording should be to enhance the aesthetic effect. It is probably better for the class to share a few instruments than for each child to have one.

Writing New Words to a Song

Children enjoy adding new words to part or all of a song that is well known.

Example One (lower elementary)

TEACHER: We have sung "How Would You Say Hello" (p. 43) in French, Spanish, and German. Let's sing it today using greetings from America. Who has suggestions for saying hello in our own country?
Suggestions: "Hi," "Howdy," "How do you do?" are offered. The song is repeated using these suggestions: "If you were a little American boy . . . I would say 'Howdy.' "

Example Two (middle elementary)

Children may collectively or individually rewrite the words for a well-known song such as "Row, Row, Row Your Boat."
Do, do, do your work,
So there will be none.
Carefully, carefully, carefully, carefully,
Soon it will be done.

Improvising Phrases

Phrases may be improvised on resonator bells (or other melody instruments) by children at all levels. The teacher must take care to shape the complexity of the task to the age and experience of the child. The phrases may be improvised as an answer to one the teacher has begun in a pentatonic scale.

Example One (early elementary)

The teacher plays on the resonator bells:

Teacher

The child may answer by playing:

Child

Younger children will accomplish this without musical notation, but middle and upper elementary children will undoubtedly be able to do it with the use of some type of musical notation. A rhymed couplet or other poetic structure might also be the inspiration for improvising phrases. In addition, tones chosen may represent those from a typical chord progression.

Example Two (upper elementary)

Couplet:
"One, two, three, four, What do you see?
Chords   I   IV   I

169

End result:
"Five, six, seven, eight,   nine bumble bees!"
Chords   V7   I

D major

One, two, three, four, What do you see?

five, six, sev - en, eight, nine bum - ble bees!

I = D F♯ A
IV = G B D
V7 = A C♯ E G

Sound Pictures

Sound pictures are written directions for a musical composition. These are well suited for small group activities (three to six children). Sound pictures may be introduced in several ways. The following are typical.

Example One (early elementary)

TEACHER: Listen carefully to this sequence of sounds. I will ask you to describe it when I am finished.

Teacher plays: Drums   **X X X X** (very loud)
                  Maracas   **x x x x**   (medium loud)
                  Clicks   with tongue x x x x (very softly)

The children then describe the sounds they heard.

TEACHER: I have several index cards describing sounds like this. In groups of three, work on the sound picture described on your index cards.

These cards are distributed. The children work on their compositions. Several are presented to the class. As the children listen, they may try to write the directions for the sound picture.

Play a high sound. Play a low sound. Now make your sound go around a corner. Bring it back again. Make it jump up and down. Play a hopping tune. Now let your sound relax and die away.	Play a walk up and down a hill. Now play a tune that runs, hops and stops.	Find a high sound. Play or sing it twice. Find a low sound. Play or sing it twice. Find 3 sounds that are between your high and low sound. Play all 5.

Find a friend to help you.
Get a △⎮ and a ⬜⧷
Make them talk softly.
They have a secret. Let them fight and then make up.

Sing a sound that looks like this.

Then play sounds that look like this.

• • • • • •

Play on a drum sounds that look like this.
——— • ———— •

Play or sing sounds that look like this. ✕ × ✕ ×

Find other sounds you like. Play or sing them.
Mix them with your
✕ × and ———• sounds.

Play or sing a sound that looks like this.

Play or sing a sound that goes around a corner. ↗

Play or sing a sound that looks like this. ⩗

Mix all your sounds together.

Example Two (middle and upper elementary)

Children are asked to write a sound picture on an index card. These cards are exchanged with other groups and performed.

On the bongo drum play one minute of sounds that uses these two rhythm patterns again and again.

$\frac{4}{4}$ ♩ ♩ ♩ ♩

$\frac{4}{4}$ ♩ 𝄽 ♩ 𝄽

Make a two-minute musical picture of "A Walk through Ghostown at Midnight," using two vocal sounds and three small instruments. Use

<⎯⎯⎯ and ⎯⎯⎯>

in your musical picture.

Recite a short nursery rhyme with the accompaniment of a small drum and a tambourine. Include a short introduction and coda as well as any musical effects you need to make the poem more interesting.

On the keyboard, make a melody with A–G–E for 30 seconds. Create harmony using the same notes for 30 seconds. Also make 30 seconds of any sounds you want on the keyboard. Conclude with 30 seconds of your melody again.

Make a two-minute sound picture which represents the sounds of a big city on a Saturday afternoon. You may use the piano, rhythm sticks, and one other instrument. Use three vocal sounds and sounds you might make with your feet.

On the piano plan one minute of sound that uses soft but high clusters. Also plan one minute of sound on the piano with the keyboard cover closed.

Example Three (upper elementary)

Movement is incorporated with the sound pictures. Sound pictures should allow children to experiment with sound as well as think about its properties.

171

Experimentation needs to be directed to develop and reinforce musical concepts.

<table>
<tr><td>

Create a composition using interesting word colors made from names of the members of your group. Give it unity.
Incorporate movements (axial) which go with the sounds.

</td><td>

Subdivide your group into 4 subgroups. Select a sound for each subgroup, order the sounds (for example, 1–2–3–4) Each subgroup may play its sound for as long as it likes, then the next begins. Play the sequence several times to shape a composition.

</td></tr>
<tr><td>

Create a sculptural group in which part of your group is placed into forms representing
ANXIETY
and part into forms representing a contrast to anxiety.
Reinforce it with sound.

</td><td>

Create a movement and sound picture of 20 seconds duration called
MOBILE
Use only body sounds but use axial and locomotive movements.
Create a short composition in which the performers take their directions from the movement of the mobile.

</td></tr>
</table>

Graphic Notation

Graphic notation is the use of nontraditional symbols to represent sounds. A loud sound might be represented as a large circle, a soft one as a small circle. A long sound might be an elongated rectangle and a short one a small square.

Children can be very creative if a few suggestions are given initially by the teacher to outline the possibilities.

A piano composition that uses low, middle, and high clusters (chords created with notes in close proximity)—all moving very slowly—could be written as:

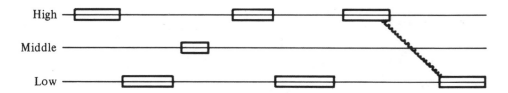

A composition written in rondo form could be:

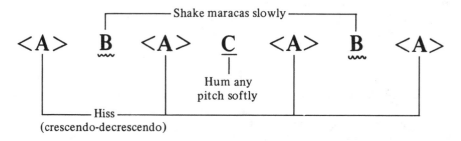

A round using only a tambourine and a vocal sound would be written as:

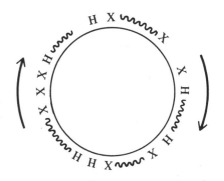

X = tapping
〜〜 = shaking
〜〜 X = shaking and tapping
H = vocal hooting

Begin at any point and proceed clockwise. Additional parts enter whenever they wish and continue clockwise. Each person in the round must make at least one complete revolution but must not perform for more than one minute.

An excellent way to start children thinking about graphic notation is to read a story or rhyme, ask the children what sound effects would enhance the story, notate these sounds graphically, and then perform the sounds from the notation without the story.* (A good source of stories is Margery Dorian and Frances Gulland's *Telling Stories Through Movement*.)

Hickory, dickory dock (**X X**)

The mouse (△ /) ran up (〜〜〜) the clock.

The clock struck one (⚙),

The mouse ran down (〜〜〜),

Hickory, dickory dock. (**X X**).

Composition

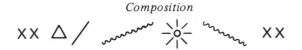

They heard footsteps softly in the distance.   **X X X X X X X**
Gradually, they could hear the person coming closer.   x x X **X**
John gulped!   ☙   He gulped again!   ☙
His heart began to pound faster and faster   **ZZZZZZZZZZZZ**
as the footsteps got louder. Finally he said: "Let's run!"
〜〜〜〜〜〜〜 Suddenly a bell rang. ◎
It startled Fred so badly that he fell down ✹ and
rolled over twice. ℳ   But they could still hear
the footsteps in the distance. **X X X X X X X X X X X X**

Composition

Another technique is to begin with a few symbols and ask the children to interpret them.

*From ideas suggested by Mary Louise Serafine in "New Directions in Creative Music for Children," a presentation at the Association for Childhood Education International Convention in St. Louis, Missouri, April 1979.

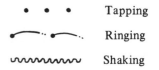

• • •   Tapping

Ringing

Shaking

The children can then use these ideas as points of departure to invent their own notation.

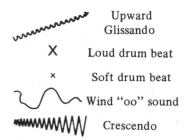

Upward Glissando

X   Loud drum beat

x   Soft drum beat

Wind "oo" sound

Crescendo

Graphic notation is used by serious composers since it represents sound in a direct way that is not possible with traditional notation. Activities of the type described above can be highly motivating to children at all levels of musical learning. Using graphic notation children can develop their creative ideas but are not limited in expressing and recording these ideas until traditional notation has been mastered. In their inventions with graphic notation, they also develop curiosity about how composers in the past have solved problems related to the notation of intensity, pitch, timbre, and duration. This stimulates interest in learning about traditional notation.

Musique Concrète

Musique concrète is electronic music created from environmental sounds that have been taped and then edited. In a classroom in which a reel-to-reel tape recorder is available, creative activities can occur through this technique. This activity is appropriate for middle and upper elementary children.

Sounds which are desired are simply collected on tape. These might be:

Sounds of nature: rain, wind, leaves rustling, a river running, the roar of the ocean, bird songs
Sounds in the house: a television, a radio, an electric mixer, an alarm clock, a toilet flushing
Industrial sounds: cars, trains, planes, machines, lawnmowers
Animal sounds: dogs barking, a rooster crowing, a cow mooing
Body sounds: a word spoken in different ways, clicking, stamping, snapping, yawning, laughing
Instrument sounds: a piano—played normally as well as by tapping on the sound board, clicking the pedals, strumming the strings, closing the lid, yelling into the strings with the sustaining pedal down.

Children should be encouraged to look for both normal and exotic sounds that would be interesting:

skidding tires
shattering glass
creaking doors
drilling oil rigs
hissing cats

roaring fires
clinking chains
ripping paper
leaking faucets
honking horns

174

Collecting the sounds on tape is a type of *musique concrète,* but editing the sounds, arranging them into a meaningful order, is a refinement of the composing process. Some editing is done during the recording process, but most editing is done by cutting the tape and reassembling the sounds in the desired order by splicing the tape back together. (Splicing tape is available in most electronics shops. Cuts on the magnetic tape should be diagonal with the splicing tape being placed on the shiny (back) side of the cut.)

Sounds can be mutated in several ways:

1. The tape may be played backwards.
2. The speed of the machine may be changed during playback from that at which it was recorded. (This change can be rerecorded at the new speed on a second machine.) Most reel-to-reel tape recorders move at 17, 36, or 74 ips (inches per second). Doubling the speed (for instance, 36 to 74) results in a recorded sound being heard at a faster tempo as well as an octave higher in pitch. Reducing the speed slows the tempo and lowers the pitch one octave.
3. Sound can be added to sound on stereo recorders that have this ability.
4. Echo and reverberation can be added on machines which have this ability.
5. Blank tape can be spliced in to create rests.
6. Volume can be altered in playback.

Collected Sounds		Recorded at
1. Playground sounds	(2 minutes)	3 3/4 inches per second
2. Horns of cars in a traffic jam	(3 minutes)	3 3/4 ips
3. Static from a radio	(1 minute)	3 3/4 ips
4. Blank tape*	(1 minute)	3 3/4 ips

Editing

The playground sounds, the static and the blank tape are cut into two-feet segments and randomly spliced together.

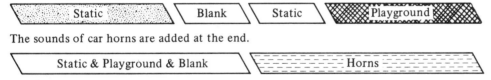

The sounds of car horns are added at the end.

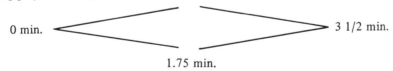

The entire composition is rewound.

Playback

The entire composition is played back at 7 1/2 ips (twice as fast). The volume is manipulated during playback (3 1/2 minutes) to simulate a

0 min. ⟨⟩ 3 1/2 min.

1.75 min.

Score in Graphic Notation

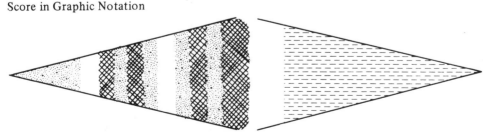

*(1 minute of blank tape is 37.5 feet at 7 1/2 ips. 18.75 feet at 3 3/4 ips 9.375 feet at 1 7/8 ips)

These are only a few suggestions for possibilities with one tape recorder in the classroom. Additional equipment allows for more sophisticated possibilities.

Students should be encouraged to create scores for *musique concrète,* thus incorporating the skills of graphic notation with the exploration of electronic music.

Writing Songs

Writing traditional tonal songs should be an activity in every classroom during the year. It is particularly important as a culminating activity. A song can be written in two ways: by beginning with a melodic rhythm and adding words and melody (and possibly accompaniment) or by beginning with words and adding the melodic rhythm and pitches.

Beginning with Rhythms   The teacher presents the class with a set of rhythms.
In the first lesson each child is asked to create a poem to fit the rhythms.

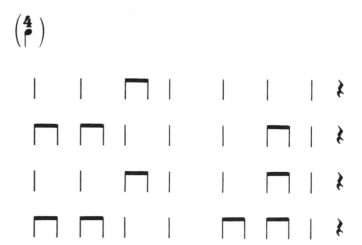

The teacher can specify rhyme schemes where desired (for example, lines 1 and 3, 2 and 4 must rhyme). Possible solutions are:

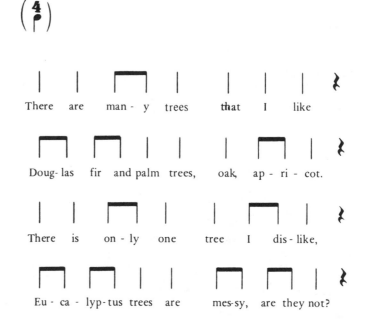

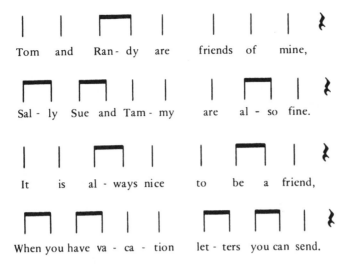

Tom and Ran- dy are friends of mine,

Sal- ly Sue and Tam- my are al - so fine.

It is al - ways nice to be a friend,

When you have va - ca - tion let - ters you can send.

The teacher may find it necessary to suggest a topic or even to write the first line of poetry to spark the creative spirit in the children and get them started on the task.

In a later lesson, pitches are added to the melodic rhythm to create a melody. Which pitches are used depends on the children's grade level. Some songs are effective with only two or three pitches, such as *la, sol,* and *mi*. Others may use a complete diatonic scale. Whether pitch names, syllables, or numbers are used depends on the system used in the classroom. Some explanation and limits set by the teacher are necessary to channel the creativity. Random use of any pitches, even within a scale, would produce an unfocused-sounding melody. Two questions should be considered:

What type of contour is desired in each phrase?
What pitches are to be used in each phrase?

Contours can be discussed with the class and outlined:

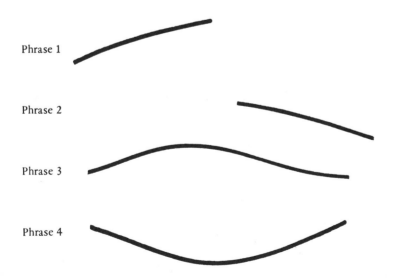

Phrase 1

Phrase 2

Phrase 3

Phrase 4

If a pentatonic scale is to be used, any tone of it may be used as long as the desired contour is followed.

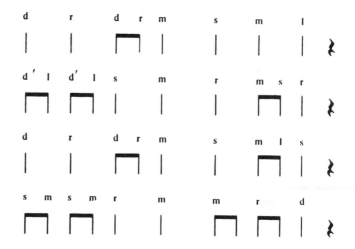

This can be notated with numbers, pitch names, or on the staff, depending upon the children's background in reading and systems.

If a diatonic melody is to be used, the teacher should assign a specific chord basis for each bar or phrase and designate the final pitch as 1 or 8 to give it a tonal flavor. The teacher should also indicate how many measures long each phrase is to be.

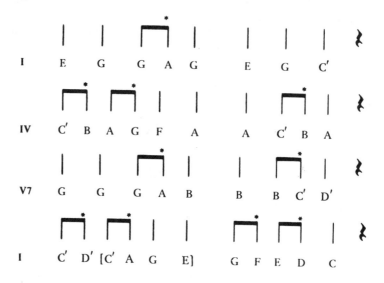

*Nonharmonic tones occuring on weak beats.

Key of C	Phrase I	I chord	(C–E–G)
	Phrase II	IV chord	(F–A–C)
	Phrase III	V7 chord	(G–B–D–F)
	Phrase IV	I chord	(C–E–G, ending on C)

Two songs written in this manner may be performed as partner songs. Since all songs in the class are of the same length and have the same chord structure, they should work well together as partner songs. If children have developed traditional notation skills from earlier experience, in a later lesson the song should be notated on the staff:

C major

Tom and Ran - dy are friends of mine,

Sal - ly Sue and Tam - my are al - so fine.

It is al - ways nice to be a friend,

When you have vac - a - tion let - ters you can send.

I = C E G
IV = F A C
V7 = G B D F

In the process of composing songs this way, some children may wish to change the words, rhythms, or even the melody of their song. This should be allowed. Artistic creation requires shaping and refining. A framework for beginning is necessary but should not be preserved indefinitely as a barrier or rule.

Beginning with Words   Writing haiku and setting it to music with ostinati is also an interesting creative music experience for children. Haiku, a type of Japanese poetry, has three lines of 5, 7, and 5 syllables, respectively. It usually deals with a subject from nature.

        1   2   3   4 5
        Beautiful sunset,

        1   2 3   4   5   6 7
        Horizon red and orange,

          1   2   3   4   5
        Night will soon be here.

A lesson in creative writing should precede setting haiku to music, one in which the children write the poems which will ultimately be set to music.

In a second lesson, each haiku should be set against a pulse. Some pulses will have more then one syllable, others will share one syllable:

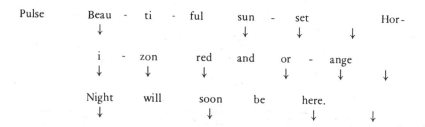

Children should read their haiku with the pulses to the class to determine if their notation is correct. Since placing the pulse also determines the word or melodic rhythm, the next step is to notate the melodic rhythm against the pulse.

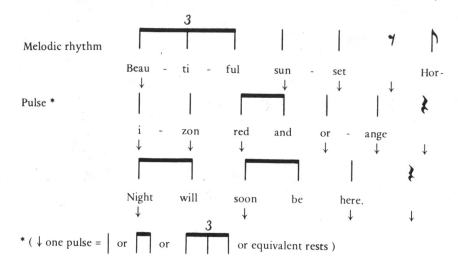

Haiku are best notated without a meter, maintaining a quarter-note pulse. However, metrical poems, when used or written, may fit into a regular accent scheme.

Children should practice and perform their haiku using rhythm instruments to tap both the melodic rhythm and the pulse as they read the text. This is a vehicle for performance and critique, essential in the creative process, as well as a chance to change and alter the words or rhythms that do not seem quite right.

The next step is to add a rhythmic ostinato. It may be derived from words of the haiku and should be evenly divisible into the total pulses used in the setting. Again, a performance of the poem in rhythm with the added ostinato is necessary.

(2 pulses divide evenly into the 14 total pulses of the original text)

A final step is to set the melodic rhythm and the ostinato to the pentatonic scale, using whatever system has been consistently developed in the classroom. (The pentatonic scale here seems compatible with the Oriental spirit of the poem, although this pentatonic scale is actually Chinese, not Japanese.)

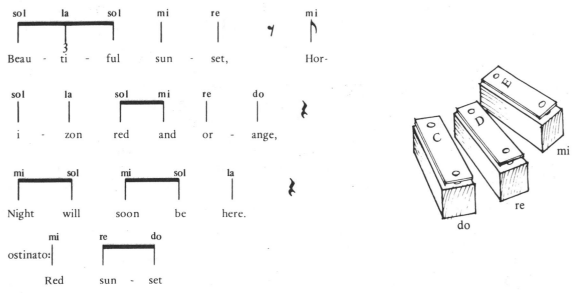

The ostinato can be used as an introduction as well as a coda. Perform-ance through singing and playing is the culminating activity, possibly even for other classes and parents. Art pictures might now be added to visualize the words of the haiku. This strategy represents several lessons, from writing the poetry to performing the end product. The entire strategy can be expanded or telescoped to allow for varying skill and conceptual levels in different class-rooms. Ultimately, the composition may be notated on the staff:

Beautiful Sunset

In summary, the two strategies for composing songs are:

Rhythm first
1. A set of rhythms is presented to the children. (Rhythms should have a clear metrical scheme and phrase structure.)
   (*Alternative strategy:* children may compose their own rhythms.)
2. A rhyme scheme is agreed upon.
3. A poem is written to the rhythm.
4. Pitches are added to the word rhythm. (Syllables, numbers, or pitch names may be used.) Pitches should be selected from the pentatonic scale or from a diatonic scale. Contour and ending tone should be considered.
5. The finished product is notated on the staff.

Words first
1. A poem is chosen or written.
2. The poem is set to a pulse (and possibly a metric scheme).
3. The melodic rhythm is notated.
4. Pitches are added.
5. The finished product is notated on the staff.
(*Alternative strategy for both:* ostinati may be added.)

Transposing a Song to a New Pitch System

Children enjoy the sound that results when a well-known song is transposed to a new scale (alike in the number of pitches but obviously not in pitch names or intervals) on the resonator bells or another melody instrument.

Example (middle–upper elementary)

First determine the key, scale, and relative position of each pitch in the melody "Are You Sleeping," p. 36.

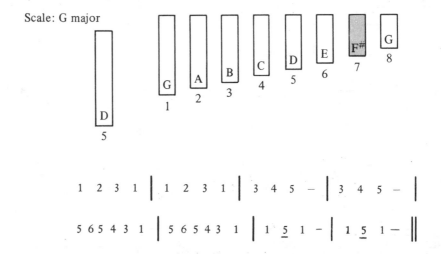

Transpose the song to another diatonic scale or a mode by interpreting the numbers in the new scale (minor, Dorian mode, or a made-up synthetic scale).
The song is then played by reading the numbers in the new scale.

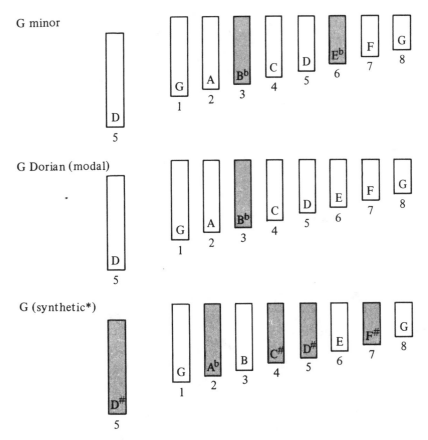

*This scale includes pitches in sequence but the sharps and flats follow no particular established formula. Some composers of the twentieth century, notably Scriabin, have done this.

Writing in Twelve Tones

Twelve-tone writing (dodecaphonic music) is an invention of the twentieth century. Its techniques were devised early in this century by the Austrian composer Arnold Schoenberg. Many other contemporary composers have used this technique. In twelve-tone music, all twelve notes of the chromatic scale are placed in a series and assigned a number. This series then becomes the basis for writing melodies.

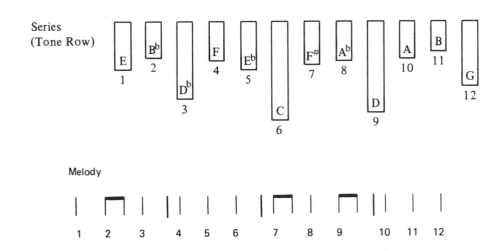

Tone rows are often played backward (retrograde) to create variations on the original row:

12 11   10   9   8   7   6   5   4   3   2   1

Children may also improvise on the tone row and create chords from it as well as add lyrics to the melodies they create.

Composing Palindromes

A palindrome is a statement or word which reads the same, backward or forward.

MADAM

ABLE WAS I ERE I SAW ELBA

A musical palindrome is one in which the rhythm or the pitches (or both) are the same forward or backward. (That is, the retrograde version is the same as the original.) Children in the middle and upper elementary levels will enjoy creating them. They can add words (perhaps also in palindrome) to their end results.

d minor

D   DEF   A   GAGAB♭   B♭ AGAG   A   F   EDD

All music lessons should be creative experiences for elementary children. Many activities are re-creative since children are singing, moving, or listening to someone else's music. Re-creative activities should be balanced with lessons of the type described in this chapter, whether composing through sound pictures, with graphic notation, through *musique concrète*, or by writing songs and lyrics, palindromes, or ostinati. It is an excellent method for accommodating individual differences and can be modified for any music-reading system used in the classroom.

The creative process is not a mysterious force that only rarely appears in a music classroom. Most children can be creative if given a format and pattern and are motivated to "create." The teacher is the catalyst who sparks the creative mind, provides a flexible framework, allows plenty of time for ideas to emerge, provides encouragement and motivation, helps shape and refine the product, and is critical without being judgmental.

Exercises and Activities

1. Create and perform a composition following guidelines provided in this section.
2. Design a lesson (or series of lessons) for a creative music experience for a chosen grade level.

Key Terms and Concepts

Couplet
Sound pictures
Graphic notation
Note clusters
Musique concrète
Editing
Ips
Haiku
Dorian mode
Synthetic scale
Twelve-tone (dodecaphonic) composition
Tone row
Retrograde
Palindrome

Professional Readings

Cope, David. *New Directions in Music*, Dubuque, Iowa: William C. Brown, 1971.

Dennis, Brian. *Experimental Music in Schools*. London: Oxford University Press, 1970.

Dorian, Margery, and Frances Gulland. *Telling Stories Through Movement*. Belmont, Calif.: Fearon Publishers, 1974.

Drake, Russel, Ronald Herder, and Anne D. Modugno. *How to Make Electronic Music*. New York: Educational Audio Visual, Inc., 1977.

Hickok, Dorothy, and James A. Smith. *Creative Teaching of Music in the Elementary School*. Boston: Allyn & Bacon, 1974.

Konowitz, Bert. *Music Improvisation as a Classroom Method*. New York: Alfred Music Company, 1973.

Marsh, Mary Val. *Explore and Discover Music*. New York: Macmillan, 1970.

————, Carroll A. Rinehart, and Edith J. Savage. *Composing Music. The Spectrum of Music and Related Arts Series*. New York: Macmillan, 1975.

May, Rollo. *The Courage to Create*. New York: Norton, 1975.

Music Educators Journal. Vol. 55, No. 3. (November 1968) Electronic Music.

Paynter, John, and Peter Aston. *Sound and Silence*. London: Cambridge University Press, 1970.

Self, George. *Make a New Sound*. London: Halston & Company, 1976.

————. *New Sounds in Class*. Bryn Mawr, Pa.: Theodore Presser Co., 1967.

Silver-Burdett Mini-Course Series. *New Music—Electronics and Sounds* (1976). *Raw Materials of Music* (1976). *Working with Sound* (1974). Palo Alto, Calif.: Silver-Burdett.

Schafer, R. Murray. *Creative Music Education: A Handbook for the Modern Music Teacher*. New York: Schirmer Books, 1976.

Schwarz, Elliott. *Electronic Music*. New York: Holt, Rinehart and Winston, 1975.

Thomas, Ronald B. *MMCP Synthesis*. (Manhattanville Music Curriculum Project). Bardonia, N.Y.: Media Materials, Inc., 1970.

————, ed. *MMCP Interaction* (Manhattanville Music Curriculum Project). Bardonia, N.Y.: Media Materials, Inc., 1970.

Wilt, Michele, and Dorothy Indenbaum. *Making Your Own Melodies (Music Discovery Activity Cards)*. West Nyack, N.Y.: The Center for Applied Research in Education, 1978.

PART FOUR

Providing Evaluation and Continuity

Measuring Music Learning

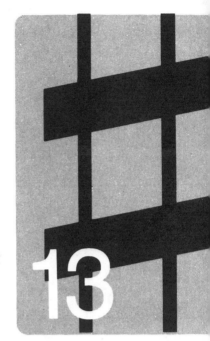

13

Learning is a change of behavior and needs to be assessed periodically to measure the amount of change. Evaluation is too frequently thought of as a pencil-and-paper test that culminates a unit of work or as questions that have only one right answer. But tests are only one type of evaluation and right-answer questions have limited use. Much music evaluation by classroom teachers is an informal assessment to determine if children have mastered a skill or acquired a concept. This is accomplished through observation to determine if a lesson objective has been met.

Objectives are the key to evaluation. If clear-cut lesson objectives are the basis for each lesson and if each of these is founded on an equally clear-cut program objective, evaluation is essentially built into the music program.

Evaluating Lesson Objectives and Activities

The behavioral objectives written for each lesson are generally stated in a measurable way: "The children will sing, tap, perform, identify, and so on." Evaluation occurs when the teacher observes whether singing, tapping, performing, identification or some other goal did occur and was reasonably and musically correct. When the objective has met whatever standard the teacher determines, the lesson can move on to something else. If the objective has not been reached, alternative strategies must be employed to achieve the desired end.

Standards for evaluation vary among educators. Trained musicians might expect so much accuracy and precision from elementary children that some objectives can never be realized. Conversely, the musically unsophisticated teacher might accept anything as musically correct if the children seem to be enjoying themselves, even when the song is sung out of tune or there is little rhythmic accuracy. These two positions represent extremes to be avoided in the reality of the music classroom. Children can only achieve musical success with a precision and musicianship compatible to the elementary school.

Each musical activity has built-in evaluation that must be considered separately.

Evaluating Singing

Objectives for this activity are usually stated as "The children will sing. . . ." Evaluation is dependent upon whether the children indeed did "sing." To establish a standard for measuring this activity, the teacher might use the following as a checklist:

1. Was the rhythm accurate? (Were the tempo and pulse maintained, the patterns sung as written?)
2. Were the pitches accurate? Did the children's voices rise and fall on pitch as they should? Was the tonality maintained?
3. Was the phrasing accurate? Did the children breathe where they should?
4. Was the tone quality of their voices pleasant and musically satisfying (rather than forced, harsh, or strident)?
5. Was the song rendered in a musically satisfying manner? (That is, were the dynamics observed?)
6. Was the harmony in tune and musically correct?

A standard must be established for each item if the teacher is to know if the objective has been met. At first, students may enjoy a music experience that is out-of-tune, disorganized, and aesthetically very poor. Enjoyment, participation, and enthusiasm are therefore not always valid ways to measure that good singing occurred. Standards of good singing must be communicated to the students so that some aesthetic criteria underlie their musical involvement and so that they work toward musical interpretations.

Evaluating Listening

Listening is no more difficult to evaluate than singing. The only difficulty is that lesson objectives for listening are harder to state. "The children will listen . . ." is not an appropriate objective. An objective that gives *evidence* of listening, however, includes:

"The children will identify . . ."
"The children will state . . ."

Obviously, what is to be identified or stated is some facet or element of the music presented. This could be:

Timbre Identification What was the instrument? Of what family was it? What type of ensemble was it? What special effects were used? What instrument was in the foreground? In the background? How did the timbres affect the overall feeling of the music?

190

Rhythm Recognition   What was the tempo? Did it change? Was there a steady pulse? Did it change? How was the pulse accented? Were there any predominant patterns? How did the rhythm affect the overall feeling of the music?

Awareness of Dynamics   Was the music generally loud? soft? Did it change? Was there a wide or narrow range of dynamics? How did the dynamics affect the overall feeling of the music?

Awareness of Pitch and Melody   Was there a melody? Was it long or short? wide or narrow in range? conjunct or disjunct? simple or ornamented? smooth or jerky? major or minor? What effect did the melodies have on the overall feeling of the music?

Awareness of Texture and Harmony   Which types of texture were used? What was the effect of texture on the overall feeling of the music? Was the harmony consonant or dissonant? How did it affect the composition?

Identification of Form   What was the overall design of the music? Did it repeat exactly? with variation? with contrast? Was it pure variation? What was the specific form?

How the facet or element is to be evaluated is the crux of measuring music learning. If one child verbally identifies the timbre or states that the music is fast, there is no guarantee the other children "listened" and observed the same thing. If children are asked to raise their hands when the A section returns, there is no guarantee they heard this independently. In order for evaluation to be more than imitation, a worksheet can be used occasionally to assess the lesson objective. This should be structured to accommodate both readers and nonreaders (see below). Worksheets may be filled out by individuals or in small groups, particularly in the middle and upper grades. Their judicious use will reflect the growing ability of the children to perceive details in listening.

Readers

Place a number in front of the instrument in the order in which it occurs in the foreground.

_____ flute

_____ clarinet

_____ trumpet

_____ trombone

_____ violin

_____ cello

Three ideas, A, B, and C, are presented in this musical composition. Place letters in the section as you listen.

(A   B   etc.) _____

Nonreaders

(Same instructions are given verbally)

(Verbal instructions are given to use O , △ , and □ to represent the three ideas heard in the composition).

_____ _____ _____ _____

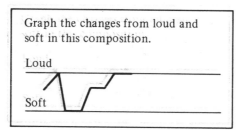

Middle Elementary

Number the family of instruments in order as they appear in the foreground.			
___ Strings	___ Woodwinds	___ Brass	___ Percussion
	___ Other*	(*piano, organ, synthesizer)	

Upper Elementary

Number the instruments in order as they appear in the foreground.			
Strings	Woodwinds	Brass	Percussion
___ Violin	___ Flute	___ Trumpet	___ Snare Drum
___ Viola	___ Oboe	___ French horn	___ Cymbals
___ Cello	___ Clarinet	___ Trombone	___ Maracas
___ Bass	___ Bassoon	___ Tuba	___ Triangle
			___ Bass drum
			___ Timpani

Evaluation of listening can also be attempted by discussing with the children how a given musical element affects the overall feeling of the music. This topic does not lend itself to written assessment. Such discussions should involve as many of the students as possible but should be objective. Such questions as "How does the music make you feel?" and "Do you like the music?" have little to do with the evaluation of listening since they are highly subjective.

Evaluating the Playing of Classroom Instruments

Objectives for playing instruments have inherent evaluation. The teacher has to determine what degree of accuracy or standard is appropriate. Considerations include:

Were the rhythms accurate?
Were the pitches correct?
Was the harmony changed at the proper time and place?
Was the entire effect musically correct and satisfying?

Evaluating Movement

The purpose of moving to music is to give physical experience to a musical concept. Movement must be evaluated on this basis, not as ballet or modern dance. Children rarely develop enough skill to use their bodies as expressive instruments. But axial and locomotive movement can develop concepts and can be used to assess this development. Evaluation occurs with the musical elements specified for movement:

Rhythm. Were the children responsive to the tempo, beat, and accent groupings?

Pitch. Were they responsive to the highness or lowness of the pitch? To the legato or staccato articulations of the melody?

Intensity. Were they responsive to the loudness and softness of the music? To the changes?

Other elements. Were they similarly responsive to the timbre, texture, and form?

Evaluation of movement is also inferred through each child's increasing awareness of these musical elements in other contexts.

Evaluating Music Reading

Music reading is best evaluated by seeing if skills have been transferred. The best evaluation is to use old notational skills in a new or different context.

Can the child who reads ⎪ ⊓ ⁊ in several well-practiced rhythms decipher a totally new line of rhythms using these same symbols? Can the child who verbalizes the meaning of *f, mf, mp,* and *p* respond correctly to these symbols when reading the directions in a "sound picture"? Can the child identify pitches as high or low using line notation, as they are played? The ultimate evaluation of music reading is not verbalizing about music symbols. This only reflects memorization. Rather, music reading is the act of translating symbols into sound. This evaluates, in whatever system the teacher uses, the understanding and aural meaning of the symbol.

Evaluating Creative Activities

Creative activities, like other activities, have no absolute measurement. However, if one child or a group of children has composed a short *musique concrète* composition, who is to say the result is not "creative"? Some may be more original than others or have a better sense of design. Particularly "good" creative results of children's activities can be used as models as long as everyone analyzes through observation why the model is particularly successful. This helps every child develop some criteria that should transfer to the next creative activity.

The role of teachers is critical here. They need to challenge the overtly creative child and encourage him or her to seek new limits. But they also need to bring the covertly creative children along, to present them a manageable task. Most children are creative in various ways, convergently and divergently, as well as in varying degrees. Evaluation has to be geared to these individual capacities.

All musical activities need to be evaluated on the basis of the lesson objective—did the children "sing, play, move, read, or create"? The standard is still left to the teacher and it should be both realistic and challenging.

In addition, certain affective behaviors give secondary evidence that a lesson did more than merely attain an objective, that it was successful because it generated a "good" feeling and was an aesthetic experience. This evidence includes the enthusiasm of the class and its willingness to participate free of reticence and embarrassment. It also includes enjoying the musical experience because it appears intrinsically motivating, something that happens over a period of time with successful musical experiences. The presence of these affective behaviors at any one time is not evidence that the music program is a success. But continued enthusiasm over a long period, coupled with a realization of most musical objectives, indeed is a strong indication of achievement.

Questions for Lesson Activities

Questions are an important part of evaluation as well as of the entire teaching process, particularly for motivation and in procedures. Teachers use questioning strategies for a variety of reasons.

Questions are crucial in motivation. A leading question about a musical instrument, song, or record can excite a child's interest particularly if the answer to the question can be found through observing the instrument or listening to the song or record.

Questions are also used to involve the children more fully in the learning process. It is more meaningful for children to participate by answering questions than merely to be told facts and figures.

Questions develop problem-solving techniques. When the teacher structures a lesson so that relationships can be understood by listening to a recording or singing a song, the children have moved closer to becoming independent learners.

Questions are also an excellent way to review a body of material, and through oral answers to questions the teacher can assess whether the class has mastered certain facts or ideas inherent in a unit of study.

Questions are sometimes used as a disciplinary measure. Children who are being disruptive or inattentive are sometimes asked a question. Often, they cannot possibly answer it because they were not attentive while it was being asked. This only serves to embarrass children and to condition the class to think they must have been misbehaving if they are asked a question. Being asked questions should be a positive, not a negative, experience. Questions should be asked not only for "correct" answers but also to stimulate more questions. Independent learners probably operate as they do because of their ability to ask the right questions and seek appropriate answers.

Types of Questions

Three basic types of questions have use for the music teacher. First is the *question of fact*, a question that has *one* right answer: "When was Beethoven born?" "How many symphonies did Mozart write?" "What is the meter signature of this song?" "What are the instruments in a string quartet?" Each of these has one correct, factual answer. An incorrect answer is not "close," "warm," or even a "good effort": it is wrong! Teachers have no difficulty asking factual questions. The difficulty comes in knowing when and why to ask factual questions.

Factual questions are appropriate when it is important that a fact be recalled, but there must be exposure to a fact before a child is asked to recall it. There is no way children would know when Beethoven was born unless they had previously been told and were expected to remember.

Factual questions do not serve well as motivators. Some teachers ask factual questions the children could not possibly answer—so the answer can be provided by the teacher: "How many symphonies did Beethoven write?" (pause) "He wrote nine." This rarely serves to create excitement among the class. Children do not say "Please, please tell us, teacher!" Rather, they learn quickly that the teacher will ultimately answer his or her own questions and that they do not need to listen. It is little better to have children guess: "When do you think Beethoven was born?" Facts are not really established by guessing.

Factual questions do not serve as good discipline measures, either. Children who have not heard the question or who would not know the answer because they were misbehaving will hardly develop a positive attitude toward strategies that utilize questions. Questions only mean trouble to them.

A second type of question is one that calls for an *opinion:* "What do you think about this composition?" "What can be said about Bobby's ostinato?" "How might we improve the song we have written?" There is no right or wrong answer to an opinion question. Questions of opinion often are followed by "Why?" to develop some factual basis or rationale for the child's opinion. This is important.

Questions of opinion can be used to provide motivation before a lesson, as well to facilitate the procedures or to evaluate the affective domain. It is important to keep a question of opinion just that, not one that overlaps into a factual area: "How many symphonies do you think Beethoven wrote?" followed by the correct answer given by the teacher is no more motivating than stating the question factually.

A third type of question is one that requires *observation* to answer. This kind of question has the widest practical use for music lessons. Music is an experiential subject, which can be observed. It lends itself to questions that can be solved through observation—by seeing or listening to the music. Examples are:

While listening to a recording,
   what are the predominant timbres?
   how many sections are there?

While singing a song,
   where do we naturally breathe?
   when does the melody skip?

While seeing a piece of music,
   where are the rests?
   what is the meter?
   how many phrases are there?

While viewing and hearing a guitar,
   how many strings are there?
   which is the highest? the lowest?

Questions of observation can lead to factual information. Children will observe that a guitar has six strings, that a song has four phrases, that a rest may indicate the end of a phrase. Discovering a fact, rather than being told, will make that fact meaningful to the children. When asked later, they can rediscover the answer in their minds because they have experienced the fact.

195

Questions of observation should be used in all facets of the lesson. They are never inappropriate.

Rhetorical questions, the fourth type, serve little purpose in the music classroom. This type of question elicits and requires no response: "That was a lovely song, wasn't it?" "Let's re-do the words to the song, O.K.?" Rhetorical questions are filler. Many teachers use them out of nervousness or habit. They do little harm, but they contribute little to the learning process.

As a general rule, remember that questions that can be solved by observation are most useful to the teacher of music. There is little need to tell children something that can be discovered through leading questions. Discovery is more meaningful to the children. True learning is self-discovery and can be implemented by the teacher through questions of observation.

Questions are useful in the classroom not only to evaluate, but also to motivate and to develop concepts. The ability to phrase appropriate, well-directed questions is the mark of a good teacher.

Evaluating Specific Program Objectives

Specific program objectives can be measured by the teacher's observation as well as by a written test. These objectives, discussed in Chapter 3, are goals for the entire year. Although there is continuing measurement throughout the school year, it is desirable both that they be achieved by year's end and that they be measured in some manner.

Typical specific program objectives cited earlier include:

Early elementary
The children will
    sing unison songs with limited ranges.
    play the basic beat on percussion instruments.
    use line notation to represent highs and lows.

Middle elementary
The children will
    sing descants and two-part harmony.
    play simple chordal accompaniment on the autoharp.
    create sound pictures.

Upper elementary
The children will
    sing partner songs.
    play syncopated rhythm patterns as ostinati.
    use conducting patterns.

Reasonable achievement of lesson objectives through the year results in a concomitant achievement of specific program objectives such as these. Some can be assessed with a written test. Others are assessed by observing the children. Few teachers could take the time to assess each child independently, although this would be ideal.

It is important to develop some type of reporting system to communicate to parents how their child is doing in music. This should cite the areas related to the program objective and not be based merely on citizenship and participation. The following document could be adapted by each teacher as a report to send home or for parent-teacher conferences:

Music Report for _____	All of the time	Most of the time	Some of the time	None of the time
Sings in tune in unison				
Sings well in harmony				
Shows good listening skills				
Plays classroom instruments correctly				
Moves appropriately to music				
Reads music correctly				
Creates music easily				
Is comfortable with music				
Has enthusiasm for music Seeks music voluntarily				
Uses a musical frame of reference outside of music				
Suggestions for improvement				

Most parents are interested in the total development of their child. Music is an important facet of this development and should be accounted for on a regular basis. A written report gives more impetus to the teacher to organize music instruction around clearly defined, measurable objectives. Accountability also gives the child a sense of progress and direction.

Standardized musical achievement tests are also used in some elementary schools. These tests are not "talent" tests to identify individuals for private instrumental instruction and should not be used for that purpose. Neither do they measure aptitude in music. Rather, they measure certain broad concepts or skills that are developed in some elementary schools.

Among the achievement tests in music, the most comprehensive are the *Music Achievement Tests* (MAT). These achievement tests are designed for use with grades three through twelve. They consist of four sections.

Test 1 measures pitch, interval, and meter discrimination. Test 2 measures the child's ability to discriminate between major and minor sounds, to hear the tonal center, and to recognize discrepancies between written music and a recorded example. Test 3 measures tonal memory as well as pitch, melody, and instrument recognition. Test 4 measures musical style, chord, and cadence recognition and additional auditory-visual discriminations. These tests are available with answer sheets, a testing manual, scoring stencils, and an audio recording.

From Test 1

PART 1—PITCH DISCRIMINATION

Subtest a (Two Tones): Compare two tones. Decide which is higher (1 or 2) or whether both tones are the same (S).

EX. A ▯ ▮ ▯ EX.B ▯ ▯ ▯   1 ▯▯▯   2 ▯▯▯   3 ▯▯▯   4 ▯▯▯   5 ▯▯▯   6 ▯▯▯

7 ▯▯▯   8 ▯▯▯   9 ▯▯▯   10 ▯▯▯   11 ▯▯▯   12 ▯▯▯   13 ▯▯▯   14 ▯▯▯   15 ▯▯▯

From Test 2

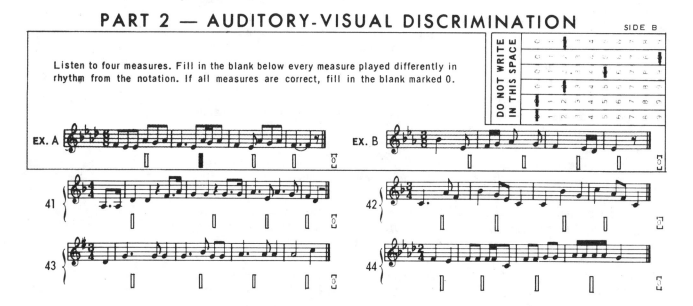

From Test 3

From Test 4

Another, much earlier musical achievement test is the *Kwalwasser–Ruch Test of Musical Achievement*. This test, designed for use with grades four through twelve, is a pencil-and-paper test that measures knowledge of musical notation in ten subtests. These include knowledge of musical symbols and terms, time signatures, syllable names, and note-rest values.

The Knuth Achievement Tests in Music have three sections of forty items each, designed respectively for Grades 3–4, Grades 5–6, and Grades 7–12. Each part presents the first and second measure of a phrase followed by four choices for the concluding two measures. The children listen to a recorded example and choose which of the four alternatives they think was the one heard.

Actually, few achievement tests are presently in print for elementary music. Most of those which are no longer available relied heavily on testing knowledge of music and of associating the sight and sound of music, both of which are limited facets of music education. The last two examples above are both structured this way. The Colwell *MAT*, probably the most comprehensive battery, relies instead on the child's perception of music as a result of training and education in the elementary years.

There may be few standardized achievement tests in music simply because there is little agreement among educators as to either the specific or broad program objectives of music. A standardized test has little validity in a music classroom if it does not measure the goals of that classroom, school, or district. For this reason, the teacher-designed test and the observation of musical behavior are undoubtedly still the best way to assess program objectives.

Exercises and Activities

1. Check several music series texts for program objectives. List those that are measurable as well as those that are not. How would each be measured?
2. Design a short written test to assess a program objective of your choice.
3. Observe a music lesson for twenty to thirty minutes and write down all questions asked. What types of questions are used and how effective are they?
4. Make up a written report form for music for a selected grade and set of program objectives.

Key Terms and Concepts

Factual questions
Opinion questions
Observation questions
Rhetorical questions

Professional Readings

Oscar K. Buros, ed. *Tests in Print II (An Index to Tests, Test Reviews and the Literature on Specific Tests)*. Highland Park, N.J.

Krathwohl, David R., Benjamin S. Bloom, and Bertram B. Mesia. *Taxonomy of Educational Objectives: Affective Domain*. New York: David McKay, 1964.

Sanders, Norris M. *Classroom Questions: What Kinds?* New York: Harper & Row, 1966.

Available Tests

Colwell, Richard. *Music Achievement Tests*. Urbana, Ill.: 1967, 1970.

Knuth, William E. *The Knuth Achievement Tests in Music*. San Francisco: Creative Arts Research Associates, 1936, 1966.

Kwalwasser, Jacob, and G. M. Ruch. *Kwalwasser-Ruch Test of Musical Achievement*. Iowa City: Bureau of Educational Research and Service, State University of Iowa, 1925, 1927.

PART FIVE

Alternative
Experiences
and
Techniques

Musical Games

The use of musical games on a frequent basis in the classroom keeps motivation at a high level. Children enjoy the challenge of a spirited game, and both friendly competition with classmates and the individual effort involved are good. Two criteria for musical games are that learning be involved which is relevant to the ongoing instruction and that the children develop (or maintain) their positive self-concept. Games can be defeating to some children, like the spelling bee which was good for the speller who was already proficient but did little to make the poor speller better. Games should enhance all children's understanding and appreciation of music. Games can also be a means of allowing practice on musical fundamentals and of evaluating many objectives.

Several games will be explained here.

Echo Clapping (all levels)
Echo clapping, discussed earlier, is a musical game of follow-the-leader.

Teacher

Class

One adaptation is to let two groups echo instead of one.

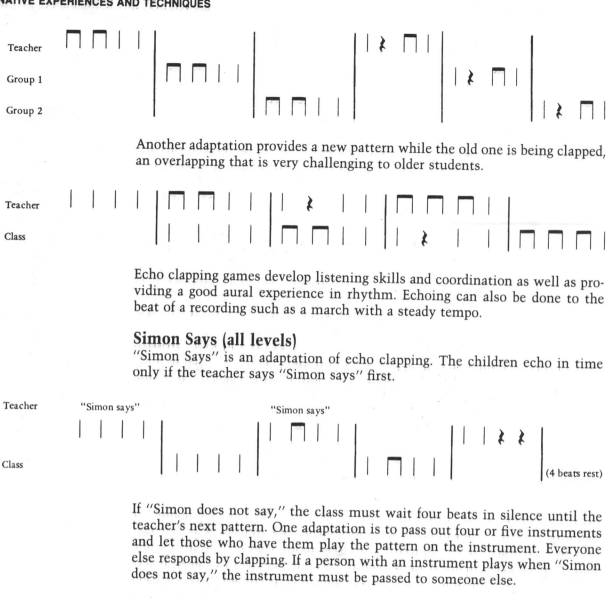

Another adaptation provides a new pattern while the old one is being clapped, an overlapping that is very challenging to older students.

Echo clapping games develop listening skills and coordination as well as providing a good aural experience in rhythm. Echoing can also be done to the beat of a recording such as a march with a steady tempo.

Simon Says (all levels)
"Simon Says" is an adaptation of echo clapping. The children echo in time only if the teacher says "Simon says" first.

If "Simon does not say," the class must wait four beats in silence until the teacher's next pattern. One adaptation is to pass out four or five instruments and let those who have them play the pattern on the instrument. Everyone else responds by clapping. If a person with an instrument plays when "Simon does not say," the instrument must be passed to someone else.

Echo Singing (all levels)
Echo singing is an extension of echo clapping. The teacher sings a syllabic pattern that is answered by the class.

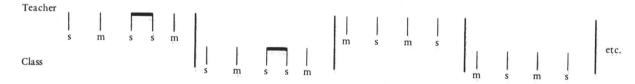

Hand signals or levels can be incorporated so children echo both in singing and with a physical motion. Echo singing can be combined with echo clapping either simultaneously or alternately. Echo singing can be incorporated with "Simon Says."

Echo Playing (middle-upper elementary)
Tonal patterns can be played on a melody instrument and echoed by the class. A recorder is good to use, but children may also echo back on a xylophone. (It is a good idea to restrict the notes to the pentatonic scale.)

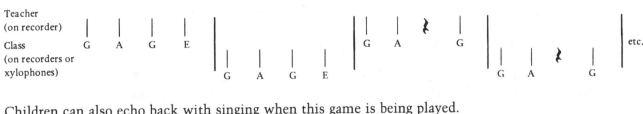

Children can also echo back with singing when this game is being played.

All Types of Echoing

Echo games can progress from simple to complex as the children gain skill in listening and in responding. Echo clapping should be extended to clicking (fingers), patschen (on thigh), and stomping (feet). Patterned movements on the floor (forward and back, left and right) can be incorporated. As the children become more proficient, patterns should be extended to eight beats.

Children may be leaders, but they should be advised to keep the patterns within a four- or eight-beat measure. It is advisable to have children write patterns they will use when they are leaders. Or each child can be given a pattern on a card to clap as the leader.

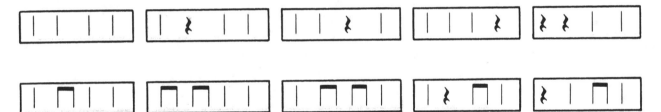

Individual differences can be accommodated by assignment of the simpler patterns to children who cannot individually clap difficult ones. Echo clapping is then achieved by letting each child be leader in turn, with all others responding. The cards can also be used as flash cards for drill in small groups at some other time.

Please Pass the Rhythm (middle elementary)

The teacher begins the game by clapping and reciting a rhyme.

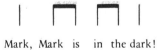

Mark, Mark is in the dark!

Mark waits four beats and then recites and claps a pattern that rhymes.

Sam, Sam, he eats jam.

Sam is "It" and continues after four beats of rest.

205

Mar-y, Mar-y eats black ber-ries.

The game continues around the room. Four beats of rest between statements gives the new person a chance to think of his or her rhyme. It also keeps the game moving in a pulselike manner.

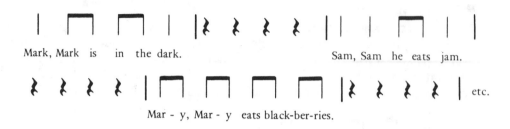

Mark, Mark is in the dark.   Sam, Sam he eats jam.

Mar - y, Mar - y eats black-ber-ries.   etc.

Children should keep the beat by tapping their toes or clapping the pulse.

The "Skeleton" Mystery Tune (middle–upper elementary)

In small groups, children are assigned (or decide to use) a song that has been sung many times in class. The song is prepared in skeleton fashion—some clap the melodic rhythm, some the accent, others the pulse:

(Mystery tune: Shoo Fly)

Melodic rhythm

Accent

Pulse

Billy Reeves

Frank Campbell

F major

Shoo, Fly, Don't Bother Me

Enthusiastically

Shoo, fly, don't both – er me, Shoo, fly, don't both – er me,

Shoo, fly, don't both – er me, For I be - long to some - bod - y.

Verse

1. I feel, I feel, I feel, I feel like a morn - ing star, I

feel,   I   feel,   I   feel,   I   feel   like   a   morn ing   star.

2. I feel, I feel, I feel, I feel, like my mother said,
   Like angels pouring 'lasses down on my little head.

I = F A C
V7 = C E G B♭

Each song is then presented to the class in its "skeleton" form. As the other children recognize the song, they must also clap along on the melodic rhythm rather than let one person guess the name. Afterward everyone sings the song while clapping the melodic rhythm.

Follow the Leader (early and middle elementary)
A recording with a steady, direct pulse is used. The teacher tells the class to think of a unique way to show the pulse (close and open your eyes, wiggle your ears or nose, click your tongue). The teacher begins and the whole class imitates at once. The teacher points to someone to be "It," with a new motion. The class imitates the child who is now "It." No motion may be repeated. The game continues with new persons leading.

Sounds from Beyond (early elementary)
One child is selected to be "It." He or she goes behind a screen and makes a sound with his or her body or with an instrument. Someone in the class must identify and imitate the sound exactly. If correct, this person now becomes "It" and goes behind the screen. When instruments are used, the same number and types must be available behind the screen as well as for the rest of the class.

Inside–Outside (early–middle elementary)
The teacher explains that singing with your "inside" voice means mentally singing the song while being silent. "Outside" singing is the regular way of singing. A song everyone knows is chosen. The children begin the song with their "outside" voices until the teacher gives a signal (says "inside," rings a bell). The class must continue to sing with their "inside" voices—silently—until the next signal, where the singing is again placed "outside." The purpose of the game is to maintain the tempo and tonality. This game develops pulse and tempo constancy as well as tonal imagery in children. It should be used only with songs they have experienced many times.

Musical Words (middle elementary)
Notes that spell words are placed on the treble or bass staff. These "words" can be placed on cards. Each child or group of children must determine what their word is as well as playing (on resonator bells, piano, or recorder) and singing it.

207

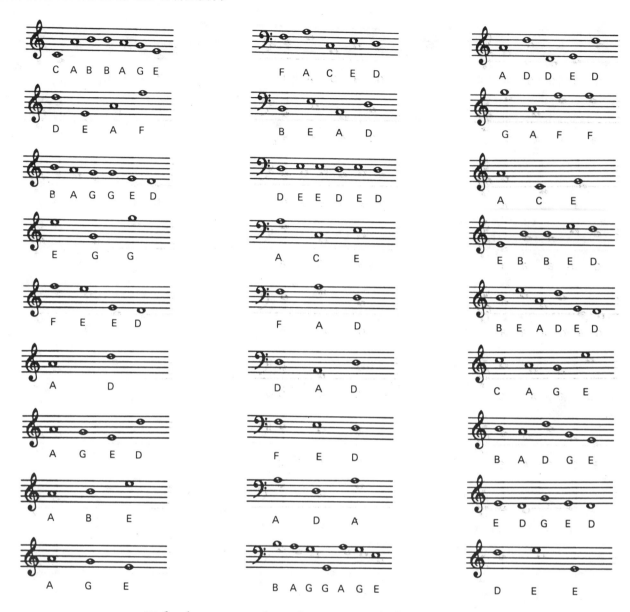

C A B B A G E	F A C E D	A D D E D
D E A F	B E A D	G A F F
B A G G E D	D E E D E D	A C E
E G G	A C E	E B B E D
F E E D	F A D	B E A D E D
A D	D A D	C A G E
A G E D	F E D	B A D G E
A B E	A D A	E D G E D
A G E	B A G G A G E	D E E

Telephone Numbers (middle–upper elementary)

A set of resonator bells, song bells, or piano keys is labeled respectively 1, 2, 3, 4, 5, 6, 7, 8, and 9 (C, D, E, F, G, A, B, C^1, D^1). Children are asked to play their telephone number on the bells (0 = rest). The rest of the class sings the tones back (with hand levels) or notates the combination (with numbers or on

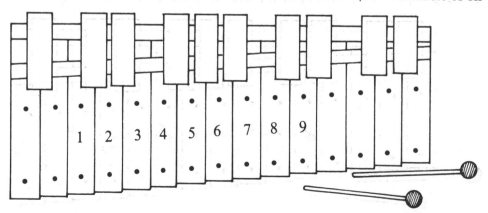

the staff). Area codes can be incorporated for long-distance calls. Street numbers, ages, identification numbers, and so forth can also be used for the game.

"One of These Beats Is Not Like the Others" (early elementary)

Two timbres, two pitches, two durations, or two intensities are chosen. These are placed out of view of the children (behind a screen or at the back of the room). A four-beat rhythm is played, using one sound on three of the beats and the other on the remaining beat.

"One of these beats is not like the others!"

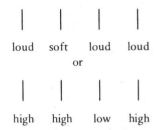

| | | | |
loud soft loud loud

or

| | | |
high high low high

After the pattern is heard, someone is called on to tell which beat was different and how—"The second beat was soft" or "The third beat was low." If the answer is correct, this child becomes "It" and plays the next pattern. As children gain skill in their perception, two or more variables, such as high and low *plus* long and short, can be combined.

Sequence (early elementary)

Five rhythm instruments are placed where they can be heard but not seen. The teacher begins by playing a simple combination of the instruments (such as drum twice and finger cymbals once). A volunteer then comes and must play the same "sequence." He then plays the next sequence.

Musical Math (all levels)

A number is tapped by the teacher on the drum. "Take × × × × ×. Add × × ×. Take away ×. Add × × ×. What is the answer?" A child taps × × × × × × × × × × and becomes the next leader. This game can include multiplication, division, squaring, and taking square-roots as well.

I'm Thinking of . . . (middle–upper elementary)

The teacher claps a rhythm, saying "I'm thinking of a state that sounds like this. What state might it be?" "Who has another state?" The game continues with a new child as the leader. "I'm thinking of . . ." can be repeated for continents, countries, presidents, world leaders, makes of automobile, fruits, classmates, and so on, with each new leader telling the category before he or she claps.

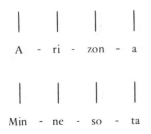

| | | |
A - ri - zon - a

| | | |
Min - ne - so - ta

XXXX (+) XXXX
(÷) 2 (+) XXX
(X) XX (+) X
(÷) XXXXX = ?
(Answer = XXX)

Days in the week
(X) XXX (+) XXXX
(÷) XXXXX
(+) XXX
(X) XXXX
(−) days in January
= ?
(Answer X)

XXXXX squared
(+) XXX
÷ XXXX
+ XXXX
(−) number of cents
    in a dime
(−) X = ?
(Answer 𝄽)

209

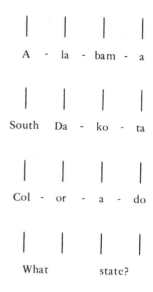

A - la - bam - a

South Da - ko - ta

Col - or - a - do

What   state?

Keep Your Cool (early–middle elementary)

An upbeat record with a strong direct pulse is played. Three or four rhythm instruments are given to children to tap the pulse. On the signal of a leader (such as a cymbal crash) the instruments must be passed to someone new *without* missing a single beat. On each subsequent signal the instrument must be given to someone who has not played it before. The game continues until everyone has played an instrument. An alternate way to play is to use a pattern instead of a pulse.

Tic-Tac-Toe (early elementary)

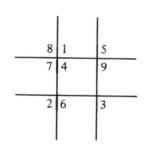

Each child is given a sheet and divides it into a tic-tac-toe board. Each child places one number from 1 to 9 randomly in each square until all nine numbers have been used. The teacher will tap a number from 1 to 9. That square may be *X*-ed or *O*-ed. The teacher continues to tap until someone can draw a line horizontally, vertically, or diagonally. That person becomes the next leader. Two children can work on one sheet in the traditional tic-tac-toe manner, alternating Xs and Os.

"Tell Me a Story" (early elementary)

A story is read by the teacher. Various instruments are assigned to provide the punctuation.

? = drum
. = wood block
! = cymbals

As the teacher reads, the story is punctuated by each instrumentalist on the basis of listening to the story and the teacher's expression.

Ringo Games (all levels)

Ringo games are like Bingo except that each square has a given rhythm, timbre sequence, or pitch (tonal) pattern. The teacher is the leader and presents the squares randomly until someone has a Ringo (diagonal, vertical, or horizontal line). As the teacher claps, the class echos back and then each child finds the square. To check the accuracy, the child with the Ringo has to play the line back to the class. He or she then becomes the leader. (Squares can be covered by beans or scraps of paper, buttons, and so on.)

Ringo charts may be drawn on white construction paper for repeated use. As in Bingo, each chart must be different. Either the teacher or the class can construct the charts initially. The sheet is divided into nine, sixteen, or twenty-five squares and one pattern placed in each square randomly. For Rhythm Ringo, the easiest list of patterns should be drawn from:

Master list of patterns using ❘ and 𝄽

For involved patterns, use the following list:

Master list of patterns using | and ⊓

For experienced students, the following list is appropriate:

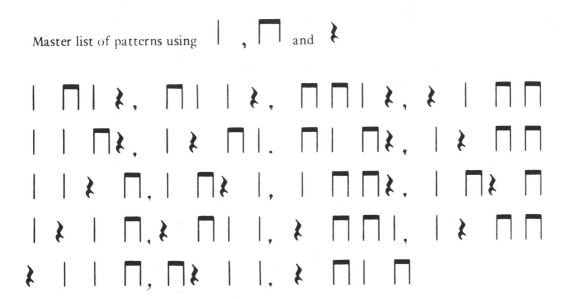

Master list of patterns using | , ⊓ and ⋌

With more advanced children, Ringo charts can incorporate the symbols for triplets and sixteenth notes as well as a variety of rests and patterns utilizing syncopation. Timbre Ringo charts can be constructed from this master list of combinations. The picture represents the timbre as well as the number of times it plays (two drums = × × on drum).

Master list of combinations using a drum, sandblocks, maracas, cymbals, sticks, triangle, jingle stick and cowbell.

Drum	Play 1,2, or 3 times	Sticks	Play 1,2, or 3 times
Sandblocks	Play 1,2, or 3 times	Triangle	Play 1,2, or 3 times
Maracas	Play 1,2, or 3 times	Jingle stick	Play 1,2, or 3 times
Cymbals	Play 1,2, or 3 times	Cowbell	Play 1,2, or 3 times

(Variation: Combine two or more instruments)

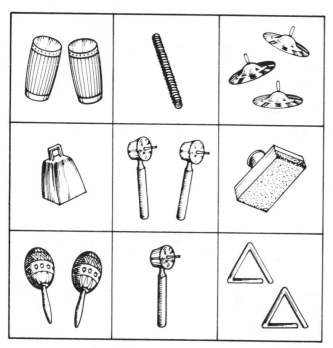 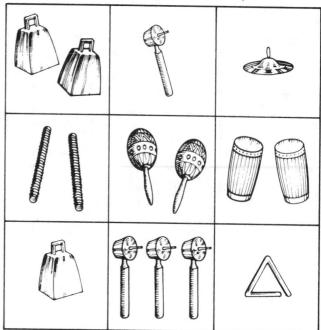

Pitch Ringo may use the following list of common tonal patterns:

Master list of common tonal patterns

d-m-s	d-s	s-d¹	d-r-m-f-s	d¹ = high do
d-s-m	s-d	s-m	s-f-m-r-d	s̲ = low sol
m-s-d	m-m	d¹-s	d-m-r-f-s	(below main
m-s-d	d-d	d¹-l	s-f-r-m-d	octave)
s-d-m	s-s		and so on	
s-m-d	d-d¹			

sol mi do	sol sol	sol do

free	sol
	mi
	    do
		sol
		    mi
		do

sol
mi
do
	sol
	    do
		sol
		 fa
		  mi
		   re
		    do

sol
 fa
  mi
 re
   do
	sol sol	sol
		 fa
		  mi
		   re
		    do

sol
do
	sol
	  mi
	  do
		sol
		mi
		do

sol
mi
  do
	free	sol
		   do

214

A pattern, representing one square, is played or sung by the teacher. Pitch Ringo can be adapted to whichever melody system is used in the classroom by adding syllables, numbers, or pitch names. Each sheet in all Ringos can also become a musical composition to be performed left to right, right to left, up to down, or in any logical way. Ringo is an excellent way to evaluate listening and reading in music.

Don't Cross Me (upper elementary)

Crossword puzzles are a way to give a written evaluation in a gamelike setting. They must be designed by the teacher to fit the achievements of the class. Nonmusical terms should be kept to a minimum.

ACROSS

1. Composer of Brandenburg Concertos
4. Part of a violin
6. A musical study
8. Many rivers (Spanish)
10. Musical idea
12. ___ tu, Brute?
13. Beginning of an opera
16. Abbreviation for Vermont
17. Musical decorations
18. Where you applaud in a musical composition
20. A type of voice
21. Gilbert ____ Sullivan

DOWN

1. Composer of 9 symphonies
2. A place of being
3. A solid shape
5. Double reed instrument
7. Before
9. Accent
11. Market
14. A large brass instrument
15. ___ium, a source of nuclear energy
19. Tonic tone

SOLUTION

Face the Music (middle-upper elementary)

Teams are chosen to see which group can find the most English expressions that utilize musical ideas. Examples:

face the music

clear as a bell

soft-pedal

keynote

theme song

put a damper on

a different drummer

play it by ear

Results can be played or acted out as charades when each group reports back to see if the other group can guess the expression. Points may be assigned to each team.

215

Games are a way to provide heightened motivation in the classroom at intervals and to evaluate selected skills and concepts in a casual way. These examples should be adapted for each teacher's specific use. Many can be modified for use in a music learning center.

Exercise and Activities

1. Choose one game cited in this chapter and list all the musical concepts that could be developed through it.
2. Adapt one of these games or devise a new one to be used in a specific setting. What does it measure? What musical learning will result?
3. Make a set of ten Ringo charts as suggested earlier in the chapter.

Professional Readings

Athey, Margaret, and Gwen Hotchkiss. *A Galaxy of Games for the Music Class*. Englewood Cliffs, N.J.: Prentice-Hall, 1975.

Bennett, Michael D. *Surviving in General Music*. Memphis: Pop Hits Publishing, 1974.

Dorian, Margery, and Frances Gulland. *Telling Stories Through Movement*. Belmont, Calif.: Fearon Publishers, 1974.

Fyfe, Joan Z. *Personalizing Music Education: A Plan for Implementation*. Sherman Oaks, Calif.: Alfred Publishing Company, 1978.

Van Witsen, Betty. *Perceptual Training Activities Handbook*, rev. ed. New York: Teachers College Press, Columbia University, 1979.

Integrating Music With Other Subjects

Music can be taught by itself or in tandem with other subjects. Children do not learn in a vacuum, nor should music be taught in one. It has both scientific and aesthetic facets that lend to its integration with many other subjects. Furthermore, young children do not tend to compartmentalize learning into distinct subjects like music, math, reading, and science as much as adults do. School to them is one big learning center, not discrete subjects and specialties.

In recent years, various attempts have been made by educators to link music effectively and equally with other subjects in the curriculum. Two movements of this type are related arts and the arts in general education (AGE).

Related Arts

Related arts are also sometimes called allied arts, correlated arts, or humanities. Whatever the label, the approach is interdisciplinary since several of the arts—music, painting, sculpture, architecture, and poetry—are somehow drawn together through one of three strategies.

Topical Approach
The topical approach is organization around a theme or idea that can include examples from several of the arts and is usually organized as a unit plan. An example might be music and dance. In this unit, the class would explore how music and dance have been combined and portrayed. This could include:

217

Ballet music (*Swan Lake, Giselle, Hoedown*)
Popular dance music (disco, Latin, country-swing)
Dance forms for listening (minuet and trio; the baroque suite with allemande,
    courante, sarabande, and gigue)
Dance themes in poetry and painting (Degas)
The art of choreography (Balanchine, Baryshnikov, Nureyev)
The use of dance in musical comedy and opera (*Oklahoma!, Aïda*)
Architecture of buildings to house dance (Lincoln Center)

The possibilities for combining music and dance would only be limited by the resources available and the teacher's imagination. "Weather and Nature Portrayed Through the Arts" could include Debussy's *La Mer*, Grofé's *Grand Canyon Suite*, Hemingway's *The Old Man and the Sea*, and Turner's portrayals of the ocean and storms. Topics united in a thematic relationship can be quite diverse as long as the topic somehow combines the arts. Additional topics include:

Satire in Art
Love Themes in Art
Art in Times of War
Social Protest Through the Arts

Topical relationships are particularly suited to the upper-elementary classroom.
There are disadvantages in relating the arts in this way. Music used must often be programmatic. There is often a tendency to simplify particular works to make them fit the selected topic. Music is often short-changed in such units. Nonetheless, occasional use of a topical unit relating the arts can be meaningful and quite motivating for children.

Common-Elements Approach
A second pattern of organization is through common elements. All of the arts share certain common elements that are manifested differently in each and include many discussed earlier in music.

Rhythm—the regular recurrence of something

Music: The pulse, accent groupings, and characteristic patterns.

I = D F♯ A
IV = G B D
V7 - A C♯ E G

English words by Margaret Fishback. © 1965 by Silver Burdett Company from *Making Music Your Own*, Book 6. Used by permission.

Poetry: The rhyme scheme, accent patterns (iambic ∪| , trochaic |∪), and number of feet (4 feet = tetrameter, 5 feet = pentameter, 6 feet = hexameter); ∪|∪|∪|∪|∪ = iambic tetrameter.

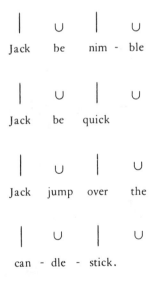

Architecture: The repetition and accents of arches, windows, doors, and surface patterns.

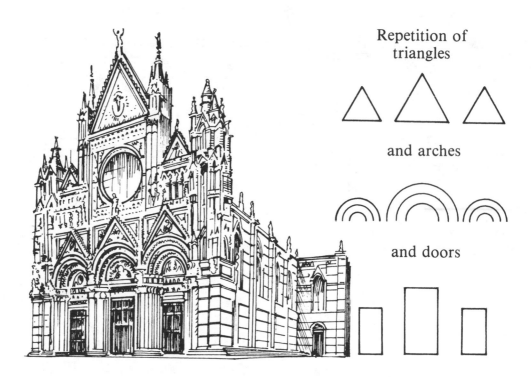

Repetition of triangles

and arches

and doors

Painting: The recurrence of ideas, lines, figures, and motives.

Line—horizontal or longitudinal organization

Music: Successive pitches are organized into melodies.

Pulse

Accent

Characteristic Pattern

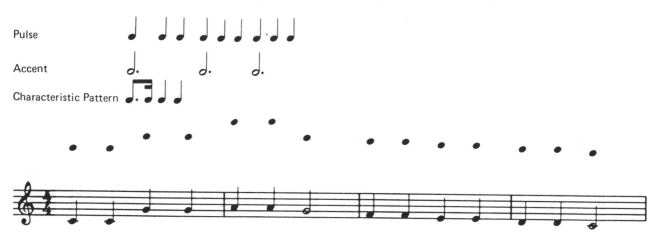

Poetry: Words are organized into phrases and sentences.
Architecture: Horizontal, vertical, and diagonal lines may be used in a building.

Painting: Lines are thick or thin, long or short, florid or simple, and they enclose space and create mass.

Design—how all the elements are placed together to
    Repeat with variation
    Repeat with contrast
    No repetition at all but only variation
All forms in all of the arts represent these qualities to some degree.

220

Other common elements frequently used to link the arts are color (timbre in music; figures of speech or words that "color" in poetry and literature; actual color used in painting, sculpture, or architecture), intensity (loudness or softness in music, saturation of color in painting), and harmony (how the elements complement each other.)

A common-elements approach, usually with one element, is appropriate even for younger elementary students. Many of the recent elementary series books contain ideas for integrating the arts in this way. There are some pitfalls, however. Music can be eclipsed by the other arts, or fallacious comparisons made between two of the arts. As with the topical approach, though, using the common-elements strategy can provide heightened meaning in the classroom.

Historical or National Approach

A third type of organization, through a historical period or national focus, has limited application in the elementary classroom. It is more appropriate for junior or senior high school. The arts are grouped together because they derive from a common historical style, such as the Renaissance or the romantic period, or because they represent the artistic efforts of one people, nation, or geographic region: "The Arts of Australia," "The Culture of the Eskimos," or "American Arts." The thesis in a historical or national integration is to find points of commonality—a philosophy, a technique, or the role of the artist. This requires an in-depth study often beyond the scope and sequence of the elementary school. Many teachers do integrate successfully this way without slighting music, and a music specialist can supplement the ongoing programs of the classroom teacher through this method.

Related arts programs have become popular as a way to bring experiences of all the arts to the classroom. They are also a product of our times, in which individual specialists—in music, art, or movement—have been replaced with a "broader" specialist. Effective instruction in all areas can still occur.

The following are examples of sample units for relating the arts in each of the three manners described:

Example One

Topical Organization

Level: middle–upper elementary
Topic: The Arts of the Hopi Indians
Overall Objective: The children will become aware of ways in which the Hopi express themselves through the arts.

Specific experiences:
1. Examining Hopi pottery
2. Creating visual designs similar to those found on Hopi pots
3. Examining Kachina dolls and learning their meaning*
4. Making Kachina dolls
5. Listening to dances of the Kachinas and exploring their social and musical significance
6. Examining Kachina masks and making papier-mâché replicas
7. Studying the dwellings of the Hopi and constructing models

*A Kachina is a supernatural person who is impersonated by a man wearing a mask.

221

Example Two

Common Elements Organization

Level: middle—upper elementary
Common Element: Line in painting, architecture, and music

Overall Objective: The children will experience line in the visual arts and in music and realize that there is a similarity between line and melody. (Line = path of a moving point; melody = path of a moving note.)

Specific experiences:
1. Drawing and observing the use of line in many paintings and realizing that lines may be

> thick
> thin
> vertical
> horizontal
> diagonal
> curved
> continuous

2. Observing the way lines are used in architecture.
3. Experiencing many types of melodies (musical lines) through singing, listening, and creating.

Ascending Melodies
Mozart, Symphony #40 (4th movement, 1st theme)

Descending Melodies
Debussy, *Clair de Lune*

Arched Melodies
Smetana, *The Moldau* (1st theme)

Stationary Melodies
Beethoven, Symphony #7 (2nd movement, 1st theme)

Example Three

Historical Organization

Level: upper elementary
Historical Period: Impressionism
Overall Objective: The children will become aware of similarities between impressionistic painting and music, including:
> **its feeling of spontaneity**

> **the emphasis on light and color (thin orchestral texture)**

> **the use of pointillism (fragmentation)**

> **the de-emphasis of form**

Specific experiences:
1. Observing paintings of Monet, Manet, Van Gogh, Degas, Renoir, Seurat, Toulouse-Lautrec, and so on.

2. Drawing and painting in an impressionistic style (light colors, short brush strokes).

3. Listening to works of Debussy and Ravel:

Debussy:	*La Mer*
	Three Nocturnes
	Prelude à l'après-midi d'un faune
Ravel:	*La Valse*
	Jeux d'Eau
	Daphnis et Chloe

The Arts in General Education

The concept of the arts in general education is a broader concept than related arts. The arts are used to promote learning in all subjects taught in elementary school; the reverse is also true. Music is used to enhance science, and science is used to enhance art. For example, although music is an expressive art, it also incorporates many scientific principles. The vibration of strings is one such example. A string vibrates at x frequency. If it is divided into two equal parts, each half vibrates at an octave higher than x, $x/2$. This 1:2 ratio of the string produces an octave. These laws of vibrating strings are largely a matter

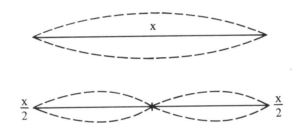

of proportion. Proportion also governs how perspective is achieved in certain paintings. Figures must be scaled down proportionally to an imaginary vanishing point to create the feeling of depth, or perspective, in a painting. "Proportion" is therefore a commonality for linking together several subject areas.

The three basic ways to relate the arts can become the framework for integrating the arts in general education as well:

Topical: The Life of the Aborigine; Birth and Death from the Artistic and Scientific Viewpoint; Weather; Rivers.

Common Elements: Spatial relationships; temporal relationships; proportions; color, line, texture.

Historical-National: A Study of Samoa; The Twentieth Century.

There is evidence that these types of integration are very important and may even change children's attitudes toward school and life. If music is integrated with other subjects, it should still develop primary values as well as non-musical concepts and skills. Integration does not equal dilution.

Exercise and Activity

Design a unit in either related arts or AGE that links several subjects together in a topical, common-elements, or historical-national manner.

Key Terms and Concepts

Related arts
Arts in General Education (AGE)
Topical approach
Common-elements approach
Poetic metres
Historical-national approach

Professional Readings

Anderson, William M., and Joy E. Lawrence. *Music and Related Arts for the Classroom.* Dubuque, Iowa: Kendall/Hunt Publishing, 1978.

Bahti, Tom. *Southwestern Indian Ceremonials.* Las Vegas: KC Publications, 1970.

Bloom, Kathryn. "Focus on Art in General Education. National–JDR 3rd Fund." *Music Educators Journal,* January 1978, pp. 41–42.

Colton, Harold S. *Hopi Kachina Dolls.* Albuquerque: University of New Mexico Press, 1959.

Cooper, Irvin. "Don't Lose Music in the Humanities Shuffle." *Music Educators Journal,* December 1968, pp. 40–41.

Fleming, William. *Art and Ideas,* 6th ed. New York: Holt, Rinehart and Winston, 1980.

Fowler, Charles. "Integral and Undiminished: the Arts in General Education." *Music Educators Journal,* January 1978, pp. 30–33.

Gingrich, Don. *Relating the Arts.* New York: The Center for Applied Research in Education, 1974.

Hipple, Walter J. "Humanities in the Secondary Schools." *Music Educators Journal,* February 1968, pp. 85–88.

Jorgenson, Dale A. "Preparing the Music Educator for Related Arts." *Music Educators Journal*, May 1970, pp. 60–66.

Karel, Leon C. "Teacher Education in the Related Arts." *Music Educators Journal*, October 1966, pp. 38–41.

Mulligan, Mary Ann. *Integrating Music into Other Studies*. New York: The Center for Applied Research in Education, 1975.

O'Brien, James P. "Packaging the One-Concept Music Period." *Music Educators Journal*, September 1973, pp. 41–43.

Saunders, Robert J. *Relating Art and Humanities to the Classroom*. Dubuque, Iowa: William C. Brown, 1977.

Wold, Milo, and Edmund Cykler. *An Introduction to Music and Art in the Western World*, 5th ed. Dubuque, Iowa: William C. Brown, 1976.

Music for the Exceptional Child

Who the exceptional child is depends on how we identify the normal child. Music for the normal child has been explored and discussed in the first fifteen chapters of this text. Normal children are in the majority in the elementary school, those who learn consistently in most areas and respond normally to the school environment. They proceed through the curriculum in the usual manner. The typical program in the school does not need to be changed to fit them since their intellectual, social, and physical abilities are typical for their age group. This does not mean they are a carbon copy of each other. One may learn math rather slowly and music quite quickly. Another may run faster than all the other children yet have problems skipping. Their strengths and weaknesses, however, do not necessitate major changes in the usual instructional pattern in his classroom. They are not exceptions.

A child who is considered exceptional does require alteration of the curriculum to suit his or her needs. The term includes

> . . . both the handicapped and the gifted child. [He or she is] . . . the child who deviates from the average or normal child (1) in mental characteristics, (2) in sensory abilities, (3) in neuromotor or physical characteristics, (4) in social behavior, (5) in communication abilities, or (6) in multiple handicaps. Such deviation must be of such an extent that the child requires a modification of school practices, or special educational services, to develop to maximum capacity.[1]

[1]Samuel A. Kirk, *Educating Exceptional Children*, 3rd ed. (Palo Alto, Calif.: Houghton Mifflin Company, 1979), p. 3.

226

Exceptional children are further classified into those with intellectual or emotional problems:

1. the mentally retarded
2. the emotionally disturbed
3. the learning handicapped

those with physical or sensory handicaps:

1. the speech handicapped
2. the visually handicapped
3. the hearing impaired
4. the physically disabled and the multiply-handicapped

and those with intellectual gifts, the gifted.

Exceptional children have received much attention in education for the past two decades. The Education for all Handicapped Children Act of 1975 (PL 94-142) mandated that local and state governments and school districts assure that each handicapped child could develop to his or her maximum potential. As a result of this bill, handicapped children have been placed in the "least restrictive" educational environment. Many handicapped children have been deinstitutionalized and taken out of special classrooms to be placed in normal classrooms, a process called *mainstreaming*. Another mandate of PL 94-142 required that IEPs (Individualized Education Programs), written statements of how the individual will meet his or her potential through school services, be provided for each child. The IEP must be devised through cooperative effort by the school, local agencies, and the parents.

Children with profound problems will continue to be in separate classes, but the 85 percent of children who are "mildly" handicapped are being mainstreamed into the normal classroom.

The advantages of mainstreaming are twofold. The handicapped probably learn more in a regular classroom and also learn to deal with the normal world rather than with a sheltered environment. There are benefits for normal children as well: they learn to understand people who are *not* "normal." They also learn how the handicapped cope with problems. One of the regular activities in which both will undoubtedly participate will be music. The teacher must become aware how handicapped children—and the gifted—can be accommodated in the music classroom. The teacher must be aware of their strengths and weaknesses as well as how they can be reached through music.

The goals of educating exceptional children through music are likewise twofold: aesthetic and therapeutic. In standard music education, the primary value lies in aesthetic awareness and development in ways described in the preceding chapters. These goals do not change simply because children may be mentally retarded, visually handicapped, or physically handicapped. All children need to be able to respond to sound—this is the province of music education. In addition, music is used as therapy with many exceptional children to help their muscular coordination, improve their speech, reduce their anxiety, or provide an extra mental challenge. These values are a viable equal to the goals of aesthetic education. Normal children respond to most areas of the curriculum, and for them music can be used primarily for aesthetic education. This is not always true for exceptional children. Music may be the only subject through which they can be educated. In such cases its purpose must be broader than for the normal child. It is academic in such circumstances to argue the issue of primary versus secondary values. The goals of

227

therapy may be more crucial than those of aesthetics. In the ideal situation, aesthetic education and therapy through music can be pursued in balance. A brief discussion of each area of exceptionality with application to both music education and music therapy follows.

Children with Intellectual and Emotional Problems

The Mentally Retarded Child

The mentally retarded are sometimes known as MR or MH (mentally handicapped) children. They are further categorized as Educable (EMR) and Trainable (TMR). Assignment to one of these groups is usually the result of intelligence testing, in which IQ (intelligence quotient) is defined as mental age divided by physical age:

$$IQ = \frac{\text{Mental age}^2}{\text{Physical age}}$$

EMR children have an IQ between 50 and 75, TMR children between 25 or 50 (on a scale in which 100, plus or minus fifteen points, is considered normal). The EMR group of children are more often mainstreamed than the TMR group. In the classroom, they often have a short attention span and can concentrate on activity for only five to ten minutes. They also have a low frustration threshold, becoming defeated easily at tasks normal children complete quickly. Their interests are at a lower grade level and they frequently choose younger playmates. In academic ability, it is much harder for EMR children to formulate concepts and to generalize. They need many more experiences than the normal child to form a category or mental grouping and to symbolize this concept. Their mental memory is not as quick as a normal child's. They find it harder to remember things they have experienced aurally and visually. Some are also very low in creative ability.

Music can be an important experience for EMR children and may be the only subject in the curriculum in which they can be successful and overcome their low threshold for frustration. It may be the only subject in which their self-concept is enhanced. For this child, the goals of music are both primary and secondary. The aesthetics of music and the elements of melody, rhythm, harmony, timbre, intensity, and form can be appreciated. Equally important, music can provide a tremendous release for all the pent-up energy the child has accumulated through years of failure. Music can facilitate motor development and coordination, both of large muscles and the small muscles of the fingers, eyes, and mouth. Music can enhance social development, providing models in songs of proper behavior, physical hygiene, and social awareness. It can develop eye-hand coordination, directionality, laterality, and even enhance language development through playing instruments and moving. The words of songs may help develop color awareness.

The key to mainstreaming EMR children in the normal classroom is to provide musical experiences in which they will be successful in front of their peers. This is not always an easy task for them or for the teacher. It requires the adaption of conventional materials and requires the child to experience concepts *many* times. It is a good idea to consider using routines again and again with EMR children, doing old things with new material as well as old

---

[2]Frequently measured by the WISC (Wechsler's Intelligence Scale for Children) or the Stanford-Binet intelligence test.

things with old material. A lesson must have variety yet not move so quickly as to overwhelm these children.

Adaptation is the principle for dealing with exceptional children. Some musical adaptations for EMR children include:

Singing Songs chosen should have a limited range (an octave or less), be conjunct, and should not involve complex rhythms. Songs that repeat words and phrases are particularly good. Sometimes words must be adapted and simplified.

D major

Mother Goose Rhyme

France

Baa, Baa, Black Sheep

Lightly

Baa, baa, black sheep have you an - y wool?

"Yes, sir, yes, sir, three bags full.

One for my mas - ter and one for my dame, And

one for the lit - tle boy who lives in the lane;"

Baa, baa, black sheep have you an - y wool?

"Yes, sir, yes, sir, three bags full."

I = D F♯ A
IV = G B D
V7 = A C♯ E G

"Baa, Baa, Black Sheep" is a good choice for younger EMR children. The contour is direct and logical and the last phrase is identical to the first in words and rhythms. Since many EMR children sing slightly lower than do their age peers, the piece can be transposed to either C or B♭.

F major

Swing Low, Sweet Chariot

Spiritual

With dedication

2. If you get there before I do, coming for to carry me home,
   Tell all my friends I'll be there, too, coming for to carry me home.

3. The brightest day I ever saw, coming for to carry me home,
   When Jesus washed my sins away, coming for to carry me home.

4. I'm sometimes up and sometimes down, coming for to carry me home,
   But still my soul feels heavenward bound, coming for to carry me home.

I = F A C
V7 = C E G B♭

     A song such as "Swing Low, Sweet Chariot" would be suitable for use with older EMR children. There are repeated phrases on which they can respond if they forget the words that change in each new verse. EMR children particularly enjoy songs that include actions—clapping, stomping, and clicking—as well as those in which only one or two words are changed in each successive verse.

Listening   Listening experiences should involve gross discriminations of

Timbre: What instrument is it?
Tempo: Is it fast or slow?
Intensity: Is it loud or soft?

In a normal class, questions concerning more difficult perceptions can be directed to children other than those who are mentally retarded. The ones above could be directed to them.

Moving   Moving should also involve only the more obvious facets of rhythm and melody—the pulse, the tempo, high–low, and loud–soft. The EMR child will also enjoy imitating whatever his or her normal classmates are doing.

Playing Instruments   EMR children particularly enjoy participation with the regular class by playing instruments. In accompaniments, they can play the pulse and, in some cases, even the accent grouping. In melody ostinati, the teacher can create a simple pattern with one, two, or three tones in it with simple rhythms that can fit the harmony of the song (See Chapter 9). Melody instruments with movable bars are good to use since the tones not to be played can be removed. Harmony instruments can be mastered too. Many teachers have success with the autoharp by color-coding chords on the instrument and in the song. (One- or two-chord songs should be used.)

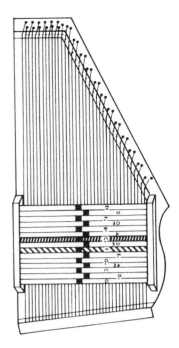

I = F A C
V7 = C E G B♭

EMR children can also participate in small groups in the creation or realization of a sound picture or special effects for a story or song.

Reading Music Reading music is a much more difficult task for an EMR child than for the normal child because of its basic conceptual nature and the need to transfer symbols to new concepts. As far as systems for melody reading are concerned, numbers are best for EMR children. Numbers have been successfully correlated with colors to enable children to read simple melodies on a set of bells. They can also notate their own melodies using this system as well in conjunction with resonator bells.

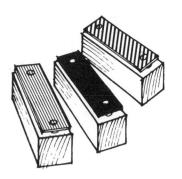

The Old Gray Goose

Mary Had A Little Lamb

Reading rhythm and durations are a bit more difficult to teach to EMR children, but a system of ⌐┐ and ♩ is a direct one that works well with them. The ♩ is represented by ▭ and ♩ by ●. The arrow under each symbol is a good reminder of the number of beats each requires. Rests are represented as ♪. This system can eventually be transferred to ♩, ♩, and ♪ and can also be combined with the pitch (number) system and colors. Normal children enjoy this too and can work back and forth between their traditional system and this highly simplified one.

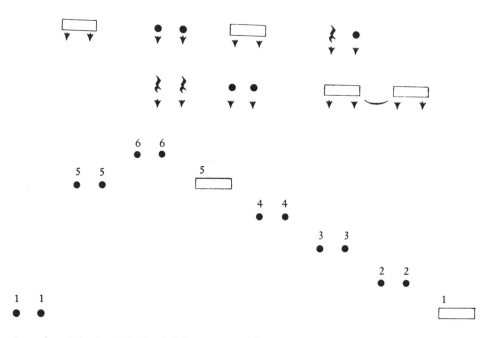

Creating Music EMR children certainly can create music. The ideas suggested in Chapter 12 can be adapted for them, particularly sound pictures, graphic notation, and *musique concrète.* Writing songs from poetry is too difficult. Sound pictures they create can be dictated to the teacher or to a child with writing ability. They can also record sound pictures on tape or devise

232

graphic notation. Although the creativity of EMR children may not be as original or involved as that of their normal peers, they can and should create. This may be merely improvising a melody on a melody instrument, even when it does not result in a completed work. Such experiences can provide a boost to ego and self-worth.

The Emotionally Disturbed Child

Emotionally disturbed (ED) children may be terribly shy and unable to adapt to social settings such as the classroom. Or they may be very social but hyperactive, thus having problems in accomplishing normal classroom tasks. They may be aggressive and destructive, full of inner torments and anxieties. These affect their own growth, and possibly the lives of those around them, since they are rarely able to control their inner feelings. Most emotionally disturbed children have difficulty building relationships with fellow classmates and teachers. Their behavior, feelings, and reactions are usually not appropriate in normal situations. All of their difficulties in learning cannot be attributed to typical handicaps or impairments. Some emotionally disturbed children are often depressed and may even develop pains and fears because of social and school problems.

The task of bringing emotionally disturbed children out of themselves or of controlling their behavior will not be the task solely of the classroom teacher or the music specialist. There may be a resource person and center in which they spend part of their day. Music can facilitate a change of behavior within these children. Like all children, they have a need to feel competent. The teacher can program musical activities in which they can be successful. These include:

Movement   Movement is essential to expel the energy many ED children have. Vigorous, energetic, and even dissonant music to which the children move freely is good, but it should be followed by gentler, more consonant music which brings the children back to a feeling of repose. The children can be advised to move as the teacher does (as if looking in a mirror). This serves to take the emphasis off the self. Using balloons to toss or scarves to move to the music is also good. Bouncing a ball on the pulse or kicking and running after it on the accent are also good ways to expel energy while the children also learn something about music. They can be asked to tense their bodies (or the neck, arm, or legs individually) as a cymbal is crashed and then gradually relax as the sound dissipates.

Singing   Songs with "happy" words may be good to use, particularly those incorporating motions and actions:
   "If you're happy and you know it, clap your hands"
                              ". . . nod your head."
                              ". . . stamp your feet."
This may help bring the shy child out of depression and give him or her a feeling of success. Songs can also be chosen because the words model appropriate social behavior—how to say hello, help a neighbor, or say thank you. Sad and melancholic songs should be included too, since these give the children an avenue for expressing the emotions they are truly feeling.

Listening   There should be use of music to match the mood of the child—isomodic (or isotempic, in case of tempo). If he or she is aggressive and hyperactive, dissonant, busy music can be matched to mood. Gradually, if the music changes to a gentler mood, he or she may become calmed. This can be combined with movement to a drumbeat as well.

The group and group activities are a vital therapy for emotionally disturbed children. Competence in music can make the difference and allow them to develop trust in and affection for classmates and teacher. As when dealing with the MR child, teachers should adapt materials for the emotionally disturbed child in the context of usual musical activities. This means creating ostinati, choosing parts, and selecting instruments with which the emotionally disturbed child will be successful. Success in music may be the reward this child needs the most.

The Learning Handicapped Child

Children with learning disabilities (LD) may exhibit a variety of characteristics. Many are hyperactive. Others have perceptual-motor impairments, performing poorly on all tasks that require visual and auditory perception. Others have attention disorders, being unable to focus and concentrate on any one task. Some have disorders of memory and thinking. Many have frequent shifts of emotional state, are impulsive, or are deficient in general coordination. Some have equivocal neurological signs and brain-wave irregularities. The LD child may have an average or even above-average intelligence, and except for the deficiencies mentioned above, may seem sufficiently bright.

Music, as a perceptual subject using multisensory approaches, can offer the LD child a great deal, even in the context of the normal classroom. These activities are appropriate:

Movement   Locomotive movement to a drumbeat helps develop large-muscle coordination. The teacher should ask the child to walk, and then match the beat to the child's walk. "Change the way you walk!" The teacher again matches the pattern on the drum to the walk. Later, the child may be asked to follow the drumbeat, with the teacher using walking (| | | |) and running (⊓ ⊓ ⊓ ⊓) patterns. Later, skipping (| ♪ | ♪) and galloping (⊓ ⊓) can be used. Movement should include many types of tempos—slow, medium, and fast—as well as changes among these. All of these movement activities can occur in the context of the normal class music lessons.

Movement through dramatization also helps the LD child develop large-muscle coordination. "Betty, sway like a tree in a gentle breeze. The breeze is turning into a strong wind. The tree is bent to the left, now to the right. It bends almost to the ground. Now the wind stops." This mime allows the child to project herself outside her immediate fears.

Echo Clapping   Remembering a sequence of sounds facilitates aural perception for the LD child. Patterns should be clapped at a moderate tempo and be short and simple (four beats using only | and ⸔). Words and syllables should be recited to the pattern to provide a verbal reinforcement:

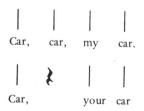

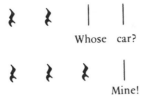

Whose car?

Mine!

Four such patterns can be repeated and linked together until all four can be said in sequence. Patterns can also be tapped on thighs and include the alternation of left and right hands if the child is able.

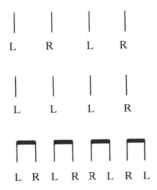

L   R   L   R

L   L   L   R

L R L R R L R L

Playing Instruments The LD child should be allowed to provide rhythm and pitch accompaniments to songs. A drum that can be hit with a large motion on the pulse (| | | |) or in a simple pattern (| ₹ | ₹) develops coordination. Playing a large xylophone with movable bars is a good experience. An ostinato should be kept simple initially, using one or two pitches. Very small instruments that require fine muscle coordination (finger cymbals, maracas) should be avoided until the child has made progress on the ones above.

C   D   C   D

Listening Skills Recorded selections should be kept short and children should be given a sheet on which to write perceptions or items to manipulate as they listen. If a listening selection is in ABABA form, they might be given two balls and three blocks to arrange as the form is revealed or five colored cards (for instance, two red and three green). They should not be expected to listen without doing something. In a lesson on timbre, they might circle or number pictures of the instruments as they are heard in the recording.

Sequencing Games Games that facilitate remembering a pattern of sounds are good for developing auditory memory. The following are suggested from Chapter 14.

All echo games
Simon Says
One of These Beats Is Not Like the Others
Sequences
Musical math

Music Reading LD children may not be able to decipher traditional notation. Large graphic symbols might be used to allow them to associate sight with sound. Particularly useful would be symbols that allow them to recognize and respond to bipolar opposites. These opposites should be introduced in pairs. Combinations of loud–soft, high–low, and long–short can be explored later. Children should be able to deal with these simplified symbols by writing their own and interpreting the works of others.

The value of music is both primary and secondary for LD children. Although they can learn about music, they can also make strides to overcome their perceptual difficulties and to find success and enjoyment from group activities. Adaptation by the teacher is as important here as it is with every area of exceptionality.

Children with Physical or Sensory Handicaps

The Speech Handicapped Child

The speech handicapped child has a speech problem that either draws undue attention toward him or her or interferes with the ability to communicate with others. This might include odd qualities in the voice, such as extreme nasality; it might include the absence of intensity levels in the voice, the incorrect articulation of words (sounds are omitted, distorted, added, or substituted in some or many words), an odd or erratic pace and rhythm in speaking, or facial distortions and grimaces while speaking. All of these affect the child's communication with others and make him or her different. The handicap may be due to physical causes such as impaired hearing, a cleft palate, or cerebral palsy. The vocal apparatus may be defective; the child may not have experienced correct speech; or he or she may be mentally retarded. The speech handicapped child can otherwise be a normal child with an average or high IQ in spite of the speech problem. Speech handicapped children may come from the entire physical, emotional, and social range. Their problems may be only temporary or may be such that they will have to deal with them all their lives. In educating the speech handicapped child, the speech therapist usually treats individual cases—but the classroom teacher or music specialist can be part of the remedial team. Music deals with many elements that are also common to speech. It utilizes dynamics—degrees of loudness or softness—that are vital to the pleasing voice. It has pitch levels, degrees of highness and lowness, also found in speech. Timbre, the sound source or tone color of music, is closely correlated to speech. Above all, there are rhythm, pacing, accentuation, and phrasing in music—all of them found in effective speech. The awareness of how these elements function in music and how they transfer to speech is an objective of music for the speech handicapped. As with all children, success in music undoubtedly has a positive transfer to other areas of the curriculum. In addition, music can develop skills of perception and listening.

Some specific suggestions include:

Singing to Experience Phrasing Songs with short phrases (two to four bars) should be sung by the teacher. Children can be asked to count the breaths, then to breathe when the teacher does, mouth the words, and finally sing along. This procedure may be repeated for many songs.

D major

Lavender's Blue

England

Merrily

1. Lav - en - der's blue, dil - ly, dil - ly, lav - en - der's green, (breath)

When I am king, dil - ly, dil - ly, you shall be queen. (breath)

Who told you so, dil - ly, dil - ly, Who told you so? (breath)

'Twas mine own heart, dil - ly, dil - ly, that told me so. (breath)

2. Call up your men, dilly, dilly, set them to work,
   Some with a hoe, dilly, dilly, some with a fork;
   Some to pitch hay, dilly dilly, some to hoe corn,
   While you and I, dilly dilly, keep ourselves warm.

I = D F♯ A
IV = G B D
V7 = A C♯ E G

Pitch Games Pitch games increase the children's awareness of pitch and intensity modulation in the children's voice. Dramatizations can be staged:

TEACHER: I'm a big giant. I walk slowly [act out] and talk loud. My voice is very low. It sounds like this: "Hello. Everyone be a big giant."

Children then imitate with their bodies and voices. The game continues with another child being something—a big bear that growls, a lion that roars, a cricket, a machine, an automobile. "Situations" can include sounds like sirens, screams, breezes, and cars shifting gears to enable the children to modulate their voices between high–low and loud–soft.

Chanting Words Choose words with a given sound to chant and clap facilitates awareness of initial or ending sounds:

"B" words

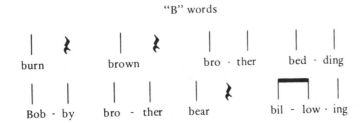

burn   brown   bro - ther   bed - ding

Bob - by   bro - ther   bear   bil - low - ing

237

Words can be suggested by the children. The teacher then writes the word and the rhythm on the chalkboard. Children then chant each several times as the teacher points to those in the list:

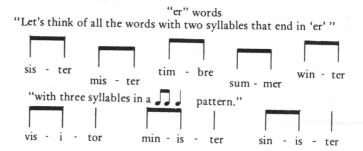

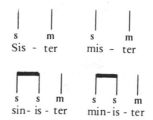

Pitches can be added. *Sol–mi* is a particularly good interval with which to begin:

Words with which children have particular difficulty should continually be incorporated with words they know and speak correctly. This reduces the likelihood the game will become just a drill and will give them a feeling of success.

Sound Pictures   Sound pictures that incorporate specific sounds a child or group of children is having difficulty with can be specifically written by the teacher:

"Make a motor sound using only the letter *p*."
"Sound like a wicked villain laughing [*H* sounds]."
"Sound like the static on the radio." (*S* and *Sh* sounds)

Chanting and Verbalization   Use every opportunity in the classroom to have the children chant and verbalize. Reading the school lunch menu in rhythm as the children echo is one way. Incorporating varying intensities, tempos, and pitch levels gives added awareness of the musical elements.

Instruments   The use of certain wind instruments can facilitate articulation. The kazoo is easy to use and enables the child to change pitch and intensity as well as to articulate the phrase length with a breath. Harmonicas, song flutes, and melodicas can also be used. (Recorders are more difficult because they are easily overblown and also have a limited dynamic range.)

Background Music   Background music can be used to see if verbalization is increased. There is some evidence that the level and rate of verbalization may be increased by using faster and louder background music.

Games   The following games from Chapter 14 are also appropriate for use with the speech handicapped child:

Echo singing
Please Pass the Rhythm
Sounds from Beyond (using vocal sounds only, particularly problem ones given to each child on a special card)
Tell Me a Story (with punctuation provided by vocal sounds that need practice)

Composition   Create vocal compositions according to the George Self notation system (Chapter 12), emphasizing vowel sounds, sibilants (s, sh, soft c, z), labials (m, n), plosives (p, b, k), and fricatives (f, th) on different occasions. Incorporate pitch and intensity as well.

Sentences   Make up a sentence using one kind of sound and sing it to sol–mi–la: "Bobby bounced both brothers briskly by the brook."

        sol   mi   sol la
        Bobby bounced both brothers

        sol   la sol mi
        briskly by the brook.

"Silly singers sing sweet serenades so they sound syrupy."

Rhyme Game   "Which doesn't belong?" The children have to think of three words (one or two syllables, as decided by teacher), two of which rhyme. The rest of the class has to say which does not belong.

Bear–tear–boat   Plea–sea–play

Word Pairs   Pairs of words that are close in sound are printed on flash cards. The teacher sings the first on sol, the class responds with the second on mi. Hand signals may be incorporated.

    sol sol   mi mi
    singing   sinking

day–they   singing–sinking
rode–wrote   sleep–slip
chip–ship   beg–bag
pig–peg   dug–duck
shoe–chew

Repeat this with words that rhyme:

pig–dig
shoe–new
sleep–deep
boat–coat
cow–now
jump–dump

The opportunities for combining speech and music are frequent for the classroom teacher since good speech has many musical qualities. It only takes awareness to allow one subject to enhance the other. Adaptation and imagination are the guiding principles.

The Visually Handicapped Child

The visually handicapped child is one who is either blind or visually impaired. Blindness, in a legal sense, has been defined as 20/200 vision, that is, the child can see at twenty feet what most people see at two hundred. Blind children typically need instruction in Braille. However, although the visually impaired have vision problems that cannot be corrected by special glasses or medical aid (unlike the normal child who wears glasses), they still can learn to read print. Both the blind and the visually impaired child may have the intelligence and school achievement of the normal child. Their social and emotional adjustment also represent a normal distribution. They are special only because of their vision.

The teacher does not have to change the content of the program to accommodate the visually handicapped, but must revise materials and adapt practices. The child should be seated in the normal classroom so he or she can take full advantage of all possible visual cues. Visuals must be large. The tactile and aural senses of the child must be used to the maximum including:

Verbalization Verbalize more than usual—explaining procedures as well as demonstrating them (for the normal child). "Hold the lower clave nested in your left hand between the valley created by your bent fingers and thumb. Tap this clave with the other one held by the right hand." Blind children may need to "feel" this position before they attempt to play the instrument.

Rote Learning Use more rote learning in the classroom, such as echo clapping and singing, rote singing, and echo playing of classroom instruments. Learning becomes a pattern of aural imitation. Constant emphasis on rote learning sharpens the visually handicapped child's pitch and rhythm memory.

Placement Place items in the music classroom so that drums, cymbals, sticks, or xylophones can always be found in the same place, whether by sight or touch.

The following modifications of teaching strategies are also suggested when teaching the visually handicapped:

1. Visuals must be large and "touchable." Particularly effective is the use on a felt board of visuals that can be touched and manipulated by the child. Felt boards can be adapted for rhythms, pitches, and timbres.

2. Instruments in which the sense of touch will facilitate understanding of the concept involved should be used. A xylophone or resonator bells—in which lower pitches are longer, higher ones shorter—is an excellent way to convey pitch concepts. The piano is not a good example for pitch learning since all white notes are the same size. The normal child can "see" the correlation between size and pitch, the visually handicapped can "feel" it. Since eye-hand coordination may be difficult for the visually impaired, a larger xylophone with movable bars and large visuals may give the child a successful experience with this task.

3. In listening lessons, the visually handicapped can convey form by manipulating objects—geometric shapes (blocks, cylinders), cards with different textures or of different sizes, and actual letters cut of plastic or cardboard.

4. Movement is needed to allow concepts to be experienced—fast and slow, loud and soft, high and low. The visually handicapped child may be a

very inward-seeking person. Movement will give an overt means to express music as well as to convey important musical concepts. (Enough space must be provided so that these children will not harm themselves.)

5. The following games from Chapter 14 are also suggested:

All types of echoing
Please Pass the Rhythm
The "Skeleton" Mystery Tune
Sequence (A good adaptation is to have children reverse the sequence.)
Musical Math
Keep Your Cool

All of these rely mostly on aural cues and provide opportunities to experience musical concepts in a casual manner. They also integrate well into the normal classroom. For individualized help, there are Braille music notation systems available.

The Hearing Impaired Child

Hearing impaired children may be those who are so deaf, either from the time of birth or as the result of an accident, that their hearing is nonfunctional as far as school and society are concerned. Or they may have a less severe impairment, being classified as "hard of hearing" with or without the use of a hearing aid. The population of hearing impaired children represents a wide distribution as far as IQ and school achievement are concerned. In special education, dealing with these children is the most technical of all fields, since the deficiency hinders the development of speech and language because of their inability to hear.

Classroom teachers can only reach hearing impaired children to a certain extent. Their education must be guided by a hearing specialist through special techniques. Even though basic communication may be through sign language, this child may be mainstreamed for music lessons. The content and expressive value of music can still be presented, but it necessitates attention to presenting music quite differently. These differences can be described in two ways:

1. The need to depend on vibration of sound to convey pitch, duration, intensity, and timbre. Normal people seldom "feel" the vibrations of an instrument, they "hear" these vibrations. The hearing impaired must rely on the sense of touch to learn these same concepts. Generally, they are most responsive to *low* and *loud* sounds. Initial experiences with music can occur with bass drums, tympani, and the largest wooden xylophones. An autoharp, held to the body where the vibrations are easily perceived, is also a good medium. Sound is best communicated in a classroom that has wooden floors. Since wood conducts sound so well, a large wooden table for the instruments is also a good way to convey vibrations.

Children should first learn the difference between sound and silence. This can be achieved by feeling vibrations (or not feeling them, which is synonymous with silence). Once the difference between sound and silence is realized, further concepts can be conveyed.

In rhythm, pulse can be seen as well as felt. Children move to the pulse of a drum, stomping their feet on a wooden floor while watching the teacher. Tempo, accent, and pattern can be conveyed in the same way. Placing their hands on a wooden table, watching and feeling as the teacher taps (| ⊓ ⊓ |) on the table, and echoing back is a way to convey pattern. Later, this can be done on instruments other than the table.

Intensity is conveyed in a similar manner. Loud sounds have a different "feel" than soft ones. Watching how the teacher strikes a drum or taps the table, seeing how much energy is utilized, conveys this feeling of intensity to the children.

Pitch concepts are more difficult to convey since, as we have noted, the child feels low and loud frequencies best. A piano, particularly with the strings exposed, can help develop broad concepts of high, middle, and low. The frequencies can be felt through the wood, but the correlation between a short, thin string and its high sound or a long, thick string with its low sound helps give visual reinforcement to the "felt" concept.

The voice is another way to help these children experience pitch. High pitches vibrate in the head and cannot be felt, but middle ones are felt in the throat, low ones in the chest. A hearing impaired child can feel the teacher sing these pitches and try to match them with his or her own body.

Children might find their singing voice once they understand the difference between high and low. Their pitch should be matched on a large wood xylophone. Once this is established, they can experience higher or lower vibrations on other keys and match their voices to them. It will be a slow process, but the voice range can be expanded by gradually adding more notes. They should also be encouraged to feel their own chests and throats for the appropriate vibrations and be given positive reinforcement when correct. A process of refinement may eventually occur.

2. There is a need for heightened visualization among hearing impaired children, who must rely much more on their eyes than hearing children. Procedures and materials must be adapted to meet this need.

Work with rhythms must include visual representation immediately. This can be in the form of the teacher pounding a drum and placing (| | | |) and the like on a chalkboard. The teacher should also use the *ta ti-ti* syllables when dealing with pulse, accent, and pattern. Lip readers can see and articulate the syllables, thus providing a multisensory way of learning that normal children routinely enjoy.

In addition, everything that is said in the music classroom can be clapped. This includes saying "Good morning," calling on students, or giving directions. Clapping heightens students' awareness of syllabication and phrasing in language.

All work with pitch must be reinforced with visual representation, using hand levels and signals and line notation. Children with hearing impairments must deal with the symbolic representations of sound earlier than normal children have to. The nature of the handicap necessitates working backward to the experience rather than in the way described in Chapter 11. This is necessary for communication and efficiency in learning.

A classroom teacher or music specialist who has signing skills can communicate with a hearing impaired child who shares this skill. In a mainstreamed classroom, the rest of the children might enjoy learning to sign too, particularly the words of their favorite songs. This heightens communication for all.

Although the deaf or hearing impaired child may not share in the music in the way the normal child can, involvement can provide feelings of competence. The emotions of the normal child in a musical endeavor are transferred to the hearing impaired child through a group empathy that defies explanation.

The Physically Disabled Child and the Multiply-Handicapped

Children who are grouped as physically disabled or multiply-handicapped are perhaps the most diverse of all those considered for "special education." It is hard to generalize about them in terms of either their handicaps or about modification in music teaching required for them. The group is so heterogeneous that each child makes individual adaptations necessary. As a group, their only homogeneity is that they all usually have problems of coordination or of perception or in cognition. They may also tend to be introspective and have social maladjustments as a result of their disabilities.

Some physically disabled children are classified as being neurologically impaired as the result of an injury to or the improper development of their central nervous system. Cerebral palsy, which is a motor disability from dysfunction of the brain, is included in this category. Cerebral palsy often results in problems connected in writing and speaking as well. Epileptic children have a neurological problem in the brain that results in various types of seizures.

The physically disabled child, however, may have an orthopedic handicap—a crippling impairment that was congenital, such as a club foot or the absence of a limb or digits, or occurred later in life as a result of polio, arthritis, muscular dystrophy, or amputation. In either case, the impairment requires special provisions in the school and in such a child's education.

The multiply-handicapped child transcends all levels of exceptionality. He or she may be deaf and blind, have cerebral palsy and a speech defect, or be gifted and orthopedically handicapped. These special obstacles require even more individualized provisions.

As far as music is concerned, modification for these children must be geared to the children themselves. Music can provide them recognition and self-actualization. Since they may be limited in other physical pursuits, music may be their *only* activity. They may have more time to work on it and to overcome their deficiencies. Music can give them a sense of worth and competence as well as provide their only interaction with normal children.

Activities offered to normal children in music should be included for these children. If they can sing, they should. If they can move, they should. If the pulse cannot be experienced by the feet, it can be registered by the eyes, the fingers, the mouth. If patterns cannot be clapped with two hands, one hand can tap it on the knee. If their hands cannot move to indicate pitch levels, perhaps the eyebrows can. If an instrument mallet is too small or slick to hold, it must be adapted. If pitches cannot be played on the xylophone, the thumb piano (kalimba) can be substituted. If instruments cannot be held and struck at the same time, they can be suspended from chairs and stands by string or clips to make playing them possible. If the child cannot sway to the three of a waltz, perhaps he or she can roll the wheelchair forward and back.

The music room must be adapted so that activities available to normal children are also available to exceptional children. Through music, these children can gain the recognition and affection they need to be whole persons. As is true with all classes of special children as well as normal ones, the individual child must be the springboard for methods and materials. Materials are chosen because the teacher knows they will meet the needs of the child and spark imagination and creativity. The materials will also provide a worthwhile outlet for hate, fear, joy, or anger. The job of music in special education is not only to provide aesthetic outlets but also to develop the child into a worthwhile, total being in society. It is a joint venture and responsibility shared by music education and music therapy.

The Gifted Child

Why are gifted children included under the discussion of exceptional children? A look at the original definition of exceptional children quickly reveals why:

Alteration is required in the school curriculum to meet their needs too.

There is no clear agreement on what being gifted means. To some, it means intellectual superiority. Others hold giftedness as associated with special aptitudes, including skill with facts, relationships, concepts, and music. It has also been defined as performance "consistently remarkable in a worthwhile type of human endeavor." As is true of all exceptional children, possessing one trait does not guarantee the possession of all others. A gifted child is not necessarily talented in music and, conversely, a musically talented child is not necessarily gifted.

The gifted have been variously categorized as possessing one or more of many traits. Among these are high IQ and physical superiority. They may have the ability to abstract easily and to remember things with which other children have difficulty. They may be a bit less sociable than other children but are usually well adjusted, self-actualizing individuals. They may be more independent and less conforming than normal children. They may think and do creatively. They are usually curious. Gifted children may need more time to withdraw and reflect on their learning than do most children.

In the past, gifted children were accelerated in public school, promoted one or two grades beyond their age peers. The problem with acceleration is a social one. Most gifted ten-year-old children still have the social needs of other ten-year-olds, even if their minds are on a collegiate level.

The alternative to acceleration is enrichment, providing in-depth coverage of school subjects rather than the usual exposure. Enrichment also means that gifted children will be leaders, not privileged members of a classroom. Because of their gifts, they are individuals from whom more is expected in better quality. Enrichment does not mean doing four pages of a workbook while the normal children do two, of reading three books to their one, however. Enrichment means *adaptation*, not *addition*. Enrichment includes:

1. Emphasizing the structure of the subject matter (how language, music, and mathematics are put together)
2. Using discovery learning rather than telling, setting up hypotheses and working from the known to the unknown
3. Emphasizing process more than product
4. Relying less on factual information and more on the analysis, synthesis, and application of knowledge
5. Allowing the child to develop high standards to evaluate his or her own work[3]

Music serves well in the education of a gifted child. The child's curiosity most often includes many subjects, among which is likely to be music. Music has a structure that can be discovered by the gifted. It also develops the ability to work independently or with a small group. The following are suggestions for enriching a child's school experience through music:

The Structure of Music

Music has much logic in its systems. The structure of music is manifest in:

1. Its rhythm system, based on an underlying pulse with values proportional to this (If a pulse = ♩ , everything is proportional to this value.)
2. Its pitch system, with values determined by the placement of a clef as a reference point (𝄞 = g)

[3]Kirk, *Educating Exceptional Children*, pp. 146–147.

3. Its harmonic system of building scales and chords, a type of formula that is applied in new keys (*d r m f s l t d'* = major scale). The normal child is concerned with knowing the absolutes in music (the spaces = F-A-C-E, a quarter note = 1 beat) but the gifted child is aware there are few absolutes. Rather, there are many principles to apply again and again like mathematical formulas.
4. Its acoustical properties, another structure of music worthy of investigation

Discovering New Ways to Organize Sound

1. The gifted will be less concerned with identifying specific timbres (It's a violin!) than with discovering all the unique ways a violin can be played (bowed, plucked, hit on back, scraped, *sul ponticello, col legno,* or with harmonics).
2. The gifted child will be interested in accent groupings beyond 2, 3, and 4—in meters of 5 and 7 as well as the meter signatures that represent these new groupings.
3. The gifted child will master concepts of major and minor scales quickly and move to other types of scales.

The gifted child may be able to transpose a song from major or minor mode into a new scale he or she has invented:

Mother Goose Rhyme — **Baa, Baa, Black Sheep** — France

Lightly

Baa, baa, black sheep have you an-y wool?
"Yes, sir, yes, sir, three bags full.
One for my mas-ter and one for my dame, And
one for the lit-tle boy who lives in the lane;"
Baa, baa, black sheep have you a-ny wool?
"Yes, sir, yes, sir, three bags full."

In addition, the following may occur:

1. The gifted child can discover how to harmonize and transpose songs with help from the teacher.
2. The gifted can listen not only for simpler elements (pulse, tempo, intensity) in music, but also for composite elements that identify a certain historical period or composer's style.
3. The gifted can compose in the ways described in Chapter 12. A point of departure should be provided for them.

"How many different ways can you play this instrument? How could you write this down?" "Compose a piece based on a calendar—or by rolling dice— or in which you shape the pitch and intensity with your hands [high–low, open–closed]." The teacher must then stand back and let the child create. The gifted child needs a great deal of variation and does not usually enjoy drill unless it is disguised as a game.

The teacher of the gifted must avoid feeling threatened by a child who perhaps grasps ideas faster and has more specialized knowledge than does the teacher. This type of child needs constant challenges, not right answers and conformity. Music can provide this challenge.

All exceptional children need alteration of the curriculum to meet their educational needs. The use of labels, as discussed in this chapter, provides a handy means of categorizing for the teacher of exceptional children. The thrust of Public Law 94-142, however, has been to avoid labels and meet the needs of exceptional children on an individualized basis. A child is not really an EMR, but someone with special needs. Music is not taught to the speech handicapped in a certain way, for example, but rather modified to meet the needs of the individual child. The guiding principles of all curriculum decisions in music for the exceptional child are *modification* and *adaptation*. They can be achieved without sacrificing the primary value of music education, aesthetic response through sound. All children have this need and right, regardless of their "exceptionality."

Many exceptional children may be talented in music and should be encouraged to study music privately, even at ages too young for the school's band or orchestra program. The classroom teacher or music specialist may need to make recommendations to parents or social agencies that such study be a part of the exceptional child's overall education.

Exercises and Activities

1. Devise a lesson plan that will provide for three types of exceptional children in the context of a normal mainstreamed classroom.
2. Interview a music specialist on the advantages and disadvantages of mainstreaming.
3. Devise a special game for a special group of children.

Key Terms and Concepts

Normal child
Exceptional child
PL 94-142 (The Education for All)

Handicapped Children Act of 1975)
Mainstreaming
IEP
MR (EMR, TMR) children
Emotionally disturbed
Isomodic (isotempic)
Learning handicapped
Speech handicapped
Visually handicapped
Legally blind
Visually impaired
Hearing impaired
Physically handicapped
Neurologically impaired
Physically disabled
Multiply-handicapped
Gifted child
Acceleration
Enrichment

Professional Readings

Alvin, Juliette. *Music for the Handicapped Child.* London: Oxford University Press, 1976

Dobbs, J. P. B. *The Slow Learner and Music.* New York: Oxford University Press, 1966.

Edwards, Eleanor. *Music Education for the Deaf.* South Waterford, Maine: Merriam-Eddy, 1974.

Graham, Richard, ed. *Music for the Exceptional Child.* Reston, Va.: Music Educators National Conference, 1975.

————, and Alice S. Beer. *Teaching Music to the Exceptional Child.* Englewood Cliffs, N.J.: Prentice-Hall, 1980.

Hardesty, Kay W. *Music for Special Education.* Palo Alto, Calif.: Silver Burdett, 1979.

Jankowski, Paul, and Frances Jankowski. *Accelerated Programs for the Gifted Music Student.* West Nyack, N.Y.: Parker Publishing Company, 1975.

Kirk, Samuel A. *Educating Exceptional Children,* 3rd ed. Boston, Mass.: Houghton, Mifflin, 1979

Kokaska, Sharon Metz. *Creative Movement for Special Education.* Belmont, Calif.: Fearon Publishers, 1974.

Krolick, Bettye. *Dictionary of Braille Music Signs.* Washington, D.C.: National Library Service for the Blind and Physically Handicapped, 1979.

Music Educators Journal, Vol. 58, No. 8 (April 1972).

Nocera, Sona D. *Reaching the Special Learner Through Music.* Morristown, New Jersey: Silver Burdett Company, 1979.

Ross, Ruth-Ellen K. *Handicapped People in Society.* Morristown, New Jersey: Silver Burdett Company, 1981.

Slyoff, Martin R. *Music for Special Education.* Fort Worth, Tex.: Harris Music Publications, 1979.

Wedemeyer, Avaril, and Joyce Cejka. *Creative Ideas for Teaching Exceptional Children.* Denver, Colo.: Love Publishing Company, 1975.

Winters, Stanley A., and Eunice W. Cox. *Competency-Based Instruction for Exceptional Children.* Springfield, Ill.: Charles C. Thomas, 1976.

Zenar, Rush. "Music in the Mainstream." *Teacher* (March 1978), 54–56.

Additional Sources of Material for the Blind.

The Lighthouse. New York: The New York Association for the Blind, 111 East 59th Street, N.Y. 10022.

Alternative Musical Approaches and Programs

In the past two decades, educators in general have questioned educational philosophy, curriculum content, and teaching practices. In music, several symposiums were held and projects established to assess the efficacy of American music education and provide alternatives. The Contemporary Music Project, begun in 1957, placed emphasis on the creativity of all students of music in the public school and provided instruction in contemporary music. The Yale Seminar of 1963 concluded that music education in America did not provide enough experiences in non-Western music and early Western music, or in the jazz, popular, and folk idioms. One important result of the Yale Seminar was the Juilliard Repertory Project, begun in 1964. This project sought to provide a variety of musical materials of high quality for use in the elementary schools. The Tanglewood Symposium of 1967 attempted further to delineate the purpose of music education in our rapidly changing society. It recommended that a variety of music of all styles (including youth music), cultures, and periods be integrated in the curriculum, that the individual student be considered in all programs, and that senior high schools give more attention to general music and humanities.

The field of music education did not change overnight as a result of these influences, but these projects and seminars did provide an awareness through which many teachers began to seek and become aware of alternative curriculums in music education. Three approaches which were developed in this period have immediate application in the elementary school: the Orff system, the Kodály approach, and the Manhattanville Music Curriculum Project (MMCP). All are the result of music educators' search for new alternatives, although only the MMCP originated in the United States.

These systems are often considered new. In reality, many strategies of Orff, Kodály, and MMCP have been used by good teachers of music for years. The innovation is that each is a developmental plan incorporating philosophy, musical concepts, objectives, and strategies. Each program also has had excellent publicity. The structure inherent in these systems developed at an opportune time, when music educators were seeking to organize instruction in a more logical, accountable manner. Good music instruction certainly occurred before their advent; conversely, their use does not guarantee a good music program will result. The individual teacher is and has always been the independent variable leading to a good educational setting and experience for children.

This book represents an eclectic approach to teaching elementary music, drawing on many sources, including the ideas of Orff, Kodály, and MMCP. Each is discussed in this chapter as an entity, providing more detail for teachers who are interested in using a system in purer form than is possible when its ideas are integrated among many others.

The Orff System

Carl Orff (1895–1982) was strongly attracted to the ideas of Émile Jaques-Dalcroze and physical movement. In 1924, Orff and Dorothea Gunther, a dancer, established in Germany a school designed to train future teachers, particularly those of physical education, in movement and creativity. Although World War II ended this experiment, Orff began to apply his ideas to early childhood education when the war was over. Orff believed that children experienced music through basic movements such as walking, running, and skipping, and that musicality in children developed as it did in primitive people, through basic word rhythms and simple chants. In the late 1940s he opened the Studio 49 workshop in Germany to build and experiment with instruments which would enhance his pedagogy. In the 1950s, he published *Schulwerk* (*Music for Children*), which summarizes his ideas and practices in five volumes. This work has been translated and modified in several countries, including the English adaptations by Doreen Hall and Arnold Walter. Walter says: "The primary purpose of music education, as Orff sees it, is the development of a child's creative facility which manifests itself in the ability to improvise."

The essence of the Orff system is play, that is, improvisation. Children are given a limited structure in which to improvise. They create compositions, however short, that are evaluated and then refined. The joy of spontaneous play in music is manifest through composition. The child is *led* to musicality; it is not explained as a finite system.

Orff's system begins with speech patterns that are derived from the words and chants children already know. These are then accompanied by bodily movements. All words become a stimulus for rhythmic activities. Children find words, which are then chanted to rhythm. Rhythms are snapped, clapped, stamped, or tapped on the thigh (patschen). They are also played on percussion instruments.

Colors

blue   yel - low   av - o - ca - do   green

clap

They are then expanded into rhymes and jingles.

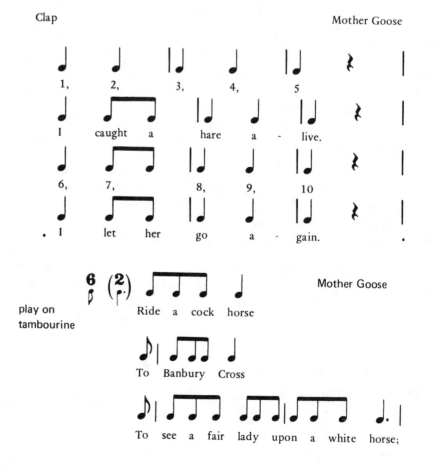

Mother Goose

The teacher and the children may adapt other classroom activities to these word rhythms and movements:

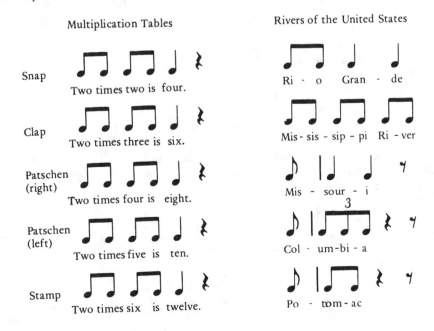

Clap and stamp   etc.

Two times se-ven is four-teen.

O - hi - o

Col - or - a - do

(Chant singly and in combinations. Add instruments.)

Today's Menu

Teacher   Class

Chant and clap

The men - u for to-day   The men - u for to-day

in - cludes   in - cludes

hot dog sand-wich-es   hot dog sand-wich-es

green sal - ad, rel - ish - es green sal - ad, rel - ish - es

one slice of bread   one slice of bread

two strips of cel - er - y   two strips of cel - er - y

jel - lo that is red.   jel - lo that is red.

An ostinato of "hot dog sandwiches"

Stamp stamp clap-clap-clap may be added throughout.

Children are encouraged to write chants and jingles that may be accompanied by rhythmic ostinati incorporating the four basic movements (snap, clap, patschen, stamp):

J. O'B.

Clap   Phoenix, Wilcox, Safford, Globe.

People have their own abode.

Ostinato*   Phoenix   Wilcox
           (snap)   (clap)

*These movements may be notated in this manner.

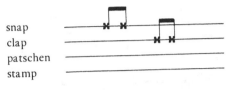

snap
clap
patschen
stamp

Phoenix   Wilcox

Word sound by itself is important and Orff liked children to experience various vowel and consonant sounds that result in interesting alliterations or assonances. Orff believed that rhythm is the strongest element in music and that song, speech, and movement form an "elemental" music, the springboard for all musical study. Meter, accent upbeat (anacrusis), and many other rhythmic concepts are introduced through speech. Phrasing, dynamics, and articulation (legato–staccato) can also be introduced in this way. Later, phrases are built into periods, sections, and forms:

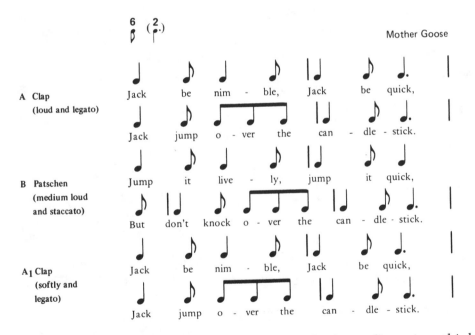

When introducing melody, Orff begins with the descending minor third (*sol–mi*):

253

Stamp, stamp, stamp your feet, stamp your feet to - geth - er.

Stamp

Rain, Rain Go Away

Doreen Hall

Rain, rain, go a - way, come a - gain some oth - er day,

come a - gain some oth - er day, lit - tle Su - sy wants to play.

He gradually adds tones

Mother Goose

Sing and clap

| sol | | | la | | sol | | mi |
| Hip | pe | ty | hop | to | the | bar | ber | shop, |

| sol | | | la | | sol | | mi |
| To | get | a | stick | of | can | | dy, |

| sol | | mi | | sol | | mi |
| One | for | you | and | one | for | me, |

| sol | | la | | sol | | mi |
| And | one | for | Sis | ter | Man | dy. |

until there is a complete pentatonic scale:

Doctor Foster

Doreen Hall

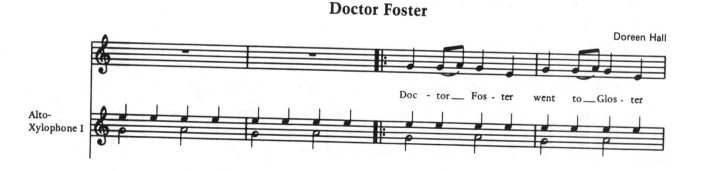

Doc - tor_ Fos - ter went to_ Glos - ter

Alto-
Xylophone I

After the pentatonic scale is experienced, a major scale is gradually incorporated, followed by modes and the minor scale.

Harmony first occurs with the use of simple fifths (borduns):

Bobby Shafto's Gone to Sea

Mother Goose words to Orff tune

sil - ver buck - les at his knee; He'll come back and mar - ry me, bon - ny Bob - by Shaf - to!

sil - ver buck - les at his knee; He'll come back and mar - ry me, bon - ny Bob - by Shaf - to!

2. Bobby Shafto's fat and fair
   Combing down his yellow hair;
   He's my love for evermore.
   Bonny Bobby Shafto!

3. Bobby Shafto's looking out,
   All his ribbons flew about
   All the ladies gave a shout
   Hey for Bobby Shafto!

These fifths eventually are used to create simple ostinati:

Bell Horses

D. H.

1. Clip, clop, clip, clop, clip, clop, clip, clop,

Shells

2. Good horses, bad horses   Three o'clock, four o'clock
   What's the time o' day?   Now fare you away.

They then become more involved with the use of additional notes of the pentatonic scale:

Peter, Peter, Pumpkin Eater

Form is continually implemented through rhythmic and pitch activities like call–response:

Canons are another way to experience form:

Melody canons

Rhythmic canons

*Part II begins when Part I is here.

Rondos are yet another form:

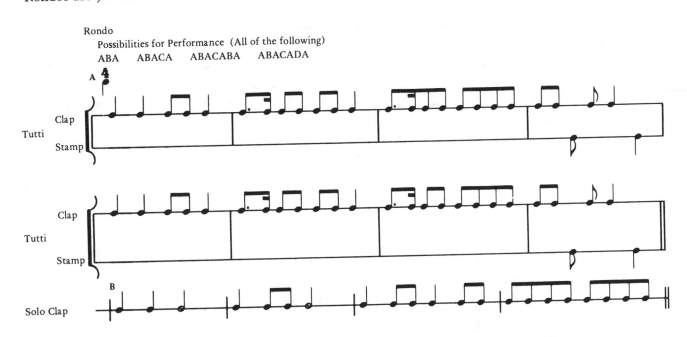

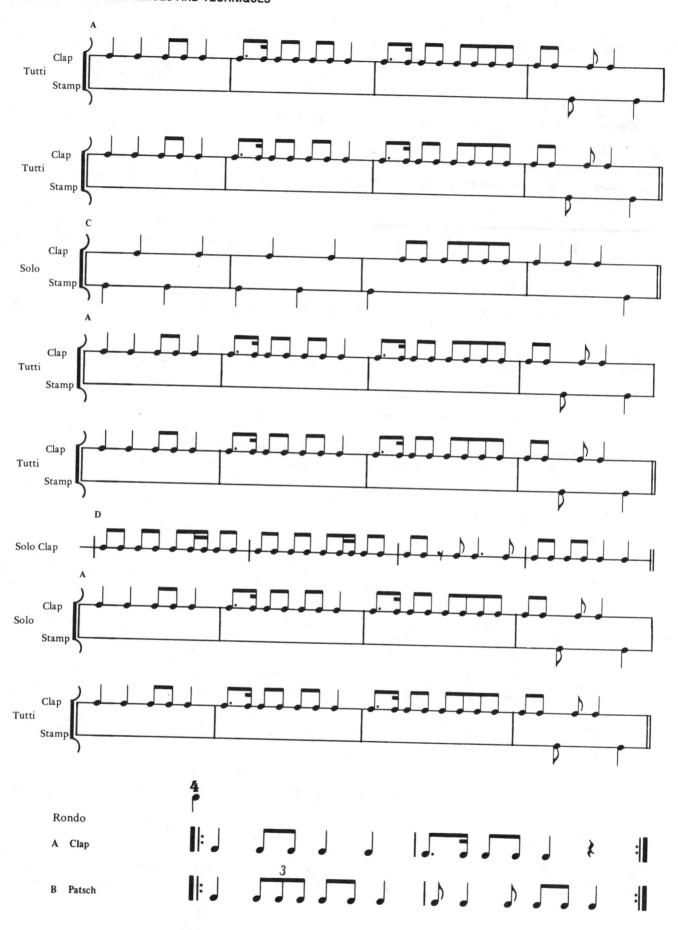

C Stamp

Possibilities for performance

ABA   ABACA   ABCA   ABACABA

First A and B = forte
All others   = piano
C   =

All of Orff's exercises are models, not prescriptions for children to follow. His *Schulwerk* is not a rigid system but rather a point of departure. According to Orff, creating music, not reading notation, is the main purpose of music education.

Instruments are integral to a child's musicianship, and Orff does not rely entirely on the voice as the core musical experience. He designed a battery of percussion instruments, of definite and indefinite pitch, that produce delicate and mellow timbres. The keyed instruments—xylophones, glockenspiels, and metallophones—all have movable tone bars over their resonating chambers. The xylophone and metallophone are constructed in three sizes—soprano, alto and bass; the glockenspiel comes in two—soprano and alto. These mallet instruments all have a range well in excess of an octave. They are pitched in C (diatonic), but have F♯ and B♭ bars that can be inserted to play in the keys of G and F Major respectively. The movable bars allow the instrument to be arranged for "success." An ostinato with only two or three notes can be programmed easily for the child. Such instruments allow individual differences to be accommodated in a musical ensemble. Drums, tympani, cymbals, and triangles complete the Orff orchestra. Recorders are also sometimes added to the complex.

However, resonator bells may be substituted in these experiences when the Orff instruments are not available.

The Orff system is one in which a high degree of creativity can occur if the teacher is also creative and allows the children to discover and experience the main facets of music in the ways envisaged by Carl Orff. Special workshops and courses are held in many areas in the U.S. to prepare teachers to perfect these techniques. In addition, the Orff system has been advanced in the United States by the AOSA (American Orff–Schulwerk Association), which was founded in 1963.

The Kodály Approach

The Kodály approach to music education was introduced to the musical world in Vienna, at the meeting of the International Society for Music Education in 1958. Since, like the Orff system, it derives from Europe, many educators tend to confuse the two. Although there are some similarities and many adaptations incorporating both systems, the Kodály system, which comes from Hungary, has some important distinctions.

Zoltán Kodály (1882–1967) was an important composer as well as a music educator. He was an excellent teacher who revolutionized music education in Hungary almost singlehandedly. His pedagogy was shaped by the principles of music education that he developed. He believed that music was accessible to everyone, particularly if exposure and teaching came at a very early age, in fact, before the first grade, in preschool or at home. The voice, he felt, is the most vital instrument. Music education must develop this vehicle through the use of folk song. Like Orff, he avoided using the half-tones of the diatonic scale (*fa* and *ti*) in early singing experiences, preferring pentatonic sounds. Unlike Orff, however, Kodály stressed music reading and literacy. Music reading is accomplished through relative solmization and hand signals (movable *do*), rhythmic syllables, and a simplified staff to read pitch. Furthermore, Kodály believed that creativity must be delayed until the children have a vocabulary of sounds and symbols with which to work. Instruments are not used initially, for the same reason.

Like Orff's system, Kodály's is developmental. There is a logical progression for introducing rhythm and melody, moving from the simple to the complex. Singing, listening, movement, and ear training are combined. There is a strong emphasis on developing music reading at all stages. The core of music education, Kodály believed, must be musical literacy, the ability to read and to write music. Just as no one could be considered literate who only *spoke* a language, neither was a person literate who could only sing or play by ear; *literacy* means fluency with musical symbols.

The rhythm system uses a system of syllables to represent each type of note. Children begin with the ♩ , usually without the note head (|), and gradually add rests and eighths (𝄽 ⊓). Later, notes of longer and shorter duration are incorporated. Each note has a word rhythm that is recited in conjunction with it:

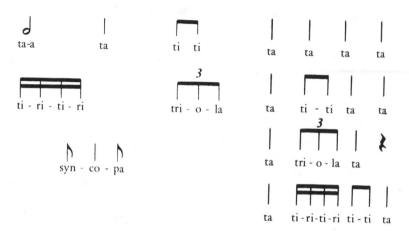

Children first experience the beat, clapping and walking to it as it occurs in songs, chants, and poems:

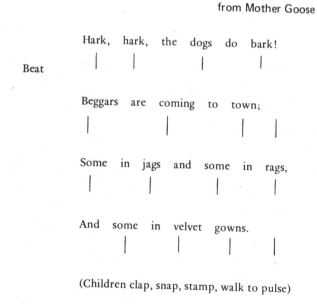

from Mother Goose

Hark, hark, the dogs do bark!

Beat

Beggars are coming to town;

Some in jags and some in rags,

And some in velvet gowns.

(Children clap, snap, stamp, walk to pulse)

Meter and accent logically follow experiences with the beat:

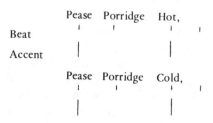

Pease Porridge Hot,

Beat
Accent

Pease Porridge Cold,

Pease   Porridge   in   the   Pot,

Nine   days   old!

[Children may clap, snap, stamp or walk to the pulse.
Accent meter may be expressed by a louder clap or a dip of the knee while walking.]

Phrasing is learned in a similar manner:

Phrase 1   The   Farmer   in   the   Dell,   the   Farmer   in   the   Dell,

Phrase 2   Heigh-ho,   the   Derry-O,   the   Farmer   in   the   Dell.

Beat = walk
Accent = Heavier stamp on "one"
Phrase = Change direction of
         walking on each phrase

Rhythmic patterns are experienced against the pulse, using the rhythm syllables to recite them:

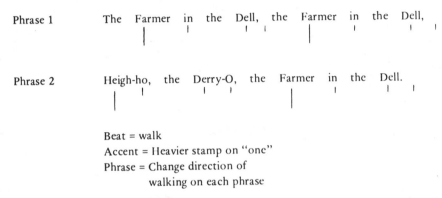

ta   ta   ta   ta   ta   ta   ta   ta

Phrase 1   Are   you   sleep - ing,   Are   you   sleep - ing,

ta   ta   ta - a   ta   ta   ta - a

Phrase 2   Bro - ther   John,   Bro - ther   John?

ti - ti   ti - ti   ta   ta   ti - ti   ti - ti   ta   ta

Phrase 3   Morn - ing bells   are   ring - ing,   Morn - ing bells   are   ring - ing,

ta   ta   ta - a   ta   ta   ta - a

Phrase 4   Ding,   ding,   dong.   Ding,   ding,   dong.

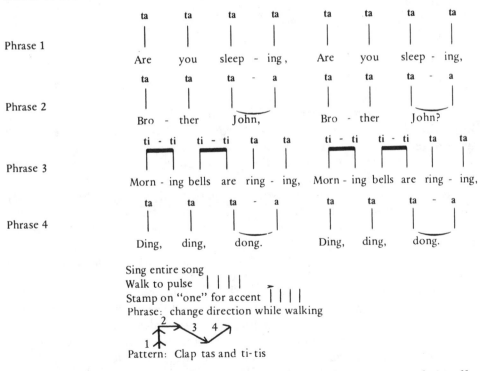

Sing entire song
Walk to pulse | | | |
Stamp on "one" for accent | | | |
Phrase: change direction while walking
Pattern: Clap tas and ti-tis

Through many of these activities children learn to experience physically all rhythmic components (pulse, accent, and pattern) plus phrasing. This is coupled with the use of rhythmic notation from the earliest experience, according to the child's level of understanding. Thus pulse and accent are notated before complicated patterns are introduced. When patterns are notated, simple, even patterns are presented before uneven (dotted) ones. Syncopated patterns occur even later. Regardless of the experience, notation is incorporated at all levels. Form and design in music are developed in the Kodály rhythm system by the use of canons, rondos and the addition of introductions and codas to these activities.

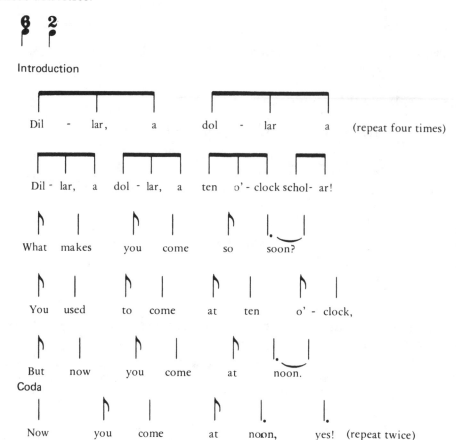

Introduction

Dil - lar, a dol - lar a (repeat four times)

Dil - lar, a dol - lar, a ten o' - clock schol- ar!

What makes you come so soon?

You used to come at ten o' - clock,

But now you come at noon.

Coda

Now you come at noon, yes! (repeat twice)

do

ti

la

sol

Initially, rhythm is introduced separately from pitch, but pitch soon follows. Kodály's pitch system is relative *sol–fa*. The syllables of *do–re–mi* are used to represent the pitches in all major and minor scales (keynote of major = *do*, keynote of minor = *la*). This allows children to grasp relationships between scale tones. No matter what the key, the distance between *sol–mi* is always a minor third, between *sol–do* a perfect fifth, and so forth. Closely aligned with this system is the use of hand signals to represent each tone, a type of pitch representation through movement. Kodály adapted the signals that John Curwen had devised in 1870, since he believed they would develop the child's inner hearing or tonal imagery—the ability to hear a melody in one's head by merely looking at the notation.

Kodály further believed the child should be introduced to a few tones at a time. These are gradually expanded to include all the tones of the pentatonic scale and eventually those of the major and minor scales as well as the modes. The diatonic major scale in its entirety, with its difficult half steps (*mi–fa* and *ti–do*) was not appropriate, he felt, as an initial experience for young children. He presented the intervals in the following order, accompanied always with hand signals:

sol-mi

268

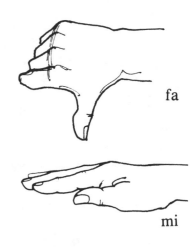

fa

sol-la-sol
  sol-la-sol-mi
   mi-re-do
    re-do
     la-sol-mi-re-do (pentatonic scale)
     sol-(la)-sol-do
     sol-do
     sol-re
     do-la
     sol-fa-mi (half-step)
     mi-fa-sol
     sol-mi-do
     do-mi-sol
     do-fa

mi

re

The syllable *ti* is not presented until much later. This represents a highly sequential developmental approach. Children learn to sight-sing each of these intervals before they move on to new ones. Their first singing experiences are naturally with songs of narrow range, expanding as wider intervals and more tones are added:

do

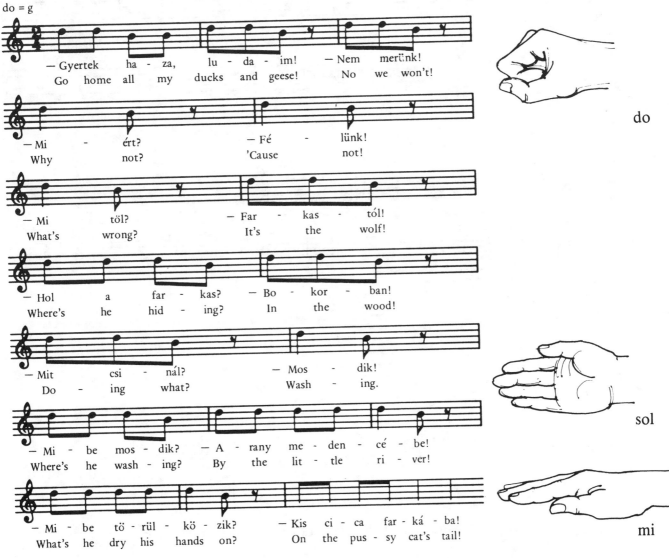

sol

mi

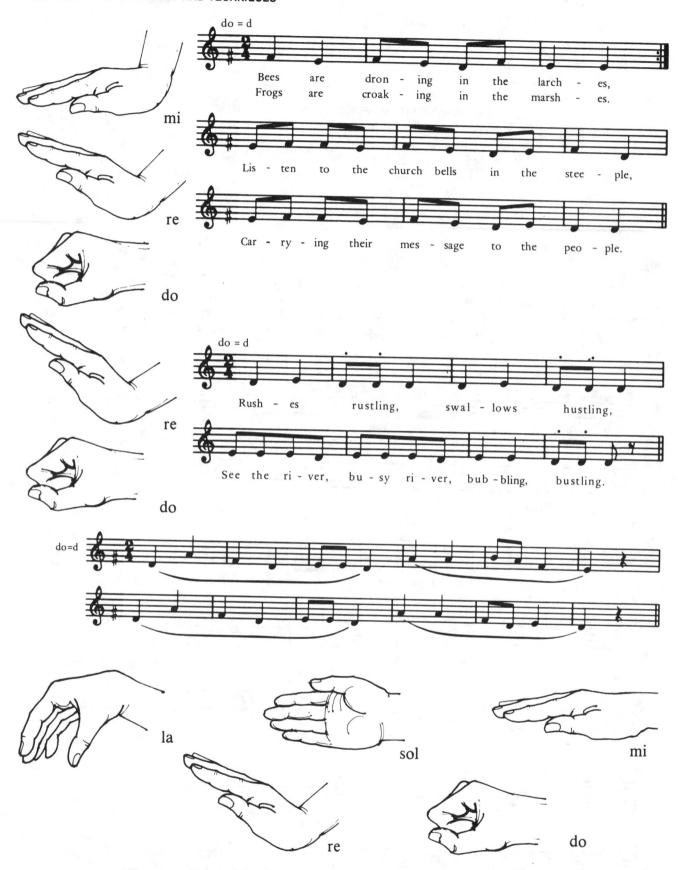

A partial staff is often used to notate these intervals in songs:

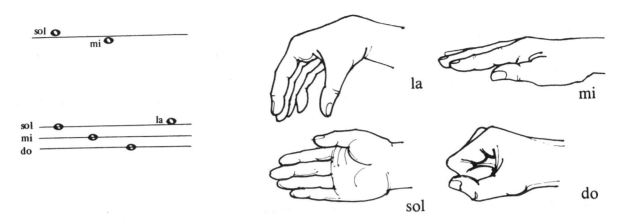

The position of *do* is continually changed to reflect the relative nature of the system:

Rhythm and pitch are soon reunited, becoming the means whereby the children can write their own compositions or complete the beginning of a phrase. They now have a notational scheme that allows them to write what they hear:

Mother Goose

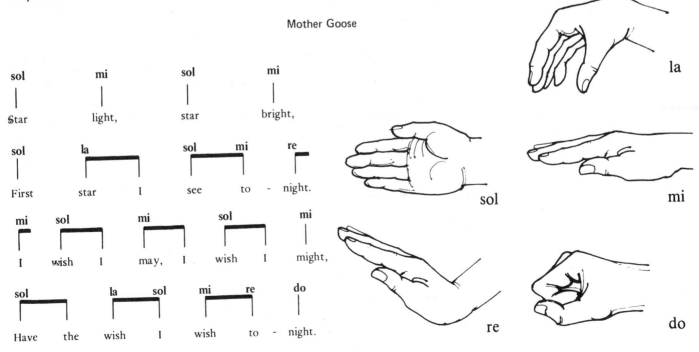

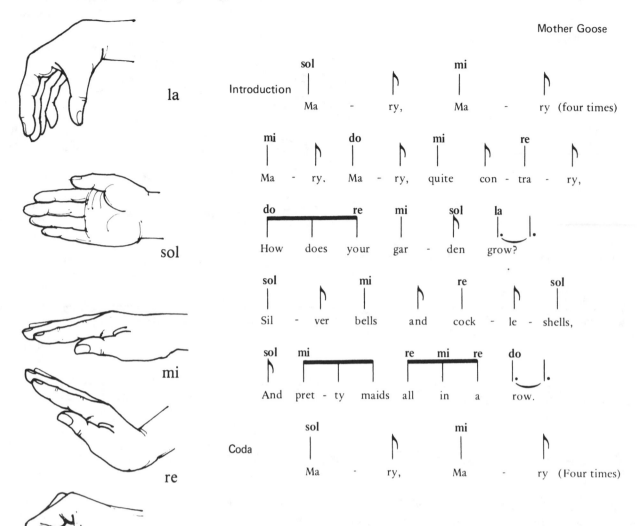

Mother Goose

Introduction

sol mi
Ma - ry, Ma - ry (four times)

mi do mi re
Ma - ry, Ma - ry, quite con - tra - ry,

do re mi sol la
How does your gar - den grow?

sol mi re sol
Sil - ver bells and cock - le - shells,

sol mi re mi re do
And pret - ty maids all in a row.

Coda

sol mi
Ma - ry, Ma - ry (Four times)

Unlike the Orff system, the Kodály system delays creativity until the child has some literacy in both pitch and rhythmic notation and therefore has a structure within which to create and notate phrases and songs. In a similar manner, the use of instruments is delayed until the child has a good command of the voice.

Like any system, Kodály's method is only as good as the teacher presenting it. Many teachers in America have been successful with this system since it presents a clear sequence of pitch and rhythm patterns leading to musical literacy. The simple intervals and rhythms used initially are sometimes not as exciting to young children as the music they hear on the radio and television. But the system does provide a variety of activities in the music classroom—singing, moving, listening, creating, and reading. It also provides an excellent conceptual framework for dealing with music.

The Kodály system has been adapted in the United States in many ways, retaining varying degrees of purity of the original system. Mary Helen Richards has popularized the works of Kodály in the United States through the use of her *Threshold to Music* and of American pentatonic songs (Hungarian folk music is much more clearly pentatonic than American music). Richards has been particularly successful in compiling sequential units on pitch and rhythm that allow the ideas of Kodály to be used without a total commitment to the entire approach. She nevertheless maintains a similar sequence of concepts. Some rhythm syllables are articulated differently and the hand signal for *fa* is changed:

fa

All of the following examples are from the *Threshold to Music* charts with suggestions for use. Most of these suggestions can be applied in varying degrees to each chart.

Developing Sound and Silence with a Steady Pulse
(| and ⁊)

Clap each drum pattern on a steady pulse such as | | | ⁊ .
Walk on | | | , pause on ⁊ .
Play a drum on the pattern | | | ⁊ .
Clap and recite "ta ta ta swish" or "drum drum drum swish" on the pattern.
Create a rhyme to recite with the patterns.

     | | | ⁊
"I can hear
     | | | ⁊
Rum tum tum

273

```
  |   |   |   ⸙
  I  can  hear
  |   |   |   ⸙
On  the  drum"
```

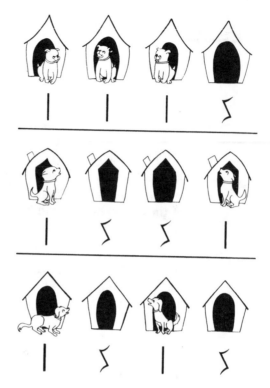

Clap each pattern.
Play the rhythm sticks on each pattern.
Recite "ta" or "swish" to the patterns.
Recite "dog" or "swish" on each pattern.

```
   |      |      |      ⸙
  dog   dog   dog   swish
```

Perform the chart as a round in three groups.
Play each pattern on a different rhythm instrument (sticks, guiro, sandblocks) and have three children or three groups do it simultaneously.
Think of a one-syllable name for a dog (Spot, Tuff, for example) and recite, using this name.

```
   |      |      |      ⸙
  Spot  Spot  Spot  swish
```

Developing Quarter- and Eighth-Note Divisions with a Steady Pulse

Clap and recite the patterns using "ta" and "ti-ti"s.
Walk on the first pattern, clap on the second, jump on the third, and so on.
Orchestrate each pattern with a different rhythm instrument while a fourth instrument keeps a steady pulse throughout (| | | |, etc.)
Perform the chart with a metronome.
Create words to fit each pattern.

wren   wren   ti-ny   wren

Ice cream soda,

Delaware punch,

Tell me the name of your

Honeybunch.

The chart may be performed as a call–response.
   Leader: Lines 1 and 3.
   Class: Lines 2 and 4.
This may be performed as round in four parts (each part begins after four beats).
New words may be created to fit the rhythms.
A different body part may be used to perform each line.
   Line one—snap fingers
   Line two—clap

Line three—patschen
Line four—stamp

Developing Concepts of Pitch

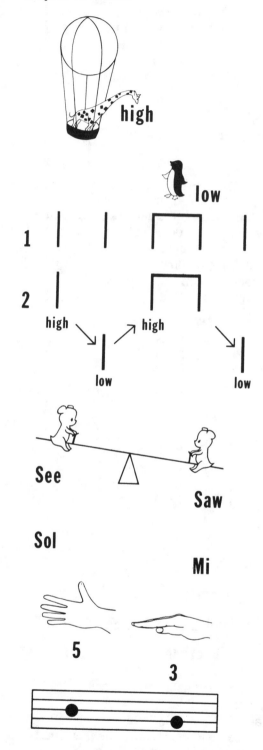

Sol and mi are introduced as high and low.
Children may crouch low on mi, stand up on sol.
Counting may be done to these two syllables using hand signals.

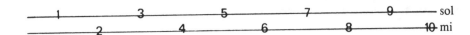

Resonator bells (or some other melody instruments) may be played to the two pitches.

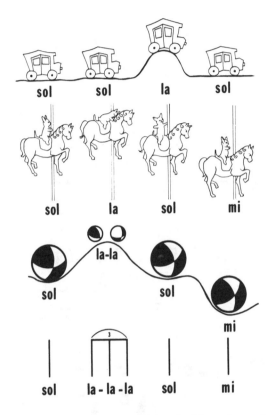

La is added to *sol* and *mi.* These are combined with various rhythm patterns. The three tones may be used in rhymes, counting, and so on.

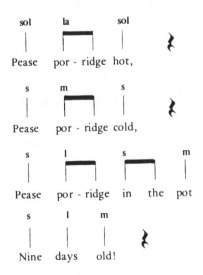

Patterns may be notated on the staff in various combinations.

Developing Additional Pitches

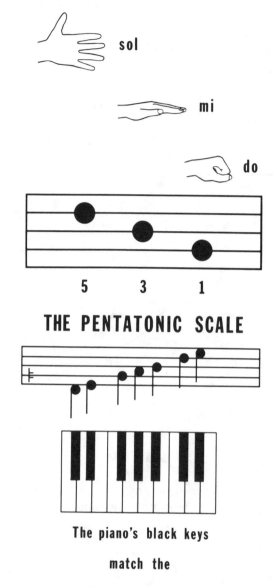

sol

mi

do

5   3   1

THE PENTATONIC SCALE

The piano's black keys

match the

Pentatonic Scale.

Additional tones (syllables and hand signals) are added until there is a complete pentatonic scale. *Do* is represented as

Developing Rhythm and Pitch Simultaneously

1

d m s   m   d

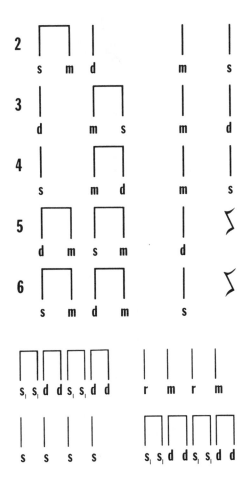

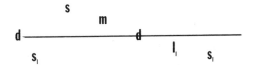

Scotland's burning!
Scotland's burning!
Look out, look out!
Fire, fire, fire, fire!
Pour on water! Pour on water!

Rhythm and pitch are continually combined through both syllable and staff notation. Rhythms may be tapped or played separately.*
Tonal patterns may be played on instruments as well as sung with hand signals.
Children should be encouraged to write their own patterns, both tonal and rhythmic,
as well as to set them to words and in staff notation. The teacher may dictate
both types of patterns.

*Below *do* = s_1 or l_1, etc.

Developing Uneven Patterns

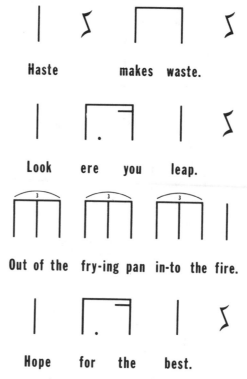

Haste   makes   waste.

Look   ere   you   leap.

Out of the   fry-ing pan   in-to   the   fire.

Hope   for   the   best.

Rhythms now include triplet divisions ▯ (triple-*ti*) and uneven patterns ▯. All rhymes like these should be sung to hand signals and notated on the staff.

Developing Form

CLAP A RONDO

CHORUS

SOLO (Make your own.)

CHORUS

SOLO (Make your own.)

CHORUS

Simple forms and contrapuntal devices (rondo and canon) may be performed rhythmically or with pitches and hand signals. Children should be encouraged to create their own canons and rondos.

All of the Richards charts may be used in a variety of ways; these suggestions are only a few. Almost every chart may be used as a singing, listening, playing, moving, reading, or creating experience if the teacher thinks creatively. The ideas suggested by the children should be incorporated as well. The basic Kodály format and sequence is maintained through these creative adaptations.

Like Orff, Kodály believed in using indigenous folk material, and American folk music must be incorporated in his system. (Mary Helen Richards has compiled suitable material.) Children learn music by making music. Good musicianship develops if instruction is sequenced logically and coherently.

Summary of Orff and Kodály Methods

Although neither system is new, both the Orff and the Kodály approaches continue to be important in the United States. The pragmatic teacher borrows and chooses, picks and adapts the best of each system for a particular situation. Both systems have sparked much interest in activity-based, multidimensional approaches to music education. Both have provided models for a logical, cohesive scope and sequence in elementary music too often missing in the past. Both, at some point in the sequence, allow creativity to emerge. Undoubtedly both systems, as adapted in the United States, will continue to be sources of methods and materials for today's music educators and classroom teachers.

The Manhattanville Music Curriculum Program

The MMCP, named after the Manhattanville College of the Sacred Heart in Purchase, New York, began in 1965. The project, funded by a grant from the U.S. Office of Education, attempted to find and provide alternatives in American music education to programs that stressed traditional values, products, and compositions. Under the leadership of Ronald B. Thomas, the program first assessed several exemplary music curriculums in the United States to find out why they were successful. It was determined that each had clear-cut objectives and a sequence of skills and concepts. In addition, teachers in these programs were facilitators of learning rather than traditional explainers or dispensers of fact. Children thus learned through discovery and exploration. Music was experiential, meeting the children's needs directly.

As the MMCP developed, these facets were incorporated into its work.

Practices were directly related to the needs and interests of the children. A spiral curriculum was developed in which each of several concepts was presented several times, becoming more specific and refined each time around. This was eventually expanded to include a precycle program for early childhood as well. The tangible results of MMCP have been published in *MMCP Synthesis*, a curriculum guide for grades three through twelve, and *MMCP Interaction*, a guide for early childhood. There were also feasibility studies including a keyboard laboratory, a science-music laboratory, an instrumental program, and pre- and in-service training programs for music teachers.

Unlike the Orff and Kodály systems, the MMCP is nontraditional. It results in nontraditional sounds. Timbres, rhythms, pitches, and intensities are explored in a manner resulting in sounds not unlike those of avant-garde music of our own time. Children learn by composing and by evaluating their own writing and performance. Like the Orff and Kodály systems, the MMCP is an attempt to arrange learning in a logical, sequential, and experiential manner.

The principles of the MMCP may be outlined as follows:

It is Composition-Oriented. Children learn about music by making their own sounds. They may use environmental sounds, or create new sounds with traditional instruments or with their own bodies. Ultimately, a composition is created by a group of students. This composition is performed for a larger group, thus incorporating performance and conducting for some, listening and evaluating for others. Children may even develop their own system of notation to record their composition.

Example:

TEACHER: Using one instrument, explore all the ways sound may be produced on it.

Group one (tambourine): The sound may be produced by shaking it hard or lightly, tappping it hard or lightly, hitting it with various types of mallets, or taping it on one's wrist, elbow, knee, and so on.

Group two (recorder): The sound may be produced by blowing through it traditionally, blowing only through the mouthpice, covering the holes in new ways such as with paper, blowing through the finger holes, and so on.

Each Composition is Evaluated for Refinement. Children may decide there are too many or too few ideas in the work, no clear design, and so on. These suggestions are incorporated by each group and their composition is refined.

Example:

TEACHER: What could we do to improve this composition? How could we integrate the sound of the bell more effectively with the triangle? Which idea is used too long? How could it be varied? Which idea seems to be too fleeting? How could it be developed? How might the burst of cymbals be better prepared? Is there a clear way to notate the recurring sound of the bongo?

The Role of the Teacher is to Facilitate. The teacher is a resource person and guide who helps direct the children's inquiries by asking the right question, never by providing the ultimate answers. He or she is a master of discovery learning, not of explanation; encouraging effort without being judgmental; and honest in critique without being threatening.

The organization of the MMCP is through the musical concepts of timbre, dynamics, pitch, form, and rhythm. For each element and level there are appropriate auditory, manual, and notational skills as well as vocabulary:

CYCLE 1*

Timbre

The quality or color of sound, the timbre, is a major factor in the expressiveness of music. The timbre may be shrill, intense, dulcet, silvery, nasal, smooth, bright, or dull. Choosing the timbre which best expresses what the composer has in mind is one of many decisions which he must make when creating music.

Dynamics

The degree of loudness or softness, the volume or the dynamics of the sound, also must be determined by the composer. Music may be loud, *forte* (f), soft, *piano* (p), or medium-loud, *mezzoforte* (mf). The volume of the music or any one part of the music will affect the total expressive result.

Pitch

The comparative highness or lowness of sounds is also determined by the composer. Initially, his choices will deal with sounds of indefinite pitch such as those produced by a triangle, a cymbal, a drum, etc. In such cases, highness or lowness often depends on preceding and/or following sounds. (A cymbal sounds low after a triangle but high after a large drum.)

Form

The plan, the shape, the order, the form of a piece of music is another determination made by the composer. Form refers to the aural design, the way the sounds are put together. The composer's plan or form is based on his expressive intent.

Rhythm

Tempo is that characteristic of music which makes it appear to go fast or slow. The pulse is the underlying beat (sometimes not heard but only sensed) that may help to create a feeling of motion in music. These items are the choice of the composer.

CYCLE 1 SKILLS

Aural

Identify the general and comparative pitch characteristics of sounds of indefinite pitch (differences between drum sounds, cluster sounds, sounds made by objects, etc.).
Identify various timbres used in the classroom and the instruments used to produce them.
Identify volume differences in student compositions and in illustrative recordings.
Identify pulse and changes in tempo.
Recognize simple sequences.

Dexterous

In performing:
Produce sounds (vocal or instrumental) at the instant they are demanded and control the ending of the sound.
Produce the desired tone quality (vocal and instrumental).
Produce sounds of three volume levels (f, p, mf) when allowed by the nature of the instrument.
Maintain the tempo when necessary.

In conducting:
Indicate precisely when to begin and when to end.
Indicate pulse, where appropriate (not meter).
Indicate desired volume.
Indicate general character of music (solemn, spirited, etc.)

Translative

Devise graphic symbols, charts, or designs of musical ideas which allow for retention and reproduction. Such visual translations should represent the overall plan, include distinguishing signs for different instruments or timbres, and relative durational factors. Volume should be indicated by the standard symbols: f, p, mf. Words designating the character of the music, such as quietly, forcefully, smoothly, or happily, should also be used.

*Reprinted from *Contemporary Music Education* by Michael L. Mark (pp. 116–22) by permission of Schirmer/Macmillan.

Vocabulary

Timbre	Form	Indefinite pitch	Volume
Dynamics	Tempo	Aural	Improvise
Forte	Pulse	Devised notation	Composer
Piano	Pitch	Cluster	Conductor
Mezzo-forte			Performer

CYCLE 1 SAMPLE STRATEGY

The Quality or Color of Sound, the Timbre, is a Major Factor in the Expressiveness of Music

Each student selects an item or object in the room with which he can produce a sound. Preferably, the item or object will be something other than a musical instrument.

After sufficient time has been allowed for students to experiment with sounds or selected objects, each student may perform his sound at the location of the item in the room.

Focus on "listening" to the distinctive qualities of sounds performed. Encourage students to explore other sound possibilities with the item of their choice.

Discuss any points of interest raised by the students. Extend the discussion by including the following questions:

How many different kinds of sounds were discovered?

Could the sounds be put into categories of description, i.e. shrill, dull, bright, intense, etc.?

After categories of sound have been established, experiment with combinations of sounds.

Is there any difference between sounds performed singly and sounds performed in combination?

In listening to the recorded examples focus on the use of timbre.

How many different kinds of sounds were used?

Could we put any of the sounds in this composition into the categories we established earlier, i.e. bright, dull, shrill, etc.?

Were there any new categories of sounds? Could we duplicate these?

Assignment

Each student should bring one small object from home on which he can produce three distinctly different sounds. The object may be a brush, a bottle, a trinket or anything made of wood, metal, plastic, etc.

Suggested Listening Examples:

"Steel Drums," Wond Steel Band; Folk 8367

"Prelude and Fugue for Percussion," Wuorinen, Charles; GC 4004

"Ballet Mechanique," Antheil, George; Urania (5) 134

The Plan, the Shape, the Order of a Piece of Music is Determined by the Composer

Each student may perform his three sounds at his own desk. Focus on "listening" to distinctive qualities of sounds performed.

Encourage students to focus attention on other exploratory possibilities by investigating the sound producing materials with greater depth.

Can you produce a sound on your object that is bright, dull, shrill, intense, etc.? How is this done?

Discuss any points of interest relative to the activity.

Extend the discussion by focusing on the following questions:

Why is silence in the room necessary for performance to be effective?

How did sounds vary or seem similar?

Which objects produced the brightest, dullest, most shrill, most intense sounds?

What makes a sound dull, bright, intense, etc.?

Divide the class into groups of 5 or 6 students. A conductor-composer should be selected by each group. He will determine the order of sounds and the overall plan of the improvisation. Conducting signals should be devised and practiced in each group so that directions will be clear.

Allow approximately 10 minutes for planning and rehearsal. At the end of the designated time each group will perform.

Tape all improvisations for playback and evaluation. Discussion should focus around the following questions:

Did the improvisation have a good plan? Did the music hold together?

What was the most satisfying factor in this piece?

How would you change the improvisation?

What are some of the conductor's concerns?

In listening to the recorded examples focus attention to the overall shape or plan of the music.

In listening to a single example two or three times students may map out a shape or a plan which represents the composition. These plans can be compared and used for repeated listenings.

Suggested Listening Examples:

"Construction in Metal," Cage, John; KO8P-1498

"Poeme Electronique," Varèse, Edgar; Col. ML5478; MS6146

The Degree of Loudness or Softness, the Volume or the Dynamics of the Sound, Will Affect the Total Expressive Result

Using the entire class as performers on object instruments, volunteer students will conduct an exploratory improvisation to investigate the effects of: sounds used singly, sounds used in combination, and dynamics. It is suggested that before the improvisation the volunteer conductors choose 3 or 4 students who will play singly when directed. Conducting cues for entrances and exits should also be established.

Tape the exploratory improvisations for immediate playback and evaluation. Discuss all perceptions verbalized by the students. Extend the discussion by including the following questions: How did volume or dynamics affect the total result?

Can all the object instruments be heard at an equal level of volume when performed in a group?

Groups consisting of 4 or 5 students will plan an improvisation. Focus attention to the quality of sounds used singly, the quality of sounds used in combination, and the expressive use of volume. Consideration for the overall shape of the piece should also be a concern.

Following a short planning and practicing period (about 10 minutes), each group will perform the improvisation for the class.

Tape the improvisations for immediate playback and evaluation. Discuss students' comments as they relate to the improvisations. Extend the discussion by focusing attention on the following questions:

What degree of loudness or softness was used most frequently by the performing groups?

Did the improvisations have an overall shape or design?

Summarize the discussion by introducing forte (f), piano (p), and mezzo-forte (mf). In listening to the recorded examples ask students to identify the dynamic level used most frequently by the composer.

Did you get any musical ideas from this composition that you might be able to use?

Suggested Listening Examples:

"Parade," Gould, Morton; Columbia CL 1533

"Te Deum, Judex Crederis," Berlioz, Hector; Columbia ML 4897

"Prelude a l'Apres-midi d'un faune," Debussy, Claude; London LS 503

The Pulse is the Underlying Beat That May Help to Create a Feeling of Motion in Music

Allow 30 seconds for each class member to think of an unusual vocal sound. The sound can be made with the throat, voice, lips, breath or tongue.

Each student may perform his/her sound for the class. Focus "listening" on the distinctive qualities of the vocal sounds performed.

Discuss any points of interest raised by the students. Extend the discussion by including some of the following questions:

Did anyone perform his/her sound long enough to communicate a feeling of motion?

How would you describe the motion?

Divide the class into groups consisting of 4 or 5 students. One person in each of the groups should be a conductor. Each group will concentrate on producing their individual sounds to the motion of an item of their choice or one which has been suggested to them, i.e. the steady motion of a carpenter hammering a nail, the steady motion of a worm crawling, the steady motion of a person jogging, the steady motion of a horse galloping, etc.

Allow approximately 10 minutes for groups to plan and practice their improvisations. At the end of the designated time each group will perform.

Tape each improvisation for immediate playback and analysis. Discuss any comments made by the students. Extend the discussion by including the following questions:

How would you describe the motion, slow, medium, fast?

Did it have a steady beat or pulse?

Summarize the discussion by introducing tempo as the characteristic which refers to the speed of music and pulse which is the underlying beat (sometimes not heard but only sensed).

In listening to the recorded examples focus attention on the use of tempo.

How would you describe the tempo, slow, medium, or fast?

Did the pulse or underlying beat change before the end of the composition? What was the effect?

Suggested Listening Examples:

"Flight of the Bumblebee," Rimski-Korsakov, Nicolai; Epic LC 3759

"String Quartet No. 79, Op. 76, No. 5, Haydn, Joseph; Turnabout TV 34012S

MMCP, like the Orff and Kodály systems, can be used totally or as one type of experience in a broadly based curriculum. Many teachers have utilized some of the ideas of MMCP in their attempts to allow children to create in the classroom. Just as painting, sketching, and writing poems and essays provide experience in the other arts, composition is a vital way to learn music. This emphasis is perhaps MMCP's most important contribution to music education.

Exercises and Activities

1. Interview a Kodály, Orff, or MMCP specialist on the advantages and disadvantages of the system.
2. Plan a lesson based on the sequence, method, or materials of either Orff, Kodály, or MMCP. Show how your lesson fits into the program objectives of the system.
3. Investigate other recent curriculum innovations that have influenced contemporary music education.

Key Terms and Concepts

Zoltán Kodály
Carl Orff
relative *sol–fa*
minor third
John Curwen
patschen
Orff instruments
    xylophone
    metallophone
    glockenspiel
improvisation
tonal imagery
anacrusis
MMCP
spiral curriculum

Professional Readings

Choksy, Lois. *The Kodály Context.* Englewood Cliffs, N.J.: Prentice-Hall, 1981.

Choksy, Lois. *The Kodály Method: Comprehensive Music Education from Infant to Adult.* Englewood Cliffs, N.J.: Prentice-Hall, 1974.

Glasgow, Robert B., and Dale Hamreus. "Study to Determine the Feasibility of Adapting the Carl Orff Approach to Elementary Schools in America." Monmouth: Oregon College of Education, May 27, 1968.

Kidd, Eleanor. *Threshold to Music,* 2nd ed. Belmont, Calif.: Fearon Publishers, 1974.

Kodály, Zoltán. *Fifteen Two-Part Exercises.* New York: Boosey & Hawkes, 1952.

Landis, Beth, and Polly Carder. *The Eclectic Curriculum in American Music Education: Contributions of Dalcroze, Kodály and Orff.* Washington, D.C.: Music Educators National Conference, 1972.

Mark, Michael L. *Contemporary Music Education.* New York: Schirmer Books, 1978.

Murphy, Judith, and Lonna Jones. *Research in Arts Education: A Federal Chapter.* Washington, D.C.: U.S. Department of Health, Education and Welfare, Publication No. (OE) 76-02000, 1976.

Nash, Grace C. *Music with Children* (Series I—Beginners to Advanced; Series II—Kindergarten through Fourth; Series III—Intermediate). La Grange, Ill.: Kitching Educational Division of Ludwig Industries, 1971.

Orff, Carl, and Gunild Keetman. *Music for Children.* English adaptation by Doreen Hall and Arnold Walter. New York: Associated Music Publishers, European-American Music, 1977.

Ribière, Raverlet J. *Musical Education in Hungary.* Paris: Alphonse Leduc, 1967. Translated by Margaret Safranek.

Richards, Mary Helen. *Threshold to Music* (separate charts for first, second, third, fourth, and higher grades). Palo Alto, Calif.: Fearon Publishers, 1964–1967.

———. *Threshold to Music.* San Francisco: Fearon Publishers, 1964.

———. *Threshold to Music, The Fourth Year.* New York: Harper & Row, 1967.

Szabo, Helga. *The Kodály Concept of Music Education.* English edition by Geoffry Russell-Smith. London: Boosey & Hawkes, 1969. (textbook with 3 LP records)

Thomas, Ronald B. *MMCP: Final Report.* "MMCP Interaction." Washington, D.C.: U.S. Office of Education, 1970.

———. *MMCP: Final Report, Part 1,* abstract. Washington, D.C.: U.S. Office of Education, ED 045 865, 1970.

Wheeler, Lawrence, and Lois Raebeck. *Orff and Kodály Adapted for the Elementary School,* 2nd ed. Dubuque, Iowa: William C. Brown, 1977.

Zemke, Sister Lorna. *The Kodály Concept.* Champaign, Ill.: Mark Foster Music Company, 1977.

Zoltán Kodály Choral Method. New York: Boosey & Hawkes, 1972.

Classroom Management 18

In a perfect classroom there would be no discipline problems. Children would always be attentive and respectful. They would enter each activity with enthusiasm and try their best at all tasks. They would get along with their classmates. There would never be pushing and shoving. Sarcastic remarks would not occur. Every lesson would proceed according to plan and there would be measurable learning for all.

In a real classroom, however, discipline is a major concern. Beginning teachers frequently say, "Why weren't we taught about the subject of discipline in college?" Discipline is not a subject, but the lack of discipline is a symptom—a symptom that something is wrong with a child, a classroom, a teacher, a lesson. Discipline means different things to different teachers. Some maintain a permissive classroom in which children interact freely with one another and with the teacher in a casual manner—and noise may result. To other teachers, such conditions would be intolerable. To them, discipline means desks in order, hands raised before speaking, and blackboards clean. Learning can occur in both situations, although there is no guarantee it will in either.

Each teacher and class evolves a distinct style. This style to a certain extent depends on the personality of the teacher as well as the nature of the subject matter. Since it is a group effort, music requires a unique approach. Singing and playing instruments at the same time requires teamwork. One child cannot choose a tempo or key different from that of the group if he or she wishes to sing or play with them. Individual will can be affirmed more in creating music or moving to it. For this reason, what constitutes good discipline in a music classroom depends on the activity.

As a general guide, those lessons which have variety and pacing appro-

1-23

"When you've finished practicing on the stool would you like to get started on the piano?"

289

priate to the task and are presented in an interesting, enthusiastic manner should result in few discipline problems. Children do not enjoy being bored. Good planning helps prevent discipline problems.

Nonetheless, even with excellent preparation on the part of the teacher, one or several children can be disruptive. No formula can guarantee that every child will be attentive and respectful 100 percent of the time. Disruptions at home or physical conditions sometimes make a child misbehave. They must be handled differently. Some principles which may help the teacher establish and maintain good discipline in a classroom include:*

1. Children want to know what you expect of them. Elementary-school children can probably adapt to any teaching style. They want to know what is acceptable and what is not. If a teacher wishes children to raise their hands before answering a question, this behavior must be established on first contact. On the other hand, if a child is free to speak out without raising a hand, the rest of the class must know they should listen and not interrupt the one who is speaking. Either style can be effective, but the teacher must establish the procedure on first contact with the class.

In the same way, there must be consistency in all classroom procedures. Children should be advised about posture. Should they sit straight or is sprawling acceptable? How are the music books and instruments distributed and collected? Are directions given once or does the teacher repeat them? There is little need for a lengthy explanation of rules and regulations. Rather, procedures and expectations can be clarified when the occasion arises. Children are more likely to remember a procedure when there is an example to reinforce it. Attention to what a teacher expects of a child and reinforcement of appropriate behavior prevents many disciplinary problems from ever arising.

2. Separate the child from the behavior. A child is not bad because he or she does something unacceptable. It is the behavior which is bad or inappropriate. The child should not be belittled. This attacks the child and lowers self-concept. Children may be disciplinary problems because they already have a low self-concept. Remarks need to be directed to the behavior. This attacks the behavior, not the child, and helps children work through their behavior. They will realize hitting another child on the head with a tambourine, for example, may hurt both the child and the instrument. For those reasons, the behavior is inappropriate.

3. Reward good behavior. When appropriate behavior occurs, there should be a reward. A positive feeling can be elicited by pointing out models of good behavior. Most rewards are verbal. Praise is something children need. The teacher should be careful to use a verbal scale of reward that is believable. If average behavior is rewarded with "That's super!" there are few superlatives left for above-average behavior. Too; if everything is "good," why should children exert effort? Rewards should involve activities that contribute to musical development. Allowing children free time to listen to "their kind of music" because they sang well merely sets up polarity between "their" music and "yours." "Yours" must be endured while "theirs" becomes special. In the same sense, allowing children to sing their favorite songs as a reward can make the usual classroom singing a punishment.

*Shirley J. O'Brien, "What About Discipline? A Learning Package for Parents" (Tuscon: Cooperative Extension Service, University of Arizona, 1976).

4. Fit the punishment to the problem. Disciplinary action can be achieved quickly without embarrassing anyone and without disrupting the class. A pause or look can bring a child back to the group. A snap of the fingers can work. It is inadvisable to use a question of content directed to the child as a means of discipline. This only embarrasses the child and rarely gets the question answered. Threats are also bad: "If you do that again, I'll. . . ." They are soon forgotten or inconsistently enforced. In extreme cases, the teacher can say "See me after class" or the child may need to be isolated—gently led by the teacher to the hall or sent to another classroom. Taking away an instrument that is being abused or changing the child's place can also help. The best disciplinary action occurs quickly and firmly.

5. Feel good about your authority as a teacher. It is senseless to worry that children will be thwarted or become frustrated if you discipline them. One child should not be allowed to disrupt the important learning of others. As the leader of the group, the teacher must not feel guilty about keeping the class in order. This is imperative, for the teacher is responsible for organizing and facilitating classroom instruction. The teacher should not worry if his or her disciplinary techniques are different from those of teachers in adjacent classrooms. Each person has his or her own style and techniques. Children can meet the expectations of many people as long as doing so does not create conflicts.

6. Provide a good model to the children. Teachers who expect children to listen to them must listen when they speak. Respect has two sides. If punctuality is important, teachers must exemplify it. If they want an enthusiastic class, they must be enthusiastic. If they wish good organization, their lessons must exemplify organization. Good behavior is learned by modeling. Children are highly influenced by the posture, attitudes, and skills of the teacher.

7. Respect children as individuals. So much instruction is accomplished in groups that children are often not thought of as individuals but as "Ms. Smith's fourth grade." This is a liability the traveling music specialist particularly faces. It is important to know children's names since disruptive behavior is easier when children think they are anonymous. A "name" makes a student an identifiable personage. Music specialists can use pictures to learn the children's names or have name tags for music each time.

Children want to be known as individuals. It helps to listen to children as well as to seek them out in nonclassroom settings—on the playground, with the physical education specialist, or even in their own homes. This allows the teacher to learn more about the child's interests and needs. This concern also reduces the incidence of behavioral problems.

The key to discipline is maintaining an orderly, consistent classroom that motivates children to want to learn music. Exciting music lessons reduce the likelihood that children will be disruptive. In addition, it is well to establish expectations with children and to reward them when these expectations are fulfilled. Children need to feel like individuals. The teacher needs to know each of them outside the group lesson. Although the disruptive behavior must be corrected, the child should not be belittled in the process. Finally, the educator must be a high example of the behavior he or she wants the children to manifest.

Exercises and Activities

1. What ten types of behavior would you not tolerate in the music classroom? How could you prevent each?

2. Observe a music classroom and notice what positive and negative things are used as disciplinary measures. What can you conclude?

Professional Readings

Canter, Lee and Marlene Canter. *Assertive Discipline.* Los Angeles: Canter and Associates, Inc., 1976.

O'Brien, Shirley J. "What About Discipline? A Learning Package for Parents." Tucson: Cooperative Extension Service, University of Arizona, 1976.

Glossary

a cappella Literally, in the style of the chapel. Refers to unaccompanied choral music, often in the Renaissance tradition.

a tempo Return to the original tempo.

accelerando An increase in tempo.

acceleration A modification of the educational program for a gifted child by moving him or her into a higher grade level.

accented beat A pulse that is slightly stressed to create a pattern of strong and weak beats. Common accent groupings are duple (Sw), triple (Sww), and quadruple (Swww).

accidental A ♭, ♯, or ♮ not in the key signature.

action songs Songs with built-in physical movements suggested in the lyrics, such as clapping, stamping, and the like.

adagio A slow, leisurely tempo that is slower than *Andante* but not as slow as *Largo*.

additive form Musical design in which nothing repeats. New ideas are added on, ABCD . . ., and so on.

aerophone An instrument whose sound is made by a vibrating air column such as clarinet, trumpet.

aesthetic listening Listening for the pure enjoyment of recognizing patterns, structures, designs, and forms in music without extramusical references.

aesthetic response Response to the sheer sound and structure of music without reliance on descriptions and narratives.

affective Concerning the feelings.

AGE (Arts in General Education). A curricular movement in which many disciplines in both science and art are related around a common concept or principle.

alla breve Cut time (2/2).

allegro A lively and fast tempo.

anacrusis A pickup beat or beats that occur before the first bar line.

andante A walking tempo; moderately slow.

andantino Slightly quicker than Andante.

animato Animated.

antecedent The first phrase in a sentence that asks a musical question.

antiphonal Descriptive of two musical groups stationed apart which perform in a call–response manner.

arco Playing a member of the string family (violin, viola, cello, or bass) with the bow.

associative listening Listening for such extramusical references in music as mood, pictures, or stories.

asymmetrical accent groupings Accent groupings of fives, sevens, and so on. Such groupings may have secondary accents (5 = 2 + 3 or 3 + 2; 7 = 2 + 3 + 2, 3 + 2 + 2, etc.).

atonality The absence of tonality, as in twelve-tone writing.

axial movement Movement in place, such as bending, swaying, or twisting.

background The sounds in music that do not generally carry the main melody but rather secondary melodies, harmonies, and the rhythmic accompaniment.

bar line The dividing line between measures.

beat A single pulse (basic duration) that is the foundation or the rhythmic structure of music.

binary form Two-part form represented as either AB or AA₁. In performance, both sections (or the first) may be repeated, AABB or AAB.

bitonality In two keys or tonalities simultaneously.

blind Description of a person with 20/200 or less vision or with a field of vision of 20 degrees or less.

blues A native American vocal form of three phrases, utilizing I, IV, and V7 harmonies with lowered third, fifth, and seventh (blue notes) tones in the major scales. Blues are usually in twelve bars, each phrase consisting of four bars.

broad program objective An objective stated for a given subject (language arts, music, math) in terms of what the child may achieve in the subject at the end of elementary school or a period longer than one grade level.

Bruner, Jerome S. An American psychologist who formulated three stages of conceptual development: enactive, iconic, and symbolic.

cadence A musical punctuation signaling the end of a phrase; a breathing point.

call–response A song or activity in which a leader or group sings one phrase or section that is answered by another group.

canon A harmonic texture created when a melody is begun by one part and then imitated by other parts with a slight time delay.

characteristic pattern (motive) The smallest unit of musical meaning, whether melodic or rhythmic, that can be identified in music. It often consists of three or four notes.

chord The basic unit of harmony, which consists of the simultaneous sounding of at least three different pitches.

chordal accompaniments Simple harmonies, usually I, IV, and V7, used to accompany a melody on the guitar, ukulele, autoharp, piano, or the like.

chordophone An instrument whose sound is made by vibrating strings, such as violin, guitar.

chromatic scale A scale built entirely of half steps.

circle of fifths An arrangement of major/relative minor keys in order of number of sharps or flats. Each successive key is a fifth higher or lower than the former.

classroom teacher The educational facilitator in an elementary classroom who is responsible for planning and directing learning experiences.

clef A sign that provides a pitch reference point on the staff. 𝄞 indicates the G above middle C, 𝄢 the F below middle C.

clusters Chords built entirely of the interval of a second (half and whole steps).

coda Added ending in a musical composition, movement, or section.

cognitive Dealing with the mind.

col legno Playing or striking the strings of a member of the violin family with the wood of the bow.

coloratura soprano A soprano voice that specializes in singing high, ornamented melodies.

common-elements approach Relating the arts through an element held in common, such as rhythm–time, color–timbre, and the like.

common time 4/4.

compound interval An interval larger than an octave (tenth, thirteenth, etc.). Compound intervals beyond the double octave (fifteenth) are not usually considered.

compound meter A meter in which the division above the beat is in threes instead of the customary twos of simple meter.

conceptual development Developing mental constructs, frameworks, or categories as the result of exposure to and experience with a given subject.

concerto A composition in three or four movements, normally for a solo instrument and orchestra.

concrete operations According to Piaget, the third stage of cognitive development, in which the child can mentally reason and solve problems as well as to conserve, center, reverse, and transform.

conjunct Melodic movement by small intervals, particularly those of a second (half or whole step); stepwise motion.

consequent The second or answering phrase in a musical sentence.

consonance A state of repose or absence of tension in music.

contour The generalized direction of a melody or series of pitches.

contrast A principle in musical design that provides variety.

conversational singer A child who cannot move his or her voice from one or two pitches, thus being unable to place his voice on the notes of a melody. He or she "speaks" the rhythm of the melody on the one or two notes in lieu of singing.

couplet Two lines of poetry which rhyme.

crescendo A gradual increase in loudness.

critical listening Listening for the technical aspects of a musical performance, such as pitch and rhythmic accuracy, intonation, and interpretation.

Curwen, John An English music educator of the nineteenth century who formulated the hand signals adapted by Zoltán Kodály.

D.C. al Fine *Da Capo al Fine.* Return to the beginning of the composition and continue until *Fine* (the finish).

da capo aria An aria in ABA form in which the final A is not written out but indicated by the repeat marks *D.C. al Fine.*

decrescendo A gradual decrease in loudness, sometimes termed *diminuendo.*

descant A second melody or part that occurs above the main melody; a countermelody.

diastematic notation Pitch notation in which high sounds are arranged in a higher position on the page and vice versa. The staff is often used to give more specific pitch placement.

295

diatonic scale An eight-tone scale that uses some combination of five whole steps and two half steps and also uses each pitch name in sequence within an octave.

discovery learning Learning through inquiry and questioning, as opposed to being told.

directional singer A child who follows the general contour of a melody but who does not sing or stay on the proper pitch or move at the correct interval from note to note.

direct symbol A musical symbol that looks like the sound it represents.

disjunct Pertaining to melodic movement by intervals larger than a second; skipwise motion.

dissonance A state of tension or "seeking" in music.

dolce Sweetly.

dominant ostinato An ostinato created around the tone the I and V7 chords have in common, *sol*, the dominant tone. (In C Major the dominant tone common to both chords is G.)

dominant seventh A chord built on the fifth tone (*sol*) of a major scale (or *mi* in the minor scale). In major it consists of *sol–ti–re–fa*. (Minor = *mi–si–ti–re*.)

dorian mode A diatonic (eight-tone) scale using this formula of whole and half steps: 1 ½ 111 ½ 1.

dot A mark used beside a note to extend its duration by half.

double bar Two bar lines, used at the end of a section of music.

dramatization A quasi-play acted out to a song, recording, or series of sounds.

drone The continuous sounding of a single pitch (or more) as an accompaniment in music.

D.S. al Fine *Dal Segno al fine*. Repeat from the sign and continue until *Fine* (the finish).

duple time A grouping of the underlying pulse in music into a strong–weak pattern.

duration The temporal element of music, which includes tempo, beat, accent, and relationship of all parts to the underlying rhythm.

dynamic markings The use of *forte* (*f*) and *piano* (*p*) in written music to indicate gradations of loudness and softness.

early elementary years Kindergarten through second grade, representing children four to seven years old.

echo songs Songs performed in call–response fashion, which generate a simple type of harmony because of the overlapping of parts.

editing In tape composition, selecting sounds, arranging them on the tape in the desired sequence, splicing the tape accordingly, and playing them back at the desired tape speed.

educable mentally retarded (EMR) Descriptive of a child whose IQ score ranges from 50 to 75 but who can obtain functional literacy and social adjustment through schooling.

electrophone An instrument whose sound source is electronically produced, such as electric organ.

electronic music Music produced by electronic means, whether by a sound synthesizer or through electronic manipulation of environmental sounds (musique concrète).

emotionally disturbed Pertaining to a child who is continually depressed, exhibits inappropriate behavior in routine situations, cannot learn (despite the absence of problems of intelligence, senses, or health), cannot relate with others, and may exhibit anxiety and physical symptoms because of problems.

enactive phase According to Bruner, the first step of conceptual development, in which a person experiences a phenomenon. It is thus an input or experiential phase of learning.

enharmonic Tones or intervals that

sound alike but are named and notated differently (F♯ and g♭)

enrichment Modification of the educational program for the gifted through offering alternatives such as more challenging activities and assignments than those given the normal child.

environmental sounds Ambient sounds.

equipment Necessary "hardware" to be used in a lesson, such as musical instruments, tape recorders, and the like.

eurhythmics A system of physical movement used to express the rhythmic components and elements of music, devised by Emil Jaques-Dalcroze early in the twentieth century.

even pattern A rhythmic pattern that either moves exactly with the underlying pulse or evenly divides two or four notes over the pulse.

exceptional child A child who requires alteration of the standard curriculum to meet his or her educational needs.

explanation Teaching by "telling" as opposed to an approach that allows students to discover relationships through inquiry.

extraneous motivation Motivation that has to do with neither the (intrinsic) process nor the (extrinsic) product of education; an arbitrary reward or payoff for learning.

extrinsic motivation Motivation that is outside the pure love of or enjoyment of learning; in which the emphasis is more on the product of learning than on the process.

factual question A question that can be answered by only one correct response—the correct fact.

F clef or staff The clef, 𝄢 , the two dots of which surround the F below middle C.

fermata (𝄐) A hold or pause.

flat (♭) Sign that lowers pitch of a note by one half step.

finger plays Songs whose words suggest small hand and finger movements.

folk dances National dances of a patterned nature performed by couples or groups.

follow-up lessons Lessons that logically follow given lessons because they use similar materials or develop similar concepts.

foreground The sounds in music that generally carry the melody, as opposed to the background accompaniments.

form The arrangement or design of musical material. Principles of form include repetition and contrast.

formal operations According to Piaget, the final stage of cognitive development, characterized by the ability to reason abstractly; adult thinking.

fugue A polyphonic composition for a set number of parts or voices (two to four are common) in which a subject (theme) is imitated by each part, entering in one and then in another. Each voice presents the subject several times.

full cadence A relatively permanent resting place at the end of a phrase, terminated most often by the progression of V7 to I.

G clef or staff The clef, 𝄞 , the curve of which circles the pitch G above middle C.

gifted child A child whose performance or IQ is positively remarkable in comparison to the normal child.

glissando A sliding up or down on a scale to give an uninterrupted flow or sweep of pitches.

grand staff The combination of the G staff and the F staff to form a continuous range of pitches.

graphic notation Musical notation that gives a general analogy of the sound it represents but not the relatively specific denotation of traditional notes.

grave Slow and solemn.

haiku Japanese poetry on subjects of nature, consisting of three lines of five, seven, and five syllables respectively.

half cadence A temporary resting place at the end of a phrase, usually on a V or IV chord.

half step The distance between two adjacent notes on the keyboard.

hand levels The use of the hand to indicate general highness or lowness of pitches in a melody.

hand signals A system of signals developed by John Curwen, in which each hand shape and level denotes a specific syllable or pitch in the diatonic scale.

harmonic minor scale A natural minor scale that has had its seventh tone (*sol*) raised one half step (*si*).

harmonics High, overtones produced on a string instrument by lightly touching the string rather than pressing it down completely.

harmony Simultaneous sounding of two or more different pitches.

harmony instruments Instruments that can provide simple harmonic accompaniments, specifically the autoharp, guitar, ukulele, and piano.

hearing impaired Descriptive of a child whose hearing is nonfunctional as far as school and society are concerned.

historical-national approach A strategy for relating the arts through the common principles and philosophy of a given national or historical style (such as Romantic art, Baroque art, and so on).

homophonic Concerning a musical texture in which a single melody is heard over a harmonic (chordal) accompaniment.

hymn tune A Protestant hymn characterized by a melody in the soprano part, with harmony provided by the alto, tenor, and bass parts.

iconic phase According to Bruner, the second stage of conceptual development, in which the learner begins to form mental categories as the result of learning experiences.

idiophone An instrument that is a self-vibrator, its own material making the sound, such as cymbals, bells, shakers.

IEP Individualized Education Program mandated by P.L. 94–142. Each handicapped child must have a specific program written to show how the individual will meet his potential through school services.

imitative canon A canon in which each part plays a similar (imitative) melody but is not an exact repetition of the first statement.

improvisation The art of creating a composition or ornamenting a melody extemporaneously.

indirect symbol A symbol in music reading that has no visual relationship to the sound involved.

interval The distance between two pitches.

intrinsic motivation Motivation that comes from the subject matter itself as well as from love of and enjoyment in learning.

inversion The position of a chord whose root is *not* the lowest sounding tone. In a C chord, E or G would be the lowest sounding tone if the chord were inverted.

IPS Inches per second, the speed with which tape passes through a tape recorder. Common speeds are 7½ ips, 3¾ ips, and 1⅞ ips.

isomodic Matching the mood of music to the mood of the child.

isotempic Matching the pace or tempo of the music to the pace of the child.

Italian tempo terms Words that describe the overall tempo and spirit of a composition. From slow to fast, common terms are *Largo— Andante— Moderato —Allegro— Presto.*

jazz improvisation The art of creating a composition or ornamenting a melody in a jazz style on the spot.

key A note of more importance within a scale to which all other notes are related and by which the scale is named.

Kodály, Zoltán (1882–1967). Hungarian composer who devised a system of music education based on folk music with pentatonic scales; his methods have been widely adapted in the United States.

largo Very slow.

learning handicapped Descriptive of a child who has extreme difficulties learning to write, spell, read, think, talk, or calculate because of a basic disorder in psychological processes involved in using written or spoken symbols.

legato A type of melodic articulation in which notes are connected in a smooth, flowing manner.

ledger line A short line added above or below the staff to show a higher or lower note, respectively, than the staff can accommodate.

lento Slow.

lesson objective A highly specific objective stated and measured for each lesson or lesson component. Lesson objectives are usually stated in behavioral terms: "The children will sing . . ."

lesson plan An organized strategy for stimulating, facilitating, and evaluating a learning task. A good lesson plan includes details of the grade level and subject, materials and equipment, objectives, motivation, procedures, and evaluation as well as ideas for follow-up lessons.

lieder Art songs; a vocal genre of the nineteenth century in which poetry is set for voice and piano.

limited staff The use of less than the traditional five lines and four spaces of the staff to represent pitches, particularly for didactic purposes.

line notation The use of two or three staff lines in a melody or tonal pattern.

locomotive movement Movement not in place, such as walking, running, or skipping.

maestoso Majestic.

mainstreaming The deinstitutionalizing of exceptional children and placing in a normal educational setting.

major A chord or tonal center built on a diatonic scale with half steps between the third and fourth and the seventh and eighth tones.

major triad A triad with a major third between its root and third, a minor third between the third and fifth.

materials The necessary "software" to be used in a lesson, such as charts, pictures, recordings, and so on.

measure A group of strong and weak beats that consistently occurs in music. Measures are separated by bar lines.

melismatic Describing a text setting for vocal music in which one syllable of the text has several notes set to it.

melodic minor scale A natural minor scale that has had its sixth (*fa*) and seventh (*sol*) tones raised one half step when ascending (to *fi* and *si*, respectively) but restored to the normal position (*fa* and *sol*) when descending.

melody A horizontal succession of pitches that forms a unity or single musical thought.

melody instruments Classroom instruments particularly suited for playing the melodic line, especially resonator bells and recorders.

melodic rhythm Generally, the rhythm of the words in a song.

membranophone An instrument whose sound is made by a vibrating membrane, such as bass drum, snare drum.

meno mosso Less movement.

mentally retarded child A child who functions intellectually below the normal range (below IQ of 85), resulting in limited learning capacity and inadequate social development.

meter The basic groupings of beats or pulses in music into strong and weak patterns. Common groupings are duple, triple, and quadruple.

meter signature The written manifestation of meter that shows the accent groupings and specifies the length of measures.

metronome A device that sounds the beats in a minute and can be adjusted to sound a variety of tempos, patented in the early nineteenth century by J. N. Maelzel.

mezzo-soprano A medium soprano, lower than a regular soprano but higher than an alto.

middle elementary years The third and fourth grades, representing children between seven and nine years old.

minor A chord or tonal center built on a diatonic scale, which, in its natural form, has half steps between its second and third and its fifth and sixth tones.

minor third The interval of one and a half steps, such as G to E (descending), C to E♭ (ascending). In the major scale, there is a minor third between the syllables *sol* and *mi*.

minor triad A triad with a minor third between its root and third, a major third between its third and fifth.

minuet and trio The third movement of the classical symphony, based on a court dance of the seventeenth century; has triple meter and is a large ABA form.

M.M. A notation indicating tempo as measured on Maelzel's metronome (M.M.) and specifying what note value equals the pulse or basic duration.

MMCP The Manhattanville Music Curriculum Program, which sought to provide an alternative music education curriculum through composition, discovery, and a spiral curriculum.

moderato A moderate tempo.

molto Very much.

monophonic Pertaining to a musical texture in which a single melody is heard without accompaniment.

motivation A stimultion for learning; a drive.

motive A brief melodic or rhythmic figure in music that is the smallest unit of musical meaning.

multiple handicapped Descriptive of a child who is classified as handicapped in more than one way, such as being both deaf and blind.

music specialist A person whose content speciality within the broad field of education is music.

musique concrète Electronic music created by using environmental sounds that are edited and mutated electronically.

muting Softening or muffling the tone of a musical instrument through the use of a special mechanical device.

natural (♮) A mark that cancels out a sharp or a flat.

natural minor scale A diatonic scale that begins and ends on *la*. It has half steps between its second and third and fifth and sixth tones.

neurologically impaired Descriptive of a child with a physical handicap due to the improper development of or injury to the central nervous system.

neurotic Pertaining to a functional nervous disorder.

non troppo Not too much.

normal child A child who does not require alteration of the standard curriculum to meet education needs.

note value The duration assigned a given note (1 beat, 2 beats, etc.) with values of all other notes being determined proportionally.

numbers The use of the numbers 1 through 8 to represent the tones in a scale.

C D E F G A B C¹
1 2 3 4 5 6 7 8

objective A statement of a goal or direction to be achieved through education. Objectives exist from the broadest ones, determined by society at large, to specific ones, stated for a single lesson.

octave An interval of eight pitch names.

Orff, Carl (1895–1982) German music educator who formulated a system of teaching based on improvisation on specifically designed instruments.

Orff instruments Keyed instruments, specifically the xylophone, glockenspiel, and metallophone, all of which have movable tone bars over a resonating chamber.

ostinato A repeated rhythmic, melodic, or harmonic pattern.

pacing The rate with which activities are presented in a classroom; the timing of the presentation, including momentum and tempo.

palindrome A word, sentence, or melody that sounds the same backward as forward.

part method A strategy for teaching a rote song in which each phrase is sung by the teacher and imitated by the class until the entire song is learned.

partner songs Two songs (or the verse and chorus of the same song) which may be sung together to produce harmony. Partner songs work together because both songs have the same harmonic structure and compatible meters.

patschen A slap on the thigh with the palm of the hand.

pentatonic scale A five-tone scale.

period A pair of phrases, the first of which is the antecedent ending on a IV or V chord, the second the consequent ending on a I chord.

phrase A group of notes in the melodic line which form a coherent unit. In singing, phrases are a "breath" length.

physically disabled Descriptive of a child with a crippling impairment that interferes with the normal functioning of the muscles, bones, and joints.

physically handicapped Descriptive of a child with a defect, whether physical (other than eyes and ears) or neurological, that inhibits the child's normal progress in school.

Piaget, Jean A Swiss educator (1896–1980) who formulated four stages of cognitive development: (1) sensorimotor intelligence, (2) preoperational thought, (3) concrete operations, and (4) formal operations.

pitch The highness or lowness of sound. Pitch depends upon frequency, the rate of vibration. The higher the frequency, the higher the pitch.

pitch names In music reading, the letters, A, B, C, D, E, F, and G (with sharps and flats) that represent pitches.

più More.

pizzicato Playing string instruments by plucking with the fingers instead of bowing (arco).

poco Little.

poetic feet The number of strong-weak (| ˘) or weak-strong (˘ |) units within a poetic line. (Dimeter = 2, trimeter = 3, tetrameter = 4, pentameter = 5, hexameter = 6, etc.)

polyphonic Pertaining to a musical texture in which two or more simultaneous melodies generate their own harmony.

301

preoperational thought According to Piaget, the second stage of cognitive development, in which children develop language and learn to represent objects with words. They are still perception-bound in this stage.

presto Very fast.

primary triads The triads built on the 1 (tonic), 4 (subdominant), and 5 (dominant) tones of a major or minor scale.

primary values Values unique to a given subject. In music, the primary value is aesthetic education and development.

problem singer A child who has difficulty matching pitches or singing because of a poor sense of pitch. This may be due to a lack of experience in singing, a poor self-concept in music, or an absence of motivation to sing.

procedure The strategy in a lesson plan for obtaining the objectives. Procedures may be "telling" (explanation) or "discovery" (inquiry).

processive form Repetition of a musical section or idea with variation.

program music Music that tells a story or conveys a setting.

psychotic Pertaining to serious mental derangement.

Public Law 94–142 The Education for All Handicapped Children Act of 1975, which mandated local and state governments to assure each handicapped child was educated to his maximum potential.

pulse The basic duration (beat) that is the foundation or the rhythmic structure in music.

pure variation Additive form.

quadrivium The medieval curriculum, which consisted of four subjects: astronomy, music, geometry, and arithmetic.

quadruple time Accent groupings in four (Swww). There may be a slight stress or secondary accent on the third count in quadruple time.

question of observation A question whose answer can be discovered or discerned by observing (seeing, listening to) a phenomenon (musical instrument, record, song). "Listen to the notes of the recorder and tell what finger placement has to do with the pitch."

question of opinion A question that has no right or wrong answer since the answer reflects only the opinion of the responder. "What do you think about Mozart's music?"

rag A piano style of jazz popular between 1890 and 1910. Rags are usually in compound binary form.

range The distance between the lowest and highest pitches in a melody. If the lowest pitch is middle C, the highest the A above, the range is a major sixth.

related arts (also allied, correlated, and interdisciplinary arts). Teaching the arts in tandem through a common element, topic, or historical period.

relative minor A minor key that has the same key signature as a major and which is built on the *la* (6) of the major scale.

relative *sol–fa* The use of solfège syllables to represent pitch names, *do* changing each time to represent the I or major keynote.

repetition Strophic form, AAAA.

repetition with contrast Return form, ABA, ABACA, and so on.

repetition with variation Processive form, $AA_1A_2A_3$, and so on.

rest values Notation for an absence of sound, each symbol being equal to its sounded counterpart.

retrograde The backward reading of a melody or rhythm.

return form A musical form in which one or several musical ideas are heard between contrasting ideas. ABA is a simple return form.

rhetorical question A question from which no answer is expected. "That's right, isn't it?"

rhythm The movement and distribution of music in time, including its tempo, pulse, accent, and pattern.

rhythm instruments Classroom instruments that do not specifically create pitch but are suitable for playing the pulse, accent, or rhythmic patterns in music.

rhythm syllables Words that represent rhythmic patterns.

ritardando A decrease in tempo.

rondo A return form in music characterized by the reappearance of an A heard after contrasting ideas. Rondos are often in the following forms: ABABA, ABACA, ABACABA, and so on.

root position The position of a chord whose root is the lowest sounding tone. In a C Major chord, it would be C.

rote-note A method of learning a song by watching the notes in a book as the teacher (or a recording) presents it.

rote songs Songs learned by imitation, without the benefit of note reading and music books.

round A strict canon in which each part sings the same melody, entering in turn at a different but set time, such as one bar, two bars, and so on.

rubato A deviation in tempo characterized by a slight increase followed immediately by a slight decrease. These deviations are minute quantities of accelerando and ritardando, respectively, representing a slight pushing and pulling in the tempo and basic pulse.

scherzando Playful and lively.

secondary value Values that are not unique to a given subject. In music, secondary values include using music to develop physical coordination or good citizenship.

sempre Always.

sensorimotor intelligence According to Piaget, the initial stage of cognitive development of children, ages 0–2, in which behavior is motivated in reflex fashion by events and objects in the environment.

sensuous listening Listening at a passive level; bathing in sound; hearing without listening.

sequences The repetition of a motive or phrase at a pitch level higher or lower than the original.

sforzando (SFZ) The direction over a note or chord to play it with special emphasis, an outburst of intensity.

shaped notes The use of specific shapes for the notehead to represent a solfège syllable.

sharp (♯) Symbol that marks raise of pitch by one half step.

simple interval An interval smaller than an octave (fourth, sixth).

simple meter A meter in which the accent grouping is 2, 3, or 4 (as reflected in the top number of the signature) and the pulse is assigned to any note duration. $\frac{2}{4}$, $\frac{3}{8}$, and $\frac{4}{2}$ are all examples of simple meter.

singing games Songs whose words suggest movment, both patterned and unpatterned, in their lyrics.

social objective The broadest level of educational goal, usually formulated by society at large, such as literacy, ability to compute, to understand democracy, and so on.

sonata allegro form A large ABA form used frequently as the first movement of a sonata, concerto, or symphony. Typically, two themes contrasted by key, contour, and intervals are presented in the A section.

song form Ternary form. It occurs as either ABA or AABA.

sostenuto Sustained.

sound picture A musical composition written in simple language and symbols for interpretation and realization by elementary children.

specific program objective An objective stated for a given subject to be achieved at the end of a specific grade level.

speech handicapped Descriptive of a child who has a speech problem that draws undue attention or interferes in communication with others.

spiral curriculum A curriculum in which key concepts or skills are introduced and then reintroduced over a series of time, allowing the concept or skill to become highly specific and refined because of the distributed exposure.

staccato A melodic articulation in which each note is performed in a detached or short manner.

staff The framework of lines and spaces (generally five and four, respectively) on which notes are written to indicate specific pitches.

stopping Inserting one's hand into the bell of a French horn to control the sound or to achieve a special effect.

strict canon A harmonic texture created when a melody is begun by one part and then exactly imitated in both pitch and rhythm by the other parts with a slight time delay. Rounds are examples of strict canons.

strophic art songs A song in which each verse of the lyrics is set to an identical melody and harmony.

strophic form Exact repetition between sections. In vocal music, words of the text may change but the form will still be strophic if the melody and harmony remain the same.

subdominant chord A chord built on the fourth note of a major scale. In major, it consists of *fa–la–do* (in minor, *re–fa–la*).

subito A qualifying musical term meaning "suddenly" or "immediately"; *subito piano* means "suddenly soft".

suite A composition with many short movements, often based on dances.

sul ponticello Bowing a string instrument near the bridge, resulting in a varied timbre.

syllabic Referring to a text setting for vocal music in which one syllable of the text has one pitch set to it.

syllables The use of *do–re–mi* syllables to represent the pitch names in a scale or melody.

symbolic phase According to Bruner, the third step of conceptual development, in which a person can deal with a category in a purely mental way.

symphony An orchestral work, most often in four movements.

syncopated pattern A rhythmic pattern in which the main accent or emphasis does not lie on the same beat as the normal accent grouping. In syncopation, the accent has been removed from where it is expected and placed where it is not expected.

synthesized sound Electronic sounds produced from the tone generators and oscillators on a synthesizer, as opposed to the mutation of environmental sounds.

synthetic scale An invented scale.

tablature A notational scheme for music that shows the position of the player's fingers rather than the actual pitches.

tempo The speed or pace of the music.

ternary Three-part form. Ternary form is most frequently a return form, ABA.

tessitura The general, average pitch level of a melody.

texture The relationship of a melody or melodies to the background accompaniment.

theme and variations A processive musical form in which a musical section (theme) is presented in transformation (variations).

through-composed art song A song in which the music changes to fit the lyrics, without repetition.

three-part harmony A melody with two supporting harmony parts.

tie A notational device in rhythm that allows the value of a second (or third, etc.) note to be added to the length of a first.

timbre The tone color of the sound generator.

tonal imagery The ability to hear mentally sounds represented visually or verbally.

tonal pattern A characteristic combination of pitches in a melody, such as *do–re–mi* or *do–sol–la*.

tone row A series of twelve notes used as the basis for twelve-tone writing.

tonic chord A chord built on the first note of a major or minor scale. In major it consists of *do–mi–sol*, in minor *la–do–mi*.

topical approach Relating the arts through a common theme, such as "War and the Arts" or "Religion and the Arts."

trainable mentally retarded (TMR) A child whose IQ score ranges from 30 to 50. Such an individual achieves social and emotional adjustment in a limited environment through schooling but rarely becomes self-supporting or is able to be unsupervised in society.

tranquillo Calm and quiet.

transposition To notate or perform a composition at a different pitch level (and thus a different key) than that at which it was originally written.

très Very.

triad A chord of three tones—the root, third, and fifth.

triple time A grouping of the underlying pulse in music into a strong-weak-weak pattern.

triplet Three notes performed in the normal time of two of the same denomination.

twelve-tone (dodecaphonic) music A system for composing music, compiled by Arnold Schoenberg, in which all twelve notes of the chromatic scale are used to form a nontonal scale or tone row.

two-part harmony A melody with a supporting harmony part.

uneven pattern A rhythmic pattern that maintains the underlying accent grouping (meter) of the music but does not move exactly with the underlying pulse. Rather, notes of uneven length follow one another. A dot is frequently the device used to create an uneven pattern.

unity Repetition in music.

upper elementary years Fifth and sixth grades, representing children nine to twelve years old.

variety Contrast in music.

visually handicapped Descriptive of children who are either visually impaired (can learn to read print) or blind (can read only in Braille).

visually impaired Descriptive of a visually handicapped child who can learn to read print.

vivace Lively and vivacious.

vive Brisk and lively.

vocal chording Singing easy chord progressions (I, IV, and V7) in three parts as an accompaniment to a melody.

whole method A strategy for teching a rote song in which the entire song is presented by the teacher and imitated by the class until the song is learned.

whole step Two half steps in the same direction.

whole-tone scale A scale in which all intervals are whole steps, such as C D E F♯ G♯ A♯ C.

An Overview of Music Fundamentals

Appendix A

I. Rhythm

Beats and Relative Duration

The beat is represented by one of the following notes:

o	*whole note*
♩ (half)	*half note*
♩	*quarter note*
♪	*eighth note*
♬	*sixteenth note*

Each type of note has a corresponding *rest*.

▬	*whole rest*
▬	*half rest*
𝄽	*quarter rest*
𝄾	*eighth rest*
𝄿	*sixteenth rest*

Each type of note or its corresponding rest is relative in value to the others. A whole note is equal in duration to two half notes, a half note to two quarters, and so on.

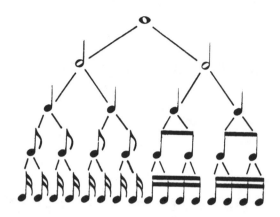

Therefore, if ○ = 4 beats, ♩ = 2 beats, ♩ = 1 beat, ♪ = ½ beat, and ♪ = ¼ beat. However, if ○ = 8 beats, ♩ = 4 beats, ♩ = 2 beats, ♪ = 1 beat, and ♪ = ½ beat.

Each type of note can occur in the proportion 3:1 through the use of a *triplet*.

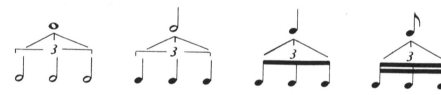

A *dot* increases the duration of a note by half its original value.

Thus if ○ = 4 beats, ○· = 6 beats. If ♩ = 1 beat, ♩· = 1½ beats.

Rests may also be dotted.

A *tie* increases the duration of a note by whatever value note is tied to it.

Thus, if ♩ = 2 beats, ♩ ♩· = 5 beats.

If ○ = 4 beats, ○ ♩· = 7 beats.

308

Tempo

Tempo may be indicated in music by a *metronome* (*M.M.*) *setting*.

M.M. ♩ = 60   (60 ♩ will occur in one minute, a slow tempo)

M.M. ♪ = 100   (100 ♪ will occur in one minute, a moderate tempo)

M.M. ♩ = 120   (120 ♩ will occur in one minute, a fast tempo)

Metronomes normally may be set from 40 to 208 beats per minute. Tempos between 80 and 100 beats are considered moderate.

Tempo is also represented by *Italian tempo terms* that suggest a speed as well as an overall style and mood. These Italian terms represent a continuum from slow to fast.

SLOW TEMPO ◄———————— MODERATE TEMPO ————————► FAST TEMPO

Largo — very slow
Lento — slow
Adagio — leisurely
Andante — walking tempo
Moderato — moderate
Allegretto — moderately fast
Allegro — quick, lively
Vivace — fast
Presto — very fast

Tempo markings are often qualified by the following terms:
Assai — very
Grazioso —gracefully
Maestoso — majestically
Meno mosso — less movement
Molto — very, much
Non troppo — not too much
Più — more
Poco — little
Sempre — always
Tranquillo — calmly
Thus
allegro non troppo = lively, but not too lively
sempre moderato = always moderately

Variations in the tempo are indicated with these terms:
Accelerando (*accel.*) — speed up gradually
Ritardando (*rit.*) or *rallentando* (*rall.*) — slow down gradually
A tempo — return to the original tempo (after a change)
Rubato —a slight speeding and slowing of the tempo

Meter

Meter is the systematic accenting of certain beats to produce a stream of strong (accented) and weak (unaccented) beats.

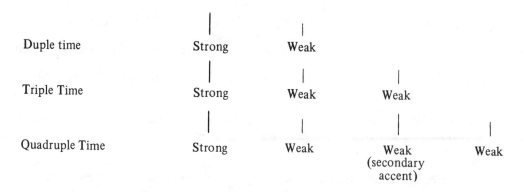

Simple meter In *simple meter*, the *meter signature* indicates the type of accent grouping in the top number. The basic beat unit is indicated in the bottom number.

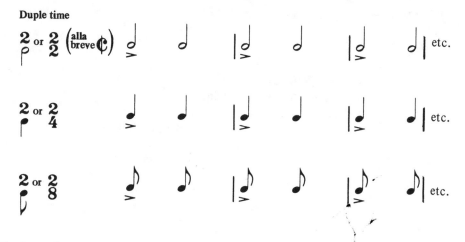

Each metric grouping is called a *measure* or *bar* and is separated from other groups by a *bar line*. A *double bar line* is frequently used to end a section or composition.

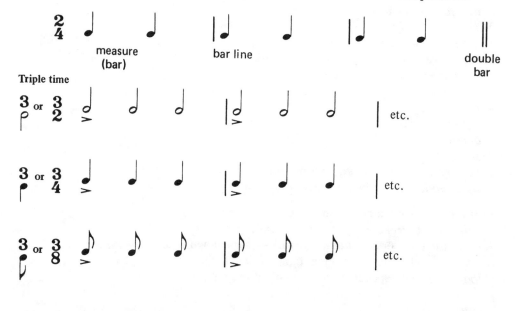

Quadruple time

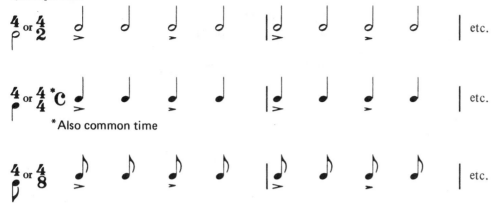

*Also common time

Compound meters

In *compound meters*, a dotted note is used as the basic beat. This allows a flow of triplets over the beat without the need to place *3* above each grouping. Therefore the true division in compound meter is found by dividing the top number by 3. The basic beat is always three times greater than the indicated bottom number.

Duple time

Triple time

Quadruple time

Asymmetrical Meters

Asymmetrical meters are commonly in five or seven with subgroupings of two or three. The basic beat may be the half, quarter, or eighth note most commonly.

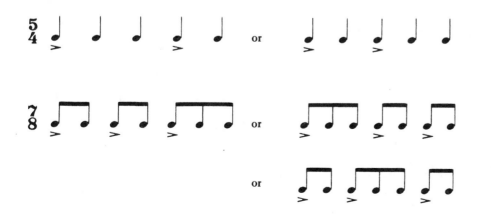

Pattern

Patterns may occur over a beat in three ways:

1. *Even pattern* (even division of the pulse or beat).

2. *Uneven pattern* (uneven division over the pulse or beat).

3. *Syncopated* (accent is shifted over the pulse or beat from where the strong beat is normally expected).

An *anacrusis* is a pick-up beat or beats that occur before the first full strong (accented) beat.

Conducting Patterns

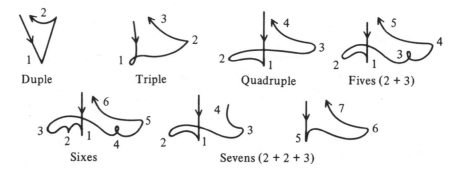

II. Dynamics (Loudness and softness of sound)

Soft ◄─────────────────────── Medium ────────────────────► Loud

Pianissimo	Piano	Mezzo piano	Mezzo forte	Forte	Fortissimo
pp	*p*	*mp*	*mf*	*f*	*ff*
(very soft)	(soft)	(medium soft)	(medium loud)	(loud)	(very loud)

 *Crescendo* (a gradual increase in loudness)

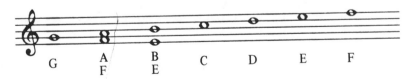 *Decrescendo* (a gradual decrease in loudness)

Subito piano = suddenly soft
Subito forte = suddenly loud
Sforzando (*sforzato*) (*sf*, *sfz*) = sudden
strong accent on one note
or combination immediately followed by soft.

III. Pitch and Melody

Pitches are designated by the *letters* A, B, C, D, E, F, and G with the addition of sharps (♯) and flats (♭).
Melody is notated by pitches placed on a five-line, four-space staff.

↑
High
|
Low
↓

A *clef* is placed on the staff to provide a reference point for pitches.
𝄞, the *treble clef* is used to designate the pitch G. Other pitches are established from the reference point on subsequent lines and spaces. The treble clef is used for higher voices and instruments.

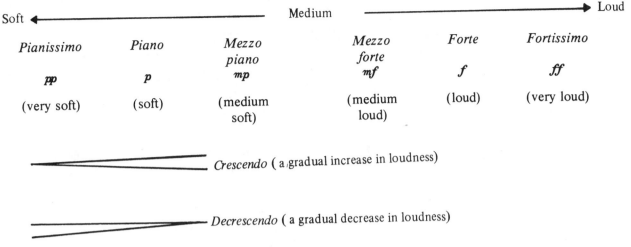

G   A   B   C   D   E   F
    F   E

𝄢, the *bass clef*, is used to designate the pitch F, other pitches being established from this reference point on subsequent lines and spaces. The bass clef is used for lower voices and instruments.

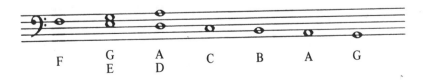

F   G   A   C   B   A   G
    E   D

313

The *grand staff* is formed when the two above staffs are placed together to form a continuous range of pitches.

G A B C D E F G A B C D E F G A B C D E F

Ledger lines are used above, between, or below these staffs to extend the range of pitches. Ledger lines are used as place holders and are written only as needed.

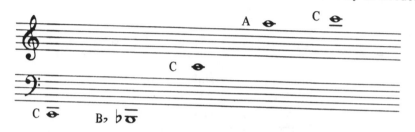

The pitches of the grand staff are represented on the piano keyboard in this manner.

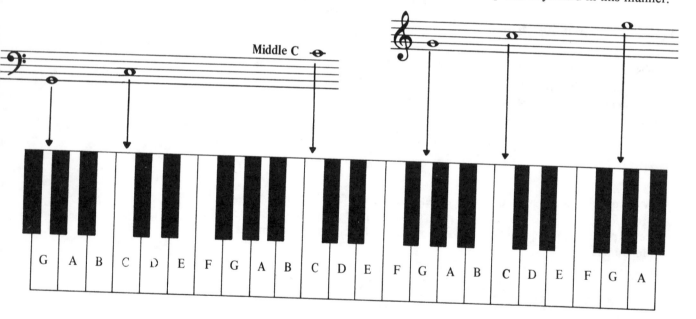

G A B C D E F G A B C D E F G A B C D E F G A

Half steps are the closest adjacent notes on the keyboard.

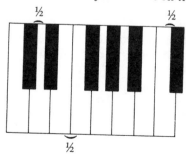

Whole steps = two half steps in the same direction.

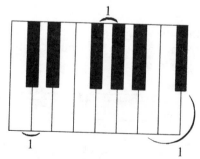

Black notes are termed either sharps (♯) or flats (♭).

A sharp (♯) raises a tone one half step.

A flat (♭) lowers a tone one half step.

A double sharp (𝄪) raises a tone one whole step.

A double flat (♭♭) lowers a tone one whole step.

A natural (♮) cancels out a sharp or flat.

A bar line cancels out an accidental such as a ♯, ♭, or ♮.

Enharmonic tones are those in which one tone may be notated or designated in two ways. For example: C♯ = D♭, E♯ = F, and A𝄪 = B.

Enharmonic tones

An *interval* is the distance between two pitches. An interval has both a *numerical* and *qualitative* designation. Numerically, intervals are called

| Unison | Second | Third | Fourth | Fifth | Sixth | Seventh | Octave |

These are *simple* intervals because they are smaller than the octave. *Compound* intervals are those which are larger than an octave.

Ninth = octave plus a second

Tenth = octave plus a third

and so on.

Intervals also have a qualitative designation, such as *perfect*, *major*, *minor*, *diminished*, or *augmented*.

The following intervals are common.*

Unison = same pitch name

Minor second = one half step

Major second = one whole step

Minor third = one and a half steps

Major third = two whole steps

Perfect fourth = two and a half steps

Augmented fourth (diminished fifth) = three whole steps

Perfect fifth = three and a half steps

Minor sixth = four whole steps

Major sixth = four and a half steps

Minor seventh = five whole steps

Major seventh = five and a half steps

Octave (perfect) = six whole steps

*Given the proper numerical designation (i.e. 2nd, 3rd, etc.).

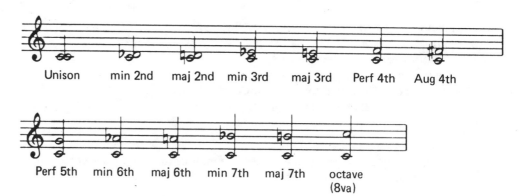

Unison   min 2nd   maj 2nd   min 3rd   maj 3rd   Perf 4th   Aug 4th

Perf 5th   min 6th   maj 6th   min 7th   maj 7th   octave (8va)

Enharmonic intervals are those that sound alike although they are spelled differently. A diminished fifth (C to G♭) is enharmonic to an augmented fourth (C to F♯).
A *scale* is a catalog of the tones used in a song or composition.
Common scales are:

Chromatic (all half steps)

Whole tone (all whole steps)

Pentatonic (Uses five tones only)
A common pentatonic scale* is

Diatonic (uses five whole steps and two half steps)
plus all pitch names in succession.

C D E F G A B C   D E F♯ G A B C♯ D

The most common diatonic scale is the **major** scale, which has half steps between its 3-4 and 7-8 notes.

1   1   ½   1   1   1   ½

Syllables are often used to represent the tones of the major scale.

do   re   mi   fa   sol   la   ti   do'

*The most common pentatonic scale eliminates the *fa* (4) and *ti* (7) of the major diatonic scale.
The black keys on the piano form this scale too.

Another common diatonic scale is the *minor scale*, which has half steps between its 2–3 and 5–6 tones. This version is known as the *natural minor scale*.

Syllables are used to represent the tones of the minor scale.

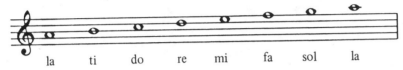

Two alternate forms of the minor scale are often used. The *harmonic minor scale* has a raised seventh tone (*sol* becomes *si*).

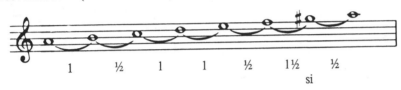

The *melodic minor scale* has raised sixth (*fa* becomes *fi*) and seventh (*sol* becomes *si*) tones as the scale ascends but the same tones as the natural minor scale when it descends.

Key signatures represent a major scale or its *relative minor*. The key of no sharps or flats is either C Major or a minor. In flat keys, the major *keynote* (*tonic*) is found by considering the last flat on the right as *fa* and counting down a fourth (or up a fifth) to locate *do* or 1. *Do* is the major keynote.

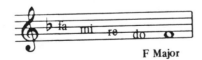

In sharp keys, the major keynote (tonic) is found by considering the last sharp on the right as *ti* and counting up a minor second (half step) to *do*. *Do* is the major keynote.

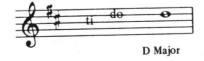

The *relative minor scale* is built on the *la* or sixth note of the major scale and has the same key signature.

The keys of the major and minor scales may be arranged in order to establish a circle of fifths (F♯ and G♭ are enharmonic keys, as are C♯–D♭ and B–C♭).

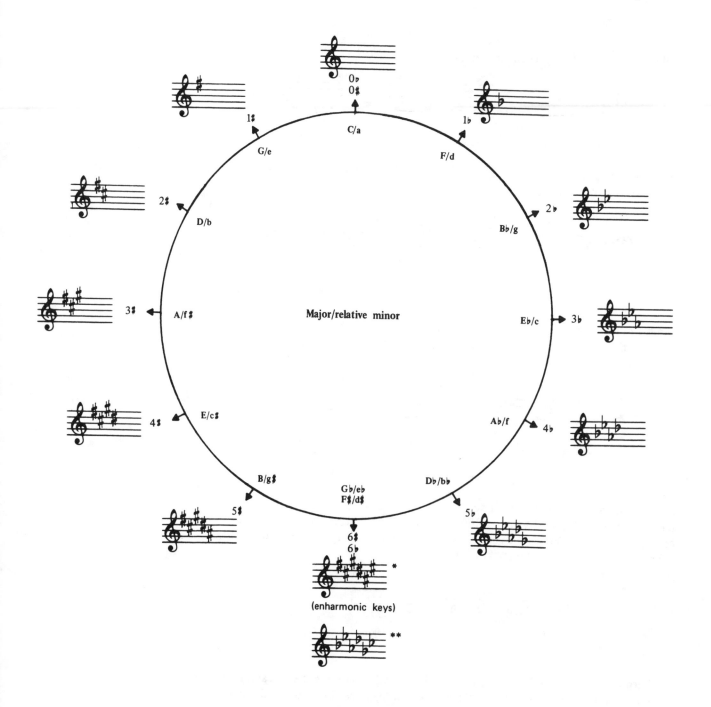

*Sharp Keys
The order of sharps is always the same in the signature:
F♯ – C♯ – G♯ – D♯ – A♯ – E♯

**Flat keys
The order of flats is always the same in the signature:
B♭ – E♭ – A♭ – D♭ – G♭ – C♭.

Transposition

Songs may need to be transposed to a new key in the classroom for several reasons·
1. To provide a range more suitable for the children's voices
2. To improve the key for a particular instrument, such as:
   a. easier piano or guitar chords
   b. chords found on the autoharp
   c. bars available on Orff instruments
   d. simplify keys for beginning instrumentalists

Steps for Transposing a Song.

Clementine

G Major   United States

Whimsically

1. In a cav - ern, in a can - yon, Ex - ca - vat - ing for a

mine, Dwelt a min - er, for - ty - nin - er, And his

daugh - ter Clem - en - tine.   Oh, my dar - ling, Oh, my

dar - ling, Oh, my dar - ling Clem - en - tine! You are

lost and gone for - ev - er, Dread - ful sor - ry, Clem - en - tine!

I = G B D
V7 = D F♯ A C

319

1. Determine the key and scale of the song. Key is determined by the key signature as well as often the last note. The beginning pitch and other predominant pitches will help reinforce this.

G major

2. Using numbers or syllables, assign each tone in the scale its respective designation.*

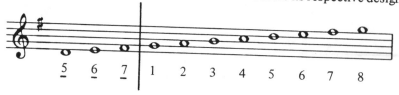

3. Determine the number or syllable of each pitch according to the scale and numbers designated in 2.

1. In a cav-ern, in a can-yon, Ex-ca-vat-ing for a

mine, Dwelt a min-er, for-ty-nin-er, And his

Chorus

daugh-ter Clem-en-tine. Oh, my dar-ling, Oh, my

dar-ling, Oh, my dar-ling Clem-en-tine! You are

lost and gone for-ev-er, Dread-ful sor-ry, Clem-en-tine!

These numbers are now the formula to be used in transposing.

*Either by numbers or syllables 1 == *do* (tonic), etc.

4. Write the scale of the key to which the song is to be transposed. Assign each tone in the scale its respective designation.

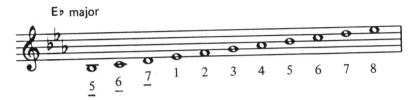

5. Rewrite the pitches by interpreting the numbers or syllables in the new key, maintaining the melodic contour of the original song.

6. Add the rhythms and chord symbols and the song is transposed.

I = E♭ G B♭
V7 = B♭ D F A♭

IV. Harmony

Chords are usually built in major on

do	(1)	the *tonic*	I
fa	(4)	the *subdominant*	IV
sol	(5)	the *dominant*	V7

The most common chords built are *triads*. Triads consist of three tones separated by the interval of a third.

The *primary triads* (those built on the tonic, subdominant, and the dominant) have a *root* (foundation note) plus a *third* and a *fifth*.

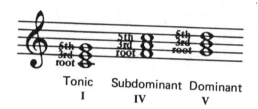

These are *major triads* since they have a major third between the root and the third plus a minor third between the third and fifth. Major triads are designated by upper-case Roman numerals (Tonic = I, Subdominant = IV, Dominant = V).

Chords in minor are built on

la	(1)	the tonic	i
re	(4)	the subdominant	iv
mi	(5)	the dominant	v

These primary triads also have a root (foundation note) plus a third and a fifth.

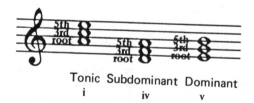

These are *minor triads* since they have a minor third between the root and third, plus a major third between the third and fifth. Minor triads are designated by lower-case Roman numerals (tonic = i, subdominant = iv, dominant = v).

The V chord in major or the v in minor usually has an added tone, a *seventh* above the root, included to create a chord that seeks resolution to the I or i chord, repectively. This is called the V7 or *Dominant 7th* chord.

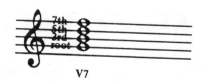

In addition, in minor, a modified scale is used for harmony (the harmonic minor scale) to create a major triad below the added seventh. As noted above, in the harmonic minor scale, the seventh tone is raised, making the root, third, and fifth a major triad with an added seventh above.

The accidental that occurs in the harmonic minor scale and its V7 chord (as the third) is never in the key signature. It must be included in each measure in which it is intended.

Chords may occur in other than *root positions*. Such positions are called *inversions*. If the third of the chord appears as its lowest sounding note, it is called a *first inversion*.

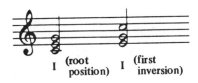

If the fifth of the chord appears as its lowest sounding note, it is called a *second inversion*.

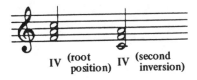

In the case of a V7 chord, where the seventh appears as the lowest sounding note, it is called a *third inversion*.

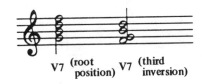

323

Steps for Harmonizing Songs

Did You Ever See a Lassie
(Ach du Lieber Augustin)

Germany

Did you ev - er see a las - sie, a las - sie, a las - sie? Did you ev - er see a las - sie do this way and that? Do this way and that way, and that way and this way; Did you ev - er see a las - sie do this way and that?

1. Determine the key and scale of the song. Again, consider, in order of importance:
Key signature
Last note
First note
Predominant pitches

F Major

2. Determine the I, IV, and V7 chords in this key.

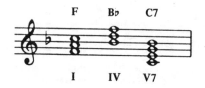

F   B♭   C7

I   IV   V7

3. Decide how often a chord is needed in the song.

Meter = $\frac{2}{4}$ usually once a bar (𝅗𝅥)

$\frac{3}{4}$ usually once a bar (𝅗𝅥.)

$\frac{4}{4}$ usually once a bar (𝅝) or twice a bar (𝅗𝅥 𝅗𝅥)

$\frac{6}{8}$ usually once a bar (𝅗𝅥.) or twice a bar (♩. ♩.)

$\frac{9}{8}$ possibly every pulse (♩.), three times a bar, but possibly only once a bar (𝅗𝅥. ♩.)

$\frac{12}{8}$ possibly every pulse (♩.), four times a bar, but possibly every other pulse (𝅗𝅥.), twice a bar.

Chord changes occur only at a place where a chord is normally expected, such as every beat, every other beat, or once per measure.

4. Analyze the melody to see which chord the predominant number of notes fall within. Songs usually begin on I and almost always end on I. Nonharmonic chords or tones should occur only on weak beats. Keep the harmony as simple as possible.

I = F A C   (F)
V7 = C E G B♭ (C7)

* = Nonharmonic (nonchord) tone

An anacrusis is rarely harmonized.
The hierarchy for selecting chords is:
I chord is the first choice.
V7 chord is the second choice.
IV chord is the third choice.

V. Melodic Structure

A *motive* is a rhythmic pattern which is used as the building block for a melody.

A *sequence* is the use of a motive at a pitch level higher or lower than the original.

Original   Sequence

A melody that progresses by half or whole steps is termed *conjunct*.

A melody that progresses by larger intervals (thirds and wider) is termed *disjunct*.

Notes of a melody played together smoothly are termed *legato*. Legato is indicated by

Notes of a melody played detached are termed *staccato*. Staccato is indicated by

A *phrase* is a distinct melodic unit with a well defined ending. In singing, a phrase is a breath's length.

Cadence

Phrases end with a feeling of repose or punctutation called a *cadence*. If the cadence is temporary, it is called a *half cadence*. Half cadences usually occur on a IV or V7 chord. If the cadence is more permanent, it is called a *full cadence*. Full cadences usually occur on the I chord when it is preceded by the V7.

Two phrases placed together may have contrasting cadences.

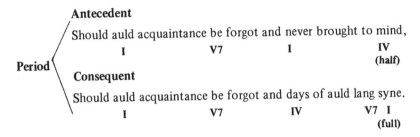

This structure of paired phrases is called a *period*. The first phrase is called an *antecedent* (question), the second a *consequent* (answer.)

Additional Symbols in Music Notation

> accent

D.C. al Fine (repeat from the end of the composition until arriving at *Fine*, the finish) the second time.

D.S. al Fine (repeat from the sign ℅) until arriving at *Fine* the second time.

‖ ‖ Repeat what occurs between the double bars.

|⁄| Repeat the preceding measure.

⌒ *Fermata* Hold (prolongation) of a note.

⌐1.⌐ ⌐2.⌐ Use the first ending on the first reading, the second ending on the second reading.

Fingerings
for the Soprano
Recorder
(Baroque System)

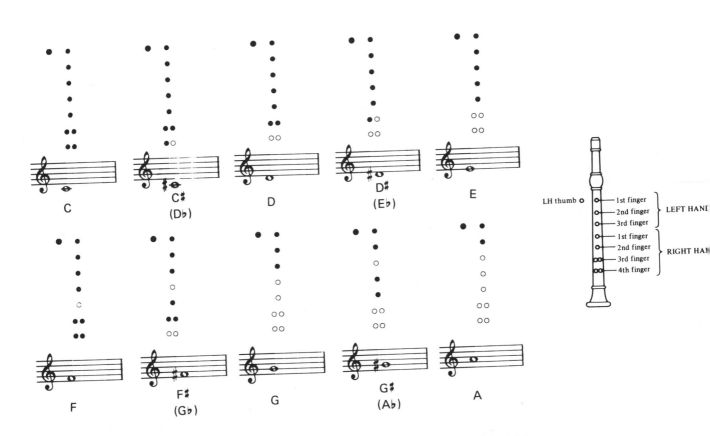

Common Guitar Chords

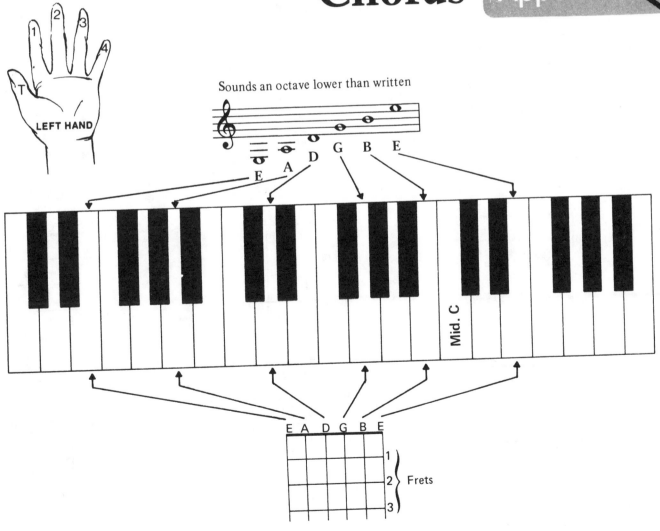

Sounds an octave lower than written

I, IV, V7 CHORDS

Appropriate Keys for Guitar
(O = open strings included in chord)
(X = string is not sounded in chord)

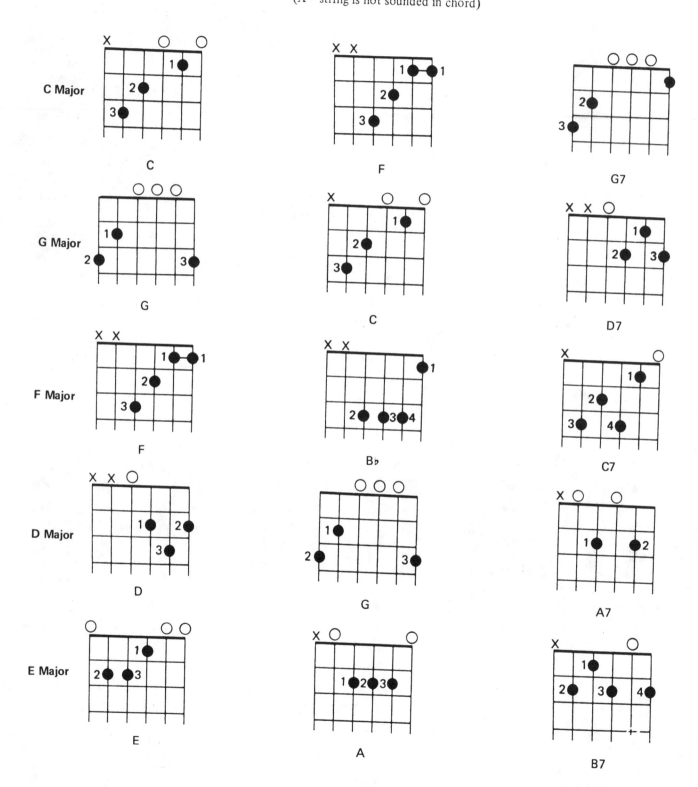

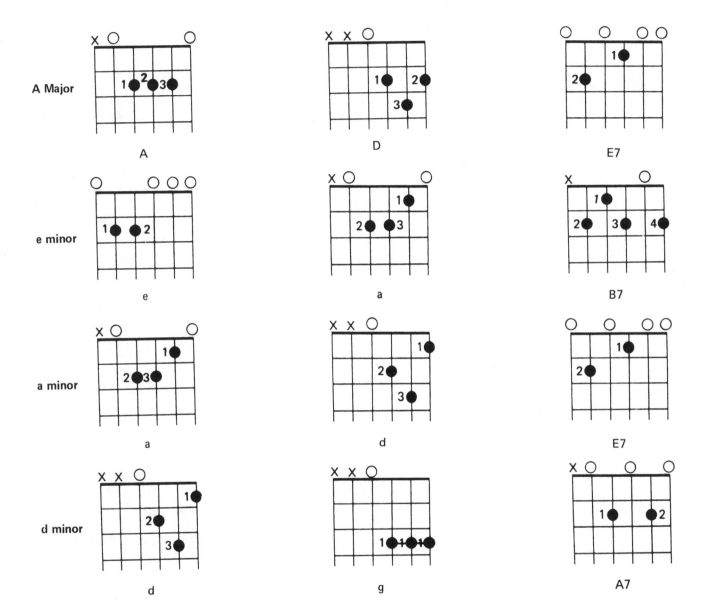

The Series Textbooks
Some Criteria for Selection and Copyright Considerations

Basic Music Series

The Comprehensive Musicianship Program, K–12. Menlo Park, CA: Addison-Wesley, 1975.

Discovering Music Together. Chicago: Follet, 1970.

The Music Book. New York: Holt, Rinehart and Winston, 1981.

Growing with Music. Englewood Cliffs, NJ: Prentice-Hall, 1970.

The Magic of Music. Boston: Ginn, 1963.

Making Music Your Own. Morristown, NJ: Silver Burdett Co., 1971.

New Dimensions in Music. New York: American Book Co., 1976.

Silver Burdett Music. Morristown, NJ: Silver Burdett, 1974.

The Spectrum of Music. New York: Macmillan, 1974.

This Is Music for Today. Boston: Allyn & Bacon, 1970.

Criteria for Selecting Music Textbooks

I. General
1. Philosophy, objectives, and content are compatible with that of the district, school, or teacher.
2. The content is accurate, interesting, varied, and in a logical sequence.
3. The authors are highly qualified in the field of elementary music education.

4. Teachers' editions are available with lesson plans and suggestions.
5. The textbook is attractive and durable.
6. The textbook is appropriate for meeting the individual needs of all students, including the normal and exceptional.
7. The cost is reasonable.
8. The textbook is free of cultural, sexual, or racial bias.

II. Specific

A. Student's copy

1. There are a variety of activities—singing (unison and harmony), listening, playing instruments, moving, reading, and creating—suitable for the intended grade level.
2. Records of most songs are available as well as selections for movement and listening. The songs are sung and accompanied in a manner appealing to children. The records are conveniently coded to the textbook.
3. Ideas from Orff, Kodály, MMCP, and other innovative curriculums are integrated.
4. There is a variety of visuals, including pictures of instruments, performers, and composers.
5. Charts of the piano keyboard, a one-octave melody bell set, and a twelve-bar autoharp are included. There is a chart of the treble staff.
6. There are alphabetical and subject indexes.

B. Teacher's copy

1. Scope and sequence charts detailing program objectives are included for each grade level.
2. Model lessons—including ideas for motivation, discovery, evaluation, follow-up, and individualizing instruction—are included.
3. There is sufficient background material on songs, recordings, instruments, composers, related arts, and the like.
4. The teacher's copy is an exact duplication of the student's book in pagination, with suggestions written in the margin.
5. The binding is suitable for placement on a music stand or piano.
6. It is suitable for use by a classroom teacher as well as by a music specialist.

Copyright Considerations

A major revision of the U.S. copyright law went into effect on January 1, 1978, clarifying what teachers may and may not do with educational material in the classroom. The following guidelines apply to music:

A. Permissible uses

1. Emergency copying to replace purchased copies which for any reason are not available for an imminent performance provided purchased replacement copies shall be substituted in due course.
2. For academic purposes other than performance, multiple copies of excerpts of works may be made, provided that the excerpts do not comprise a part of the whole which would constitute a performable unit such as a section, movement, or aria but in no case more than 10 percent of the whole work. The number of copies shall not exceed one copy per pupil.
3. Printed copies which have been purchased may be edited OR simplified provided that the fundamental character of the work is not distorted or the lyrics, if any, altered or lyrics added if none exist.

4. A single copy of recordings or performances by students may be made for evaluation or rehearsal purposes and may be retained by the educational institution or individual teacher.

5. A single copy of a sound recording (such as a tape, disc, or cassette) or copyrighted music may be made from sound recordings owned by an educational institution or an individual teacher for the purpose of constructing aural exercises or examinations and may be retained by the educational institution or individual teacher. (This pertains only to the copyright of the music itself and not to any copyright which may exist in the sound recording.)

B. Prohibitions

1. Copying to create or replace or substitute for anthologies, compilations, or collective works.

2. Copying of or from works intended to be "consumable" in the course of study or teaching such as workbooks, exercises, standard tests, and answer sheets and like material.

3. Copying for the purpose of performance except as in A1 above.

4. Copying for the purpose of substituting for the purchase of music except as in A1 and A2 above.

5. Copying without inclusion of the copyright notice which appears on the printed copy.

Resource Lists | Appendix E

Listening Collections

Bowmar Orchestral Library

BOL #51 ANIMALS AND CIRCUS
Saint-Saëns, CARNIVAL OF THE ANIMALS
    Introduction, Royal March of the Lion, Hens and Cocks, Fleet-Footed Animals,
    Turtles, The Elephant, Kangaroos, Aquarium, Long-Eared Personages, Cuckoo in
    the Deep Woods, Aviary, Pianists, Fossils, The Swan, Finale
Stravinsky, CIRCUS POLKA
Donaldson, UNDER THE BIG TOP
    Marching Band, Acrobats, Juggler, Merry-Go-Round, Elephants, Clowns, Camels,
    Tightrope Walker, Pony Trot, Marching Band

BOL #52 NATURE AND MAKE-BELIEVE
Grieg, MARCH OF THE DWARFS
Donaldson, ONCE UPON A TIME SUITE
    Chicken Little, Three Billy Goats Gruff, Little Train, Hare and the Tortoise
Tchaikovsky, THE LARK SONG (Scenes of Youth)
Grieg, LITTLE BIRD (Vöglein)
Liadov, DANCE OF THE MOSQUITO
Rimsky-Korsakov, FLIGHT OF THE BUMBLEBEE
Donaldson, SEASON FANTASIES
    Magic Piper, The Poet and His Lyre, The Anxious Leaf, The Snowmaiden
Torjussen, TO THE RISING SUN (Fjord and Mountain, Norwegian Suite #2)
Debussy, CLAIR DE LUNE

BOL #53 PICTURES AND PATTERNS
Rossini–Respighi, PIZZICATO (Fantastic Toyshop)
Bizet, MARCH—TRUMPET AND DRUM (Jeux d'Enfants)
    IMPROMPTU—THE TOP (Jeux d'Enfants)

Lecocq, POLKA (Mlle. Angot Suite)
  GAVOTTE (Mlle. Angot Suite)
Kabalevsky, INTERMEZZO (The Comedians)
Schumann–Glazounov, GERMAN WALTZ—PAGANINI (Carnaval)
Donaldson, BALLET PETIT
Mozart, MINUET
Handel, A GROUND
Schumann–Glazounov, CHOPIN (Carnaval)
Liadov, VILLAGE DANCE
Debussy, EN BATEAU (IN A BOAT) (Petite Suite)
Donaldson, HARBOR VIGNETTES
  Fog and Storm, Song of the Bell Buoy, Sailing

BOL #54 MARCHES
Pierné, ENTRANCE OF THE LITTLE FAUNS (Cydalise Suite No. 1)
Prokofieff, MARCH
Elgar, POMP AND CIRCUMSTANCE #1
Berlioz, HUNGARIAN MARCH (Rakoczy)
Alford, COL. BOGEY MARCH
Pierné, MARCH OF THE LITTLE LEAD SOLDIERS
Prokofiev, MARCH (Love for Three Oranges)
Ippolitov-Ivanov, CORTEGE OF THE SARDAR
  (Caucasian Sketches)
Schubert, MARCHE MILITAIRE
Sousa, STARS AND STRIPES FOREVER
Rodgers, THE MARCH OF THE SIAMESE CHILDREN (The King and I)

BOL #55 DANCES, Part I
Wolf-Ferrari, DANCE OF THE CAMORRISTI
Guarnieri, DANÇA BRASILEIRA
Kabalevsky, GAVOTTE
Dvořák, SLAVONIC DANCE #1
Copland, HOE-DOWN (Rodeo)
Walton, FAÇADE SUITE
  Polka, Country Dance, Popular Song
Brahms, HUNGARIAN DANCE #5
Waldteufel, SKATERS' WALTZ
Khatchaturian, MAZURKA (Masquerade Suite)
Khatchaturian, GALOP (Masquerade Suite)

BOL #56 DANCES, Part II
Vaughan-Williams, FOLK DANCES FROM SOMERSET (English Folk Song Suite)
Benjamin, JAMAICAN RUMBA
Corelli, BADINÈRIE
Smetana, DANCE OF THE COMEDIANS
Lecocq, CAN-CAN (Mlle. Angot Suite)
Lecocq, GRAND WALTZ (Mlle. Angot Suite)
Strauss, TRITSCH-TRATSCH POLKA
Rossini–Respighi, TARANTELLA (Fantastic Toyshop)
Rossini–Respighi, WALTZ (Fantastic Toyshop)
Waldteufel, ESPAÑA WALTZ
Guion, ARKANSAS TRAVELER
Khatchaturian, RUSSIAN DANCE (Gayne Suite #2)

BOL #57 FAIRY TALES IN MUSIC
Coates, CINDERELLA
Mendelssohn, SCHERZO (Midsummer Night's Dream)
Ravel, MOTHER GOOSE SUITE
  Pavane of the Sleeping Beauty, Hop o' My Thumb, Laideronette, Empress of the Pagodas, The Conversations of Beauty and the Beast, The Fairy Garden

BOL #58 STORIES IN BALLET AND OPERA
Menotti, SUITE FROM AMAHL AND THE NIGHT VISITORS
    Introduction, March of the Three Kings, Dance of the Shepherds
Humperdinck, HÄNSEL AND GRETEL OVERTURE
Tchaikovsky, NUTCRACKER SUITE
    Overture Miniature
    March, Dance of the Sugar-Plum Fairy, Trepak, Arabian Dance, Chinese Dance,
    Dance of the Toy Flutes, Waltz of the Flowers

BOL #59 LEGENDS IN MUSIC
Saint-Saëns, DANSE MACABRE
Grieg, PEER GYNT SUITE #1
    Morning, Asa's Death, Anitra's Dance, In the Hall of the Mountain King
Dukas, SORCERER'S APPRENTICE
Saint-Saëns, PHAETON

BOL #60 UNDER MANY FLAGS
Smetana, THE MOLDAU
Torjussen, LAPLAND IDYLL (Fjord and Mountain, Norwegian Suite #2)
Torjussen, FOLK SONG (Fjord and Mountain, Norwegian Suite #2)
Grainger, LONDONDERRY AIR
Sibelius, FINLANDIA
Coates, LONDON SUITE
    Covent Garden, Westminster, Knightsbridge March

BOL #61 AMERICAN SCENES
Grofé, GRAND CANYON SUITE
    Sunrise, Painted Desert, On the Trail
    Sunset, Cloudburst
Grofé, MISSISSIPPI SUITE
    Father of Waters, Huckleberry Finn, Old Creole Days, Mardi Gras

BOL #62 MASTERS OF MUSIC
Bach, JESU, JOY OF MAN'S DESIRING
Handel, BOURRÉE (from Royal Fireworks Music)
Haydn, VARIATIONS (from "Surprise" Symphony)
Mozart, MINUET (from Symphony #40)
Beethoven, SCHERZO (from Symphony #7)
Grieg, WEDDING DAY AT TROLDHAUGEN
Schubert, MINUET (from Symphony #5)
Wagner, RIDE OF THE VALKYRIES
Verdi, TRIUMPHAL MARCH (Aïda)
Brahms, HUNGARIAN DANCE #6
Mahler, SECOND MOVEMENT, SYMPHONY #1

BOL #63 CONCERT MATINEE
Debussy, CHILDREN'S CORNER SUITE
    Doctor Gradus ad Parnassum, Jimbo's Lullaby, Serenade for the Doll, The Snow
    Is Dancing, The Little Shepherd, Golliwog's Cakewalk
Corelli-Pinelli, SUITE FOR STRING ORCHESTRA
    Sarabande, Gigue, Badinèrie
Haydn, MINUET ("Surprise" Symphony)
Verdi, ANVIL CHORUS (Il Trovatore)
Grieg, NORWEGIAN DANCE IN A (#2)
Schumann, TRÄUMEREI (Scenes from Childhood)

BOL #64 MINIATURES IN MUSIC
Zador, CHILDREN'S SYMPHONY
Schubert, THE BEE
Haydn, GYPSY RONDO
Schumann, WILD HORSEMEN, HAPPY FARMER (Album for the Young)

Couperin, LITTLE WINDMILLS
Leo, ARIETTA
Liadov, MUSIC BOX
Gounod, FUNERAL MARCH OF THE MARIONETTE
Elwell, DANCE OF THE MERRY DWARFS (Happy Hypocrite)
Villa-Lobos, LITTLE TRAIN OF THE CAIPIRA (Bachianas Brasileiras No. 2)

BOL #65 MUSIC, USA
Copland, SHAKER TUNE (Appalachian Spring)
Thomson, CATTLE & BLUES (Plow That Broke the Plains), FUGUE AND CHORALE ON
      YANKEE DOODLE (Tuesday in November)
McBride, PUMPKIN-EATER'S LITTLE FUGUE
Gould, AMERICAN SALUTE
Cailliet, VARIATIONS ON "POP! GOES THE WEASEL"
Ives, LAST MOVEMENT, SYMPHONY #2

BOL #66 ORIENTAL SCENES
Koyama, WOODCUTTER'S SONG
Donaldson, THE EMPEROR'S NIGHTINGALE
Folk tune, SAKURA

BOL #67 FANTASY IN MUSIC
Coates, THE THREE BEARS
Prokofiev, CINDERELLA
      Sewing Scene, Cinderella's Gavotte, Midnight Waltz, Fairy Godmother
Donaldson, MOON LEGEND
Tchaikovsky, SLEEPING BEAUTY WALTZ

BOL #68 CLASSROOM CONCERT
Tchaikovsky, ALBUM FOR THE YOUNG
Stravinsky, DEVIL DANCE
Bartók, THREE COMPOSITIONS
Pinto, MEMORIES OF CHILDHOOD

BOL #69 MUSIC OF THE DANCE: STRAVINSKY
FIREBIRD SUITE:
      Koschai's Enchanted Garden, Dance of the Firebird, Dance of the Princesses,
      Infernal Dance of Koschai, Magic Sleep of the Princess Tzarevna, Finale: Escape
      of Koschai's Captives
SACRIFICIAL DANCE (The Rite of Spring)
VILLAGE FESTIVAL (The Fairy's Kiss)
PALACE OF THE CHINESE EMPEROR (The Nightingale)
TANGO, WALTZ AND RAGTIME (The Soldier's Tale)

BOL #70 MUSIC OF THE SEA AND SKY
Debussy, CLOUDS, FESTIVALS
Holst, MERCURY (The Planets)
Wagner, OVERTURE (The Flying Dutchman)
Thomson, SEA PIECE WITH BIRDS
Debussy, DIALOGUE OF THE WIND AND THE SEA (The Sea)

BOL #71 SYMPHONIC MOVEMENTS, NO. 1
Tchaikovsky, THIRD MOVEMENT, SYMPHONY #4
Beethoven, SECOND MOVEMENT, SYMPHONY #8
Mozart, FIRST MOVEMENT, SYMPHONY #40
Schumann, SECOND MOVEMENT, SYMPHONY #4
Brahms, THIRD MOVEMENT, SYMPHONY #3
Saint-Saëns, FOURTH MOVEMENT, SYMPHONY #3

BOL #72 SYMPHONIC MOVEMENTS, No. 2
Dvořák, FIRST MOVEMENT, SYMPHONY #9 (From the New World)

342

Beethoven, FIRST MOVEMENT, SYMPHONY #5
Britten, FIRST MOVEMENT, Boisterous Bourrée (A Simple Symphony)
Hanson, SECOND MOVEMENT, SYMPHONY #2 (Romantic)
Sibelius, FIRST MOVEMENT, SYMPHONY #2

BOL #73 SYMPHONIC STYLES
Haydn, SYMPHONY #99 (Imperial)
Prokofiev, CLASSICAL SYMPHONY

BOL #74 TWENTIETH-CENTURY AMERICA
Copland, EL SALON MEXICO
Bernstein, DANZON (Fancy Free), SYMPHONIC DANCES (excerpts) (West Side Story)
Gershwin, AN AMERICAN IN PARIS

BOL #75 U.S. HISTORY IN MUSIC
Copland, A LINCOLN PORTRAIT
Schuman, CHESTER (New England Triptych)
Ives, PUTNAM'S CAMP (Three Places in New England)
Harris, INTERLUDE (Folk Song Symphony)
Phillips, MIDNIGHT RIDE OF PAUL REVERE (Selections from McGuffey's Readers)

BOL #76 OVERTURES
Strauss, OVERTURE (The Bat)
Brahms, ACADEMIC FESTIVAL OVERTURE
Mozart, OVERTURE (The Marriage of Figaro)
Berlioz, ROMAN CARNIVAL OVERTURE
Rossini, OVERTURE (William Tell)

BOL #77 SCHEHERAZADE BY RIMSKY-KORSAKOV

BOL #78 MUSICAL KALEIDOSCOPE
Borodin, ON THE STEPPES OF CENTRAL ASIA
Ippolitov-Ivanov, IN THE VILLAGE (Caucasian Sketches)
Borodin, POLOVTSIAN DANCES (excerpts) (Prince Igor)
Glière, RUSSIAN SAILORS' DANCE (The Red Poppy)
Bizet, CARILLON, MINUET (L'Arlésienne Suite No. 1), FARANDOLE (L'Arlésienne Suite
    No. 2), PRELUDE TO ACT I (Carmen)
Berlioz, MARCH TO THE SCAFFOLD (Symphony Fantastique)

BOL #79 MUSIC OF THE DRAMA: WAGNER
LOHENGRIN
    Overture to Act I, Prelude to Act 3
THE TWILIGHT OF THE GODS
    Siegfried's Rhine Journey
THE MASTERSINGERS OF NUREMBERG
    Prelude, Dance of the Apprentices, and Entrance of the Mastersingers
TRISTAN AND ISOLDE
    Love Death

BOL #80 PETROUCHKA BY STRAVINSKY (Complete ballet score with narration)

BOL #81 ROGUES IN MUSIC
Strauss, TILL EULENSPIEGEL
Prokofiev, LIEUTENANT KIJE SUITE
    Birth of Kije, Troika
Kodály, HÁRY JANOS SUITE
    Viennese Musical Clock, Battle and Defeat of Napoleon, Intermezzo, Entrance of
    the Emperor

BOL #82 MUSICAL PICTURES
MOUSSORGSKY, Pictures at an Exhibition, Night on Bald Mountain

BOL #83 ENSEMBLES, LARGE AND SMALL
Britten, YOUNG PERSON'S GUIDE TO THE ORCHESTRA
Gabrieli, CANZONA IN C MAJOR FOR BRASS ENSEMBLE AND ORGAN
Bach, CHORALE: AWAKE, THOU WINTRY EARTH
Schubert, FOURTH MOVEMENT, "TROUT" QUINTET
Kraft, THEME AND VARIATIONS FOR PERCUSSION QUARTET
Mozart, THEME AND VARIATIONS (Serenade for Wind Instruments, K361)

BOL #84 CONCERTOS
Grieg, FIRST MOVEMENT, PIANO CONCERTO
Brahms, FOURTH MOVEMENT, PIANO CONCERTO #2
Mendelssohn, THIRD MOVEMENT, VIOLIN CONCERTO
Castelnuovo-Tedesco, SECOND MOVEMENT, GUITAR CONCERTO
Vivaldi, THIRD MOVEMENT, CONCERTO IN C FOR TWO TRUMPETS

BOL #85 MUSICAL IMPRESSIONS
RESPIGHI, Pines of Rome, Fountains of Rome, The Birds (Prelude)

BOL #86 FASHIONS IN MUSIC
Tchaikovsky, ROMEO AND JULIET (Fantasy-Overture)
Bach, LITTLE FUGUE IN G MINOR
Ravel, DAPHNIS AND CHLOE, Suite No. 2
Mozart, ROMANZE (A Little Night Music)
Schoenberg, PERIPETIA (Five Pieces for Orchestra)

Pop Hits Listening Guide (Pop Hits)
Includes guide, 45 rpm record, student worksheets sent monthly.

Adventures in Listening (RCA)

Grade 1
Vol. 1
Gluck, AIR GAI (Iphigenie in Aulis)
Massenet, ARAGONAISE (Le Cid)
Bizet, THE BALL (Children's Games)
Berlioz, BALLET OF THE SYLPHS (The Damnation of Faust)
Moussorgsky, BALLET OF THE UNHATCHED CHICKS (Pictures at an Exhibition)
Stravinsky, BERCEUSE (The Firebird Suite)
Bizet, CRADLE SONG (Children's Games)
Tchaikovsky, DANCE OF THE LITTLE SWANS (Swan Lake)
J. S. Bach, GIGUE (Suite No. 3 in D)
Grétry, GIGUE (Céphale et Procris)
Bizet, LEAP FROG (Children's Games)
Rossini–Britten, MARCH (Soirées Musicales)
Prokofiev, MARCH (Summer Day Suite)
Kabalevsky, PANTOMIME (The Comedians)
Ibert, PARADE (Divertissement)
Shostakovich, PIZZICATO POLKA (Ballet Suite No. 1)
Thomson, WALKING SONG (Acadian Songs and Dances)
Delibes, WALTZ OF THE DOLL (Coppélia)

Grade 1
Vol. 2
Grieg, ANITRA'S DANCE (Peer Gynt Suite No. 1)
Hanson, BELLS (For the First Time)
Liadov, BERCEUSE (Eight Russian Folk Songs)
Tchaikovsky, DANCE OF THE REED PIPES (Nutcracker Suite, Op. 71a)
Khachaturian, DANCE OF THE ROSE MAIDENS (Gayne Ballet Suite)
Tchaikovsky, DANCE OF THE SUGAR PLUM FAIRY (Nutcracker Suite, Op. 71a)
Saint-Saëns, THE ELEPHANT (Carnival of the Animals)

Bartók, FROM THE DIARY OF A FLY (Mikrokosmos Suite for Orchestra)
Arnold, GRAZIOSO (English Dances)
Moore, HARVEST SONG (Farm Journal)
Delibes, LESQUERCARDE (The King Is Amused)
Menotti, MARCH OF THE KINGS (Amahl and the Night Visitors)
Milhaud, MODERE NO. 1 (Suite Provençale)
German, MORRIS DANCE (Henry VIII Suite)
Mozart, NO. 8 (The Little Nothings)
McBride, PONY EXPRESS (Punch and the Judy)
Moussorgsky, PROMENADE (Pictures at an Exhibition)
Stravinsky, RUSSIAN DANCE (Petrouchka)
Rossini–Britten, WALTZ (Matinées Musicales)
Kabalevsky, WALTZ (The Comedians)

Grade 2
Vol. 1
Fauré, BERCEUSE (Dolly)
Moussorgsky, BYDLO (Pictures at an Exhibition)
Rossini, CAN-CAN (The Fantastic Toyshop)
McDonald, THIRD MOVEMENT, CHILDREN'S SYMPHONY
Prokofiev, DEPARTURE (Winter Holiday)
Elgar, FOUNTAIN DANCE (Wand of Youth Suite No. 2)
Handel, HORNPIPE (Water Music)
Bartók, JACK-IN-THE-BOX (Mikrokosmos Suite No. 2)
Milhaud, LARANJEIRAS (Saudades do Brasil)
Ibert, THE LITTLE WHITE DONKEY (Histoires No. 2)
Herbert, MARCH OF THE TOYS (Babes in Toyland)
Shostakovich, PETITE BALLERINA (Ballet Suite No. 1)
Grétry, TAMBOURIN (Céphale et Procris)
Kodály, VIENNESE MUSICAL CLOCK (Háry János Suite)
Meyerbeer, WALTZ (Les Patineurs)

Grade 2
Vol. 2
Arnold, ALLEGRO NON TROPPO (English Dances)
Rossini–Britten, BOLERO (Soirées Musicales)
Rimsky-Korsakoff, DANCE OF THE BUFFOONS (The Snow Maiden)
Bizet, THE DRAGOONS OF ALCALA (Carmen Suite)
Copland, DREAM MARCH (The Red Pony Suite)
Pierné, ENTRANCE OF THE LITTLE FAUNS (Cydalise Suite No. 1)
Gluck, MUSETTE (Armide Ballet Suite)
Cimarosa–Malipiero, NON TROPPO MOSSO (Cimarosiana)
Respighi, PRELUDE (The Birds)
McBride, PUMPKIN EATER'S LITTLE FUGUE
J. S. Bach, RONDEAU (Suite No. 2 in B Minor)
Howe, SAND
Webern, SEHR LANGSAM (Five Movements for String Orchestra)
Elgar, SUN DANCE (The Wand of Youth Suite No. 1)
Delibes, SWANHILDE'S WALTZ (Coppélia)
Prokofiev, TROIKA (Lieutenant Kije Suite)
Schuller, THE TWITTERING MACHINE (Seven Studies on Themes of Paul Klee)

Grade 3
Vol. 1
J. S. Bach, BADINÈRIE (Suite No. 2 in B Minor)
Offenbach, BARCAROLLE (The Tales of Hoffmann)
Hanson, CHILDREN'S DANCE (Merry Mount Suite)
Copland, CIRCUS MUSIC (The Red Pony)
Herbert, DAGGER DANCE (Natoma)

Elgar, FAIRIES AND GIANTS (Wand of Youth Suite No. 1)
Rossini, FINALE (William Tell Overture)
Villa-Lobos, THE LITTLE TRAIN OF THE CAIPIRA (Bachianas Brasileiras No. 2)
Kabalevsky, MARCH AND COMEDIANS' GALLOP (The Comedians)
Vaughan Williams, MARCH PAST OF THE KITCHEN UTENSILS (The Wasps)
Tchaikovsky, PUSS-IN-BOOTS AND THE WHITE CAT (The Sleeping Beauty)
Debussy, THE SNOW IS DANCING (Children's Corner)
Gounod, WALTZ (DANCE OF THE NUBIANS) (Faust Ballet Music)

Grade 3
Vol. 2
Thomson, THE ALLIGATOR AND THE 'COON (Acadian Songs and Dances)
Bartók, BEAR DANCE (Hungarian Sketches)
Handel, BOURRÉE AND MENUET II (Royal Fireworks Music)
Bizet, THE CHANGING OF THE GUARD (Carmen Suite No. 2)
McDonald, FIRST MOVEMENT, CHILDREN'S SYMPHONY
Taylor, THE GARDEN OF LIVE FLOWERS (Through the Looking Glass Suite)
Grieg, IN THE HALL OF THE MOUNTAIN KING (Peer Gynt Suite No. 1)
Lully, MARCHE (Ballet Suite)
Sousa, SEMPER FIDELIS
Saint-Saëns, THE SWAN (Carnival of the Animals)
Rossini–Respighi, TARANTELLA (The Fantastic Toyshop)
Prokofiev, WALTZ ON THE ICE (Winter Holiday)

Grade 4
Vol. 1
Lecuona, ANDALUCIA (Suite Andalucia)
Rimsky-Korsakov, BRIDAL PROCESSION (Le Coq d'Or Suite)
Grofé, DESERT WATER HOLE (Death Valley Suite)
Chabrier, MARCHE JOYEUSE
Grieg, NORWEGIAN RUSTIC MARCH (Lyric Suite)
Respighi, THE PINES OF THE VILLA BORGHESE (The Pines of Rome)
Mozart, ROMANZE (A Little Night Music)
Cailliet, VARIATIONS ON "POP! GOES THE WEASEL"
Tchaikovsky, WALTZ (The Sleeping Beauty)
Ginastera, WHEAT DANCE (Estancia)

Grade 4
Vol. 2.
Milhaud, COPACABANA (Saudades do Brasil)
Kodály, ENTRANCE OF THE EMPEROR AND HIS COURT (Háry János Suite)
Ravel, LAIDERONNETTE, EMPRESS OF THE PAGODAS (Mother Goose Suite)
Grainger (arr.), LONDONDERRY AIR (Irish Tune from County Derry)
Bizet, MINUETTO (L'Arlésienne Suite No. 1)
D. Scarlatti, NON PRESTO (The Good-Humored Ladies)
Menotti, SHERHERDS' DANCE (Amahl and the Night Visitors)
Dvořák, SLAVONIC DANCE No. 7
Sousa, THE STARS AND STRIPES FOREVER
Schumann, TRÄUMEREI (Scenes from Childhood)
Khachaturian, WALTZ (Masquerade Suite)

Grade 5
Vol. 1
Sibelius, ALLA MARCIA (Karelia Suite)
Gould, AMERICAN SALUTE
Ravel, THE CONVERSATIONS OF BEAUTY AND THE BEAST (Mother Goose Suite)
Chabrier, ESPAÑA (Rhapsody for Orchestra)
Schubert, FIRST MOVEMENT, SYMPHONY #5
Gottschalk–Kay, GRAND WALKAROUND (Cakewalk Ballet Suite)

MacDowell, IN WAR-TIME (Suite No. 2 [Indian])
Bach, JESU, JOY OF MAN'S DESIRING (Cantata No. 147)
Charpentier, ON MULEBACK (Impressions of Italy)

Grade 5
Vol. 2
Respighi, DANZA (Brazilian Impressions)
Bartók, AN EVENING IN THE VILLAGE (Hungarian Sketches)
Anderson, THE GIRL I LEFT BEHIND ME (Irish Suite)
Copland, HOE-DOWN (Rodeo)
Brahms, HUNGARIAN DANCE #1
Carpenter, THE HURDY-GURDY (Adventures in a Perambulator)
Stravinsky, INFERNAL DANCE OF KING KATSCHEI (The Firebird Suite)
Coates, KNIGHTSBRIDGE MARCH (London Suite)
Mozart, MENUETTO (Divertimento No. 17 in D)
Humperdinck, PRELUDE (Hänsel and Gretel)

Grade 6
Vol. 1
Bizet, FARANDOLE (L'Arlésienne Suite No. 2)
Borodin, IN THE STEPPES OF CENTRAL ASIA
J. S. Bach, LITTLE FUGUE IN G MINOR
Wagner, PRELUDE TO ACT III: LOHENGRIN
R. Strauss, ROSENKAVALIER SUITE (Der Rosenkavalier)
Beethoven, SECOND MOVEMENT, SYMPHONY NO. 8
Falla, SPANISH DANCE #1 (La Vida Breve)
Copland, STREET IN A FRONTIER TOWN (Billy the Kid)
Griffes, THE WHITE PEACOCK

Grade 6
Vol. 2
Guarnieri, BRAZILIAN DANCE (Three Dances for Orchestra)
Smetana, DANCE OF THE COMEDIANS (The Bartered Bride)
Vaughan Williams, FANTASIA ON "GREENSLEEVES"
Tchaikovsky, FOURTH MOVEMENT, SYMPHONY #4
Debussy, THE PLAY OF THE WAVES (The Sea)
Glière, RUSSIAN SAILORS' DANCE (The Red Poppy Suite)
Corelli–Pinelli, SARABANDE (Suite for Strings)
Holst, THE SPIRITS OF THE EARTH (The Perfect Fool—Ballet Suite)
Walton, VALSE (Façade Suite)

Select Discography for World Musics

General Collection

Music of the World's Peoples
  Folkways Records FE 4504, 4505, 4507. Notes and introduction by Henry Cowell.

Africa

  African Musical Instruments
  ASCH Records AH8460

  African Music
  Folkways Records FW 8852

China

  China's Instrumental Heritage
  Lyrichord Discs LL 92

Chinese Classical Instrumental Music
Folkways Records FW 6812

Chinese Classical Music
Lyrichord Discs LL 72

India

Classical Music of India
Nonesuch Records H-72014

Indian Folk Music
The Columbia World Library of Folk and Primitive Music, Volume XIII, Edited and compiled by Alan Lomax (Columbia Masterworks KL-215).

Music of India: Traditional and Classical
Folkways Records FE 4422

List of Suppliers

Record Companies

Activity Records
Educational Activities, Inc.
Freeport, New York 11520

Bowmar Records, Inc.
4563 Colorado Blvd.
Los Angeles, California 90039
(*Meet the Instruments*)

Bowmar/Noble Publishers, Inc.
4563 Colorado Boulevard
Los Angeles, California 90039
(Bowmar Orchestral Library)

Capitol Records
Educational Department, Capitol Tower
1750 North Vine Street
Hollywood, California 90028
(Capitol and Angel Records Educational Catalog)

Columbia Records, Inc.
Educational Department
799 Seventh Avenue
New York, New York 10019

Decca Records
MCA, Inc.
445 Park Avenue
New York, New York 10022

Educational Records Sales
157 Chambers Street
New York, New York 10007

Folkways/Scholastic Records
50 West 44 Street
New York, New York 10036

The Franson Corporation
Institutional Trade Division
100 Avenue of the Americas
New York, New York 10013
(Distributors of Children's Record Guild
and Young People's Records)

Keyboard Junior Publications, Inc.
1346 Chapel Street
New Haven, Connecticut 06511

Pop Hits
3149 Southern Avenue
Memphis, Tennessee 38111

RCA Records
P.O. Box 1999
Indianapolis, Indiana 46291
(*Adventures in Listening*)

RCA Victor Educational Sales
155 East 24 Street
New York, New York 10010
(*RCA Victor Basic Record Library*)

Classroom Music Instruments and Equipment

M. Hohner, Inc.
545 Busse Road
Elk Grove Village, Illinois 60007
(Orff Instruments)

Hughes Dulcimer Company
8665 West 13th Avenue
Denver, Colorado 80215

Magnamusic-Baton, Inc.
10370 Page Industrial Boulevard
St. Louis, Missouri 63132

Music Education Group
P.O. Box 1501
Union, New Jersey 07083

Peterson Electro-Musical Products
Worth, Illinois 60482

RadioMatic of America, Inc.
760 Ramsey Avenue
Hillside, New Jersey 07205

Rhythm Band, Inc.
P.O. Box 126
Fort Worth, Texas 76101

Silver Burdett Company
P.O. Box 2000
Morristown, New Jersey 07960

Terminal Music
166 West 48 Street
New York, New York 10036

Wurlitzer Educational Products
WEPCO, Inc.
1700 Pleasant Street
De Kalb, Illinois 60115

School Music Supplies

Gamble's Musical Merchandise Catalog
Gamble Music Company
312 South Wabash Avenue
Chicago, Illinois 60604

Lyons Band
530 Riverview Avenue
Elkhart, Indiana 46514

Peripole
Browns Mills, New Jersey 08015

Copyrights and Acknowledgments

28, 88 "The Birch Tree" from *This Is Music*, Book 4 by William R. Sur et al. Copyright © 1967 by Allyn and Bacon, Inc., Boston. Reprinted with permission.

35 "Leo the Lion" from *Growing with Music*, Book 1 by Wilson et al. Englewood Cliffs, N.J.: Prentice Hall, Inc. 1963.

39 "I Caught a Rabbit" collected by Jean Thomas, the "Traipsin' Woman" from *Making Music Your Own*, Book 3. © 1964 by Silver Burdett Company. Used by permission.

68 "My little Red Drum" from *The Magic of Music*, Book Two by Watters et al. © 1970, 1965 by Ginn and Company (Xerox Corporation). Used with permission.

80, 81 "There's Work To Be Done" and "No Need to Hurry" from *New Dimension in Music*, 3rd edition, Book 3, *Expressing Music* by Robert Choate et al. © 1980. Reprinted by permission of D. C. Heath.

110 "Mary Ann" from *Growing with Music*, Book 8, by Wilson et al. Englewood Cliffs, N.J.: Prentice-Hall, Inc., 1963.

130 Raindrops from the *Small Singer*. Copyright 1969 by Bellwin-Mills Publishing Corporation of Melville, New York. All rights reserved. Used by permission.

133 "Put Your Finger in the Air," words and music by Woody Guthrie. TRO © Copyright 1954 and renewed 1982 Folkways Music Publishers, Inc., New York, N.Y.

134 "The Cuckoo from *Around the World in Two Hours*. Copyright © 1951, World Around Songs, Burnsville, N.C. Used by permission. English translation by Katherine F. Rohrbough. "Chair, Chair, Chair" from the *Birchard Music Series*, Book 4. © 1962. Reprinted by permission of Summy-Birchard Music.

148 "Camptown Races" from *Songs in Motion* by Mary Helen Richards. Copyright © 1965 by Fearon Publishers, Inc. Reprinted by permission of Pitman Learning, Inc., Belmont, California.

159 "Taffy" from *Exploring Music*, Book I by Eunice Boardman and Beth Landis. Copyright © 1966 by Holt, Rinehart and Winston, Publishers.

206 "Shoo Fly Don't Bother Me" from *Rhythm and Dances for Elementary School* by Dorothy LaSalle. Copyright © 1951. Reprinted by permission of John Wiley & Sons, Inc.

253–264 "Clap clap your hands," Raindrops," Bobby Shafto," "Bell Horses," "Peter, Peter Pumpkin Eater," melody canons, rhythmic canons, rondo and instrumental exercise from *Schulwerk*,

Music for Children, I by Carl Orff (and Gunild Keetman, English translation by Doreen Hall and Arnold Walter, 1955). Copyright © 1956 by B. Schott's Söhne, Mainz. Used by permission of European American Music Distributors Corp., sole U.S. agent for B. Schott's Söhne, Mainz.
266 Kodály rhythm symbols from The Kodály Method by Lois Chosky, pp. 18–23. © 1974. Reprinted by permission of Prentice-Hall, Inc., Englewood Cliffs, New Jersey.
269 "Gyertek" from *Kodály Concept of Music Education* (Szabo). © 1969 by Boosey & Hawkes Music Publishers, Ltd. Reprinted by permission of Boosey & Hawkes Inc.
270 (top and middle) Excerpts from *Fifty Nursery Songs* by Zoltan Kodály. © 1962 by Zoltan Kodály. © assigned 1963 to Boosey & Hawkes Music Publishers Ltd. English edition © 1964 by Boosey & Hawkes Music Publishers Ltd. Reprinted by permission of Boosey & Hawkes Inc.
270 (bottom) and **271** (middle) Exercises from *333 Elementary Exercises* by Zoltan Kodály. © 1941 by Zoltan Kodály. © assigned 1957 to Boosey & Co. Ltd.; English edition © 1963 by Boosey & Co., Ltd. Reprinted by permission of Boosey & Hawkes Inc.
273–280 Charts from *Threshold to Music* by Mary Helen Richards. Copyright © 1964 by Fearon Publishers, Inc. Reprinted by permission of Pitman Learning Inc., Belmont, California.
281 "Ring Ring de Banjo" from *Songs in Motion* by Mary Helen Richards. Copyright © 1965 by Fearon Publishers, Inc. Reprinted by permission of Pitman Learning Inc., Belmont, California.
284 Reprinted with permission of Macmillan Publishing Co., Inc. from *Contemporary Music Education* by Michael L. Mark. Copyright © 1979 by Schirmer Books, a Division of Macmillan Publishing Co., Inc.

Motion stories, *Clap My Hands*, page 130, and *Percussion Walk*, page 137, from Creative Movement for the Developing Child, Revised Edition by Clare Cherry. Copyright © 1971 by Fearon Publishers, Inc. Reprinted by permission of Pitman Learning, Inc., Belmont, California.
Photographs of musical instruments on pages 102, 113 and 116 courtesy of Rhythm Band Inc., Fort Worth, Texas.
Cartoon on page 289: *The Family Circus* by Bill Keane. Reprinted courtesy of The Register and Tribune Syndicate Inc.

Song Index

TITLE	KEY	METER	CHORDS	PAGE
Raindrops	G major	$\frac{4}{4}$	I, V7	130–131
Rain, Rain, Go Away	C pentatonic	$\frac{4}{4}$		254
Ring, Ring de Banjo	C pentatonic	$\frac{4}{4}$		281
Rocka My Soul	F major	$\frac{4}{4}$	I, V7	80
Row, Row, Row Your Boat	C major	$\frac{6}{8}$	I	82, 153
Rushes Rustling	D pentatonic	$\frac{2}{4}$		270
Sally Go Round the Sun	F major	$\frac{6}{8}$	I, V7	47
Shoo, Fly, Don't Bother Me	F major	$\frac{2}{4}$	I, V7	59, 136, 206–207
Springfield Mountain	G major	$\frac{3}{4}$	I, V7	87
Star Light, Star Bright	D pentatonic	$\frac{4}{4}$		83
Swing Low, Sweet Chariot	F major	$\frac{2}{4}$	I, V7	230
Taffy	C major	$\frac{4}{4}$	I, IV, V7	159
Tailor and the Mouse, The	a minor	$\frac{4}{4}$	i, V7, III, V7/III	62–63
The More We Get Together	F major	$\frac{3}{4}$	I, V7	160–161
There's Work To Be Done	C major	$\frac{4}{4}$	I, IV, V7	80–81
Three Blind Mice	C major	$\frac{6}{8}$	I	117
Turn the Glasses Over	F pentatonic	$\frac{4}{4}$		114
Wiggle Song, The	G major	$\frac{6}{8}$	I, IV, V7	129–130

Subject Index

Page numbers in italics refer to the glossary.